STELLA HAMBERG

Moritz Woelk

STELLA HAMBERG

HIRMER

The works of stella Hamberg are surely among the exceptions in present-day sculpture, inasmuch as they interpret the oldest subject of this physical, three-dimensional medium, the figure, in a distinctly elementary yet keenly intellectualised manner.

The works collected in this book date from 2004 to 2017 – from the end of her studies at Dresden's Hochschule für bildende Künste to some of her newest projects. In this period, one can see an impressive development, yet one marked by artistic themes and structural features that can be traced like common threads through all her work. Many features of her earlier sculptures becomes more clearly recognisable in retrospect, and her newest works seem so immediate that it would be presumptuous to try to characterise their role in an artistic career whose further development we cannot yet know. The following attempts to illuminate two aspects: the vitality and consistency in the evolution of her work, and the range of her artistic approaches.

Much as Hamberg's work to date has exhibited the originality and individuality of its creator, it did not arise from nowhere, but rather against the background of a millennia-old history of the medium down to the present day, one to which the artist is as attentively attuned as to life itself. This two-pronged reference is also part of the strength of her art. She occupies herself with both existential and formal questions, and problems that were also of concern, if in other ways, to Matthias Grünewald, Michelangelo, and Rodin, and to sculptors of antiquity and the Middle Ages. The result in her own work is not so much a question of dependency or a literal use of "models," but rather a kind of musical counterpoint with voices from this great tradition – an aspect of her oeuvre that represents a special delight to all who are interested not only in contemporary art but also in ancient art, even though precisely what is absolutely new in her work stands out all the more clearly against this background.

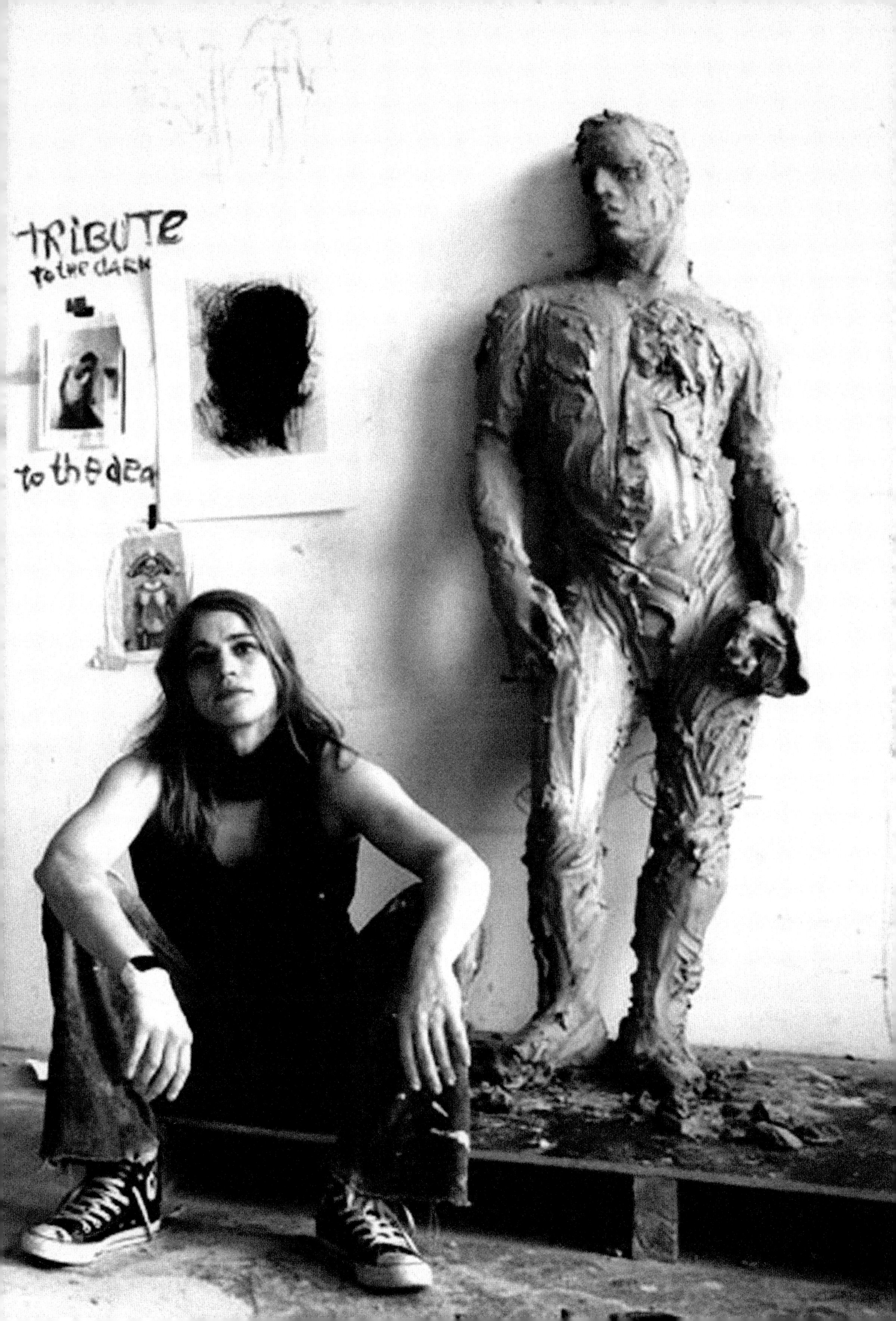
TRIBUTE
to the dark
to the dea

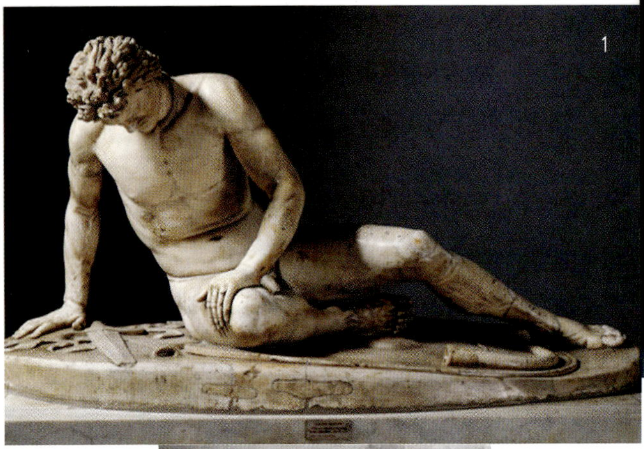

1

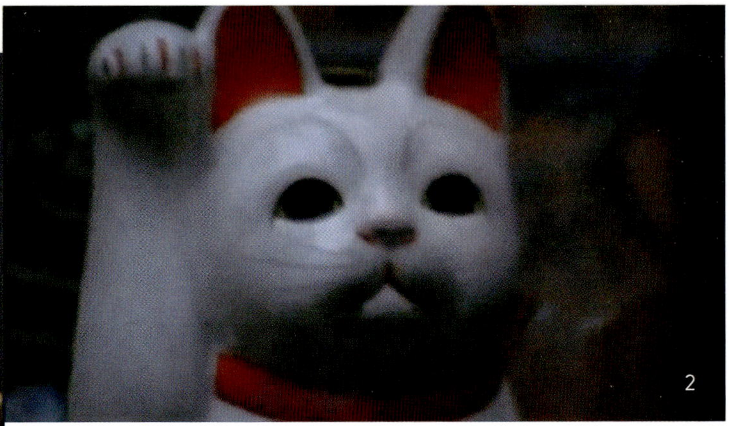

2

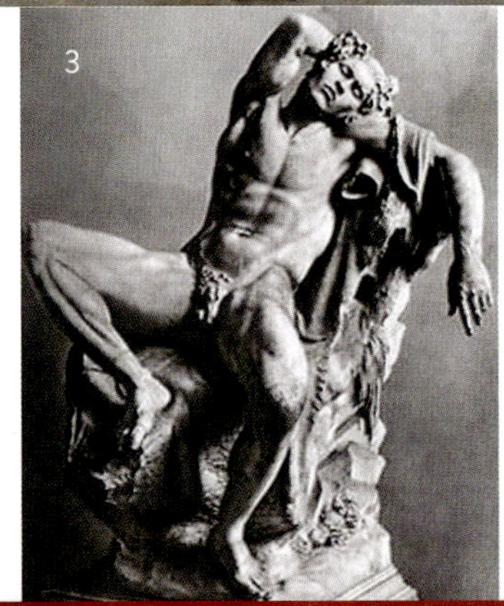

3

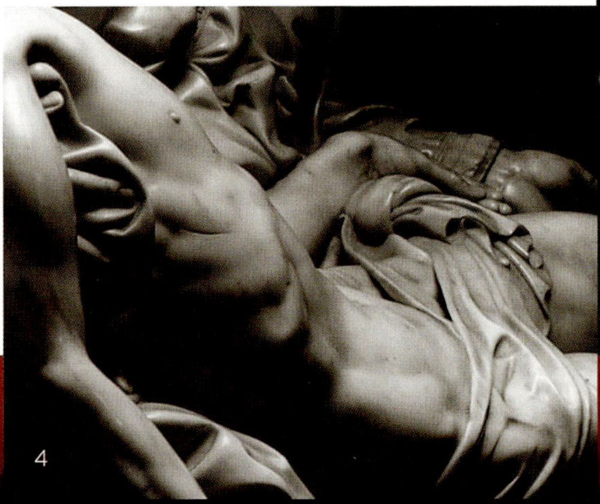

4

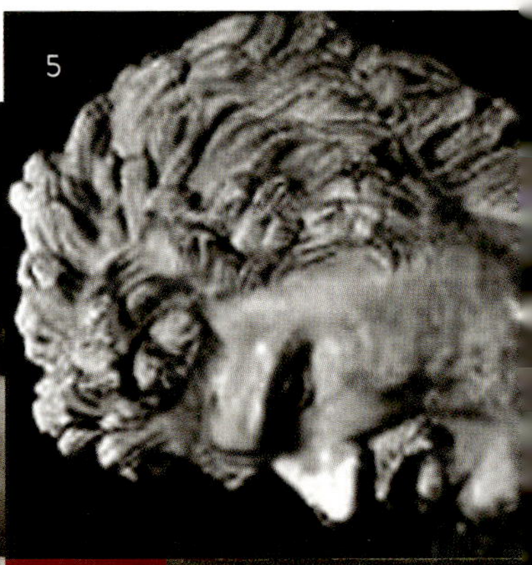

5

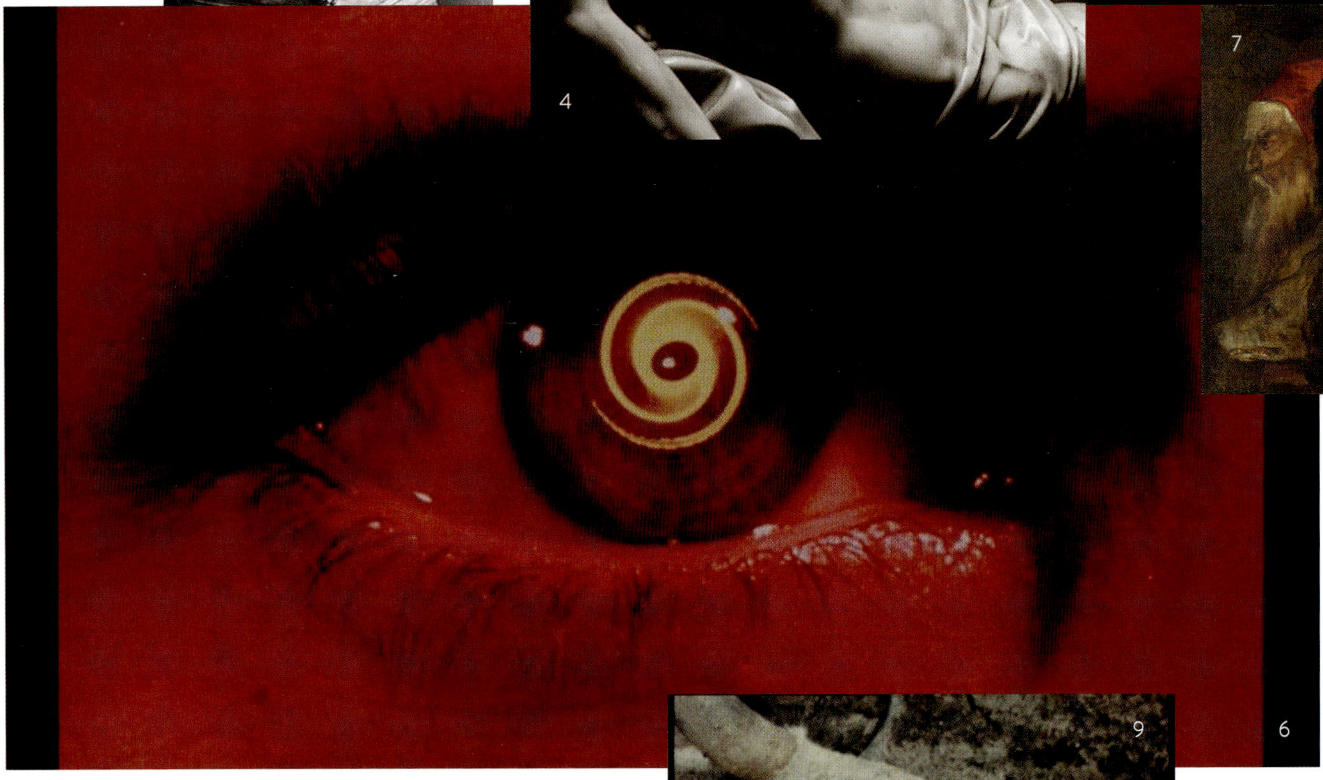

6

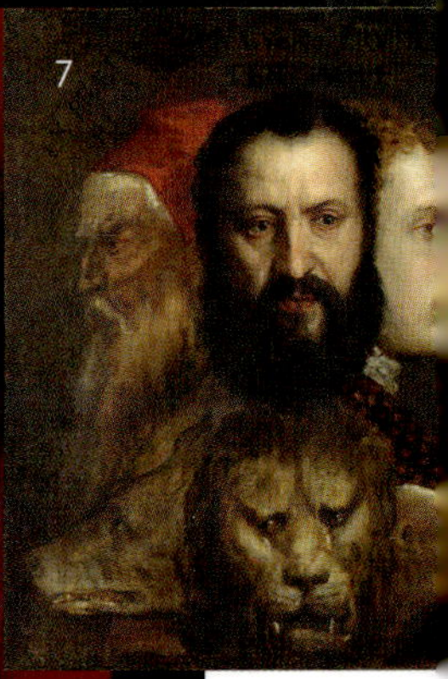

7

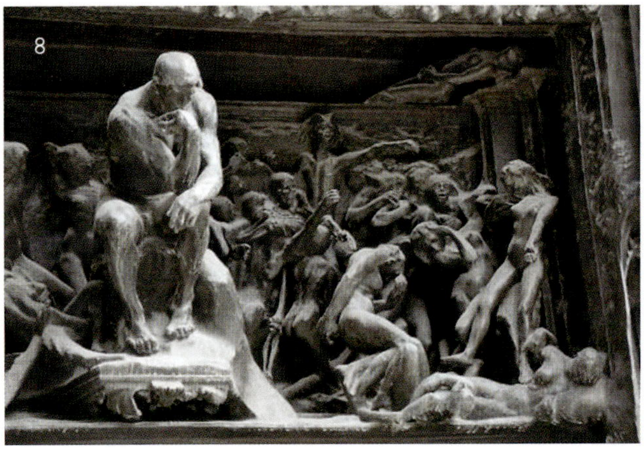

8

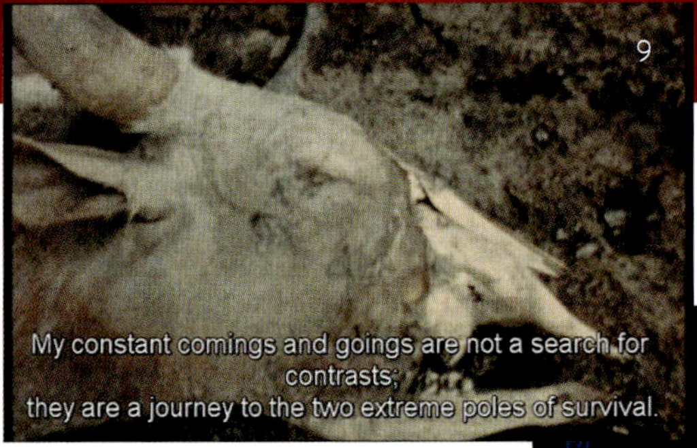

9

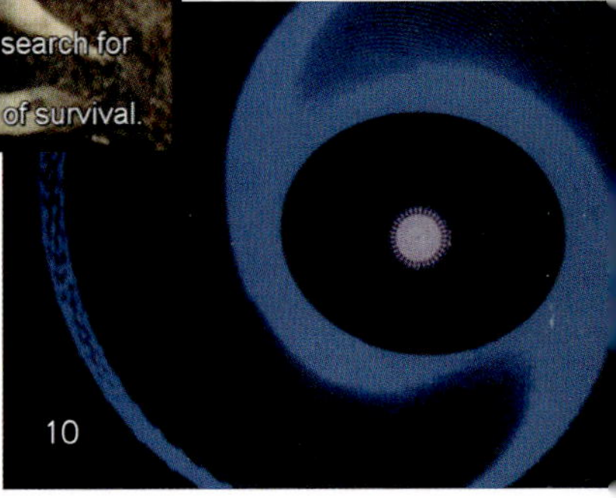

10

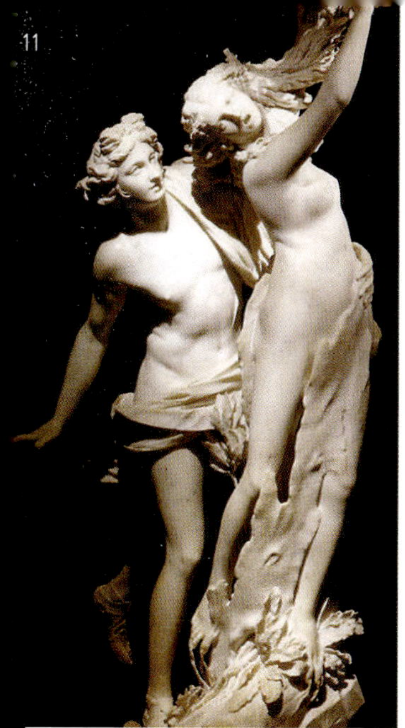

11

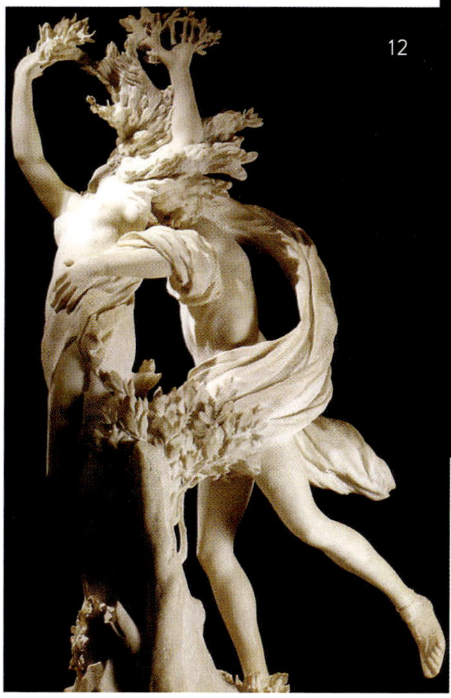

12

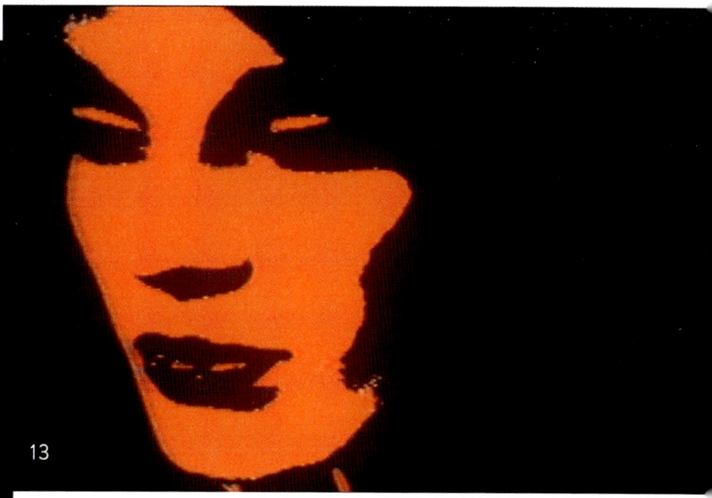

13

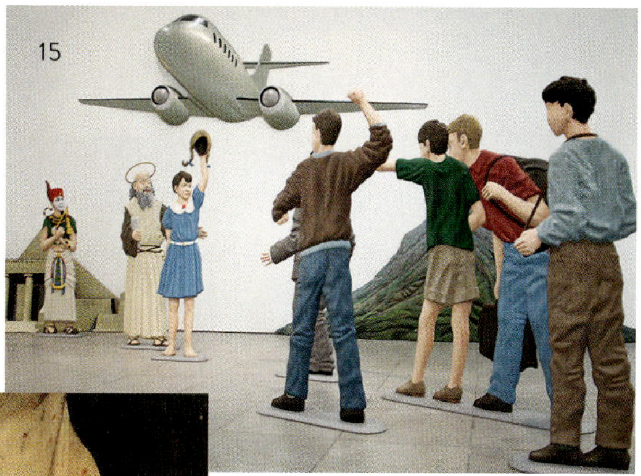

15

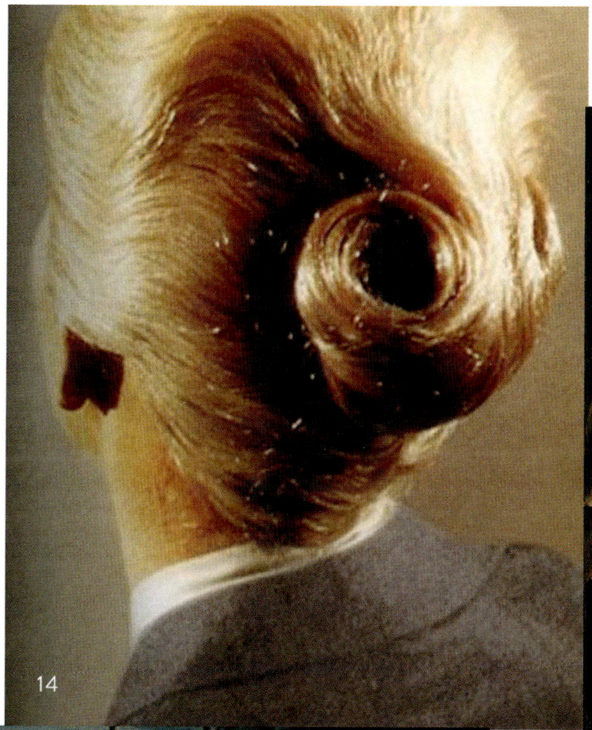

14

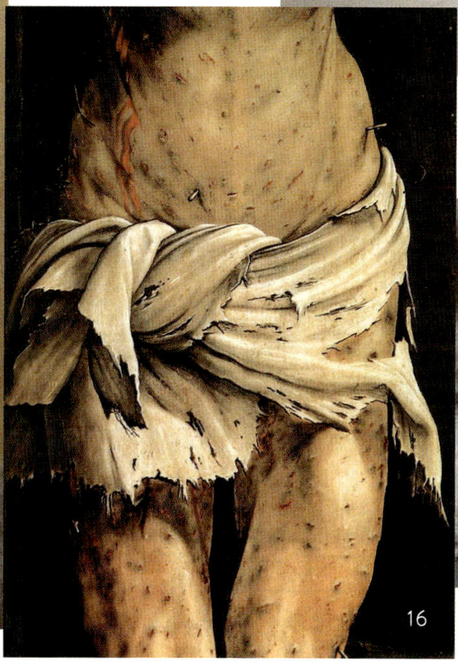

16

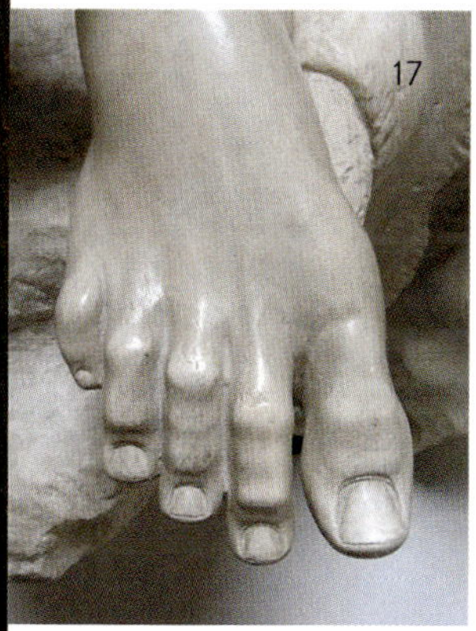

17

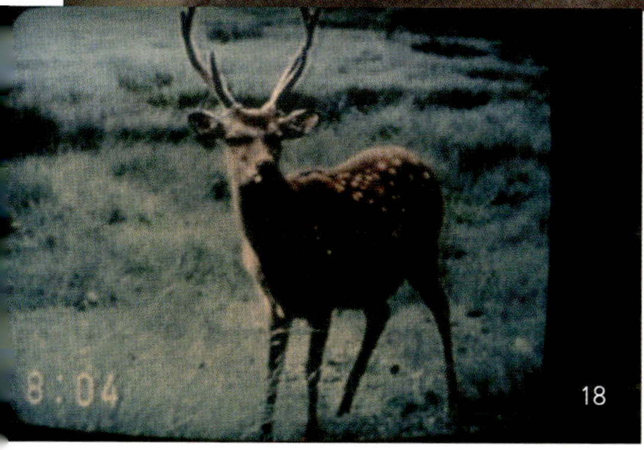

18

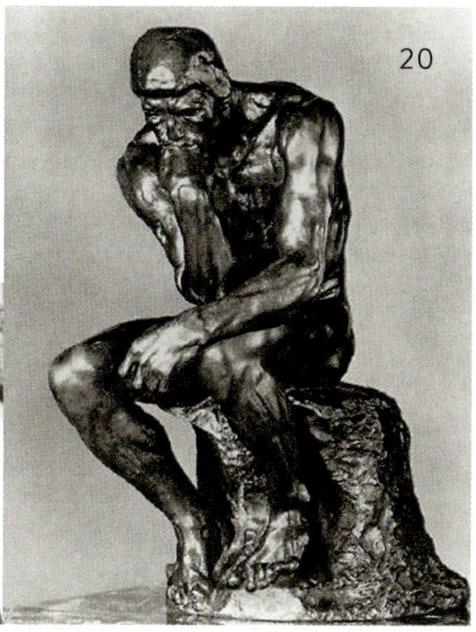

20

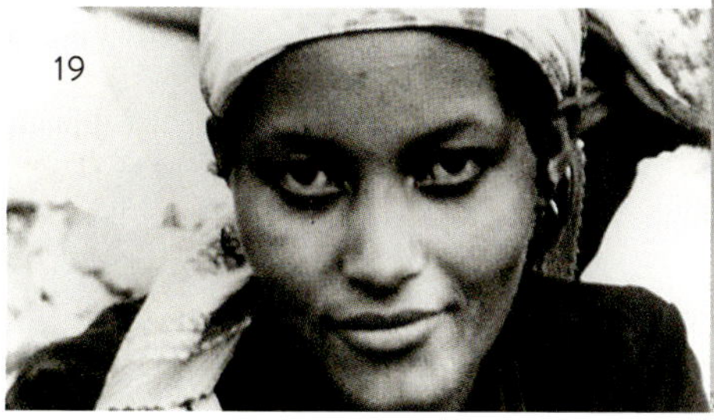

19

1+5 Dying Gaul
2, 6, 9, 10, 13, 18, 19 Chris Marker, Sans Soleil, Filmstills
3+17 Barberini Faun
4 Michelangelo Buonarroti, Pietà
7 Titian, Allegory of Prudence
8 August Rodin, Gates of Hell, The Thinker, detail
11+12 Gian Lorenzo Bernini, Apollo and Daphne
14 Alfred Hitchcock, Vertigo, Hair knot
15 Martin Honert, Flying Classroom
16 Matthias Grünewald, Isenheim Altar, detail
20 August Rodin, The Thinker

SCULPTURE AS PICTURE – COMPOSITE SCULPTURES 2004 TO 2006

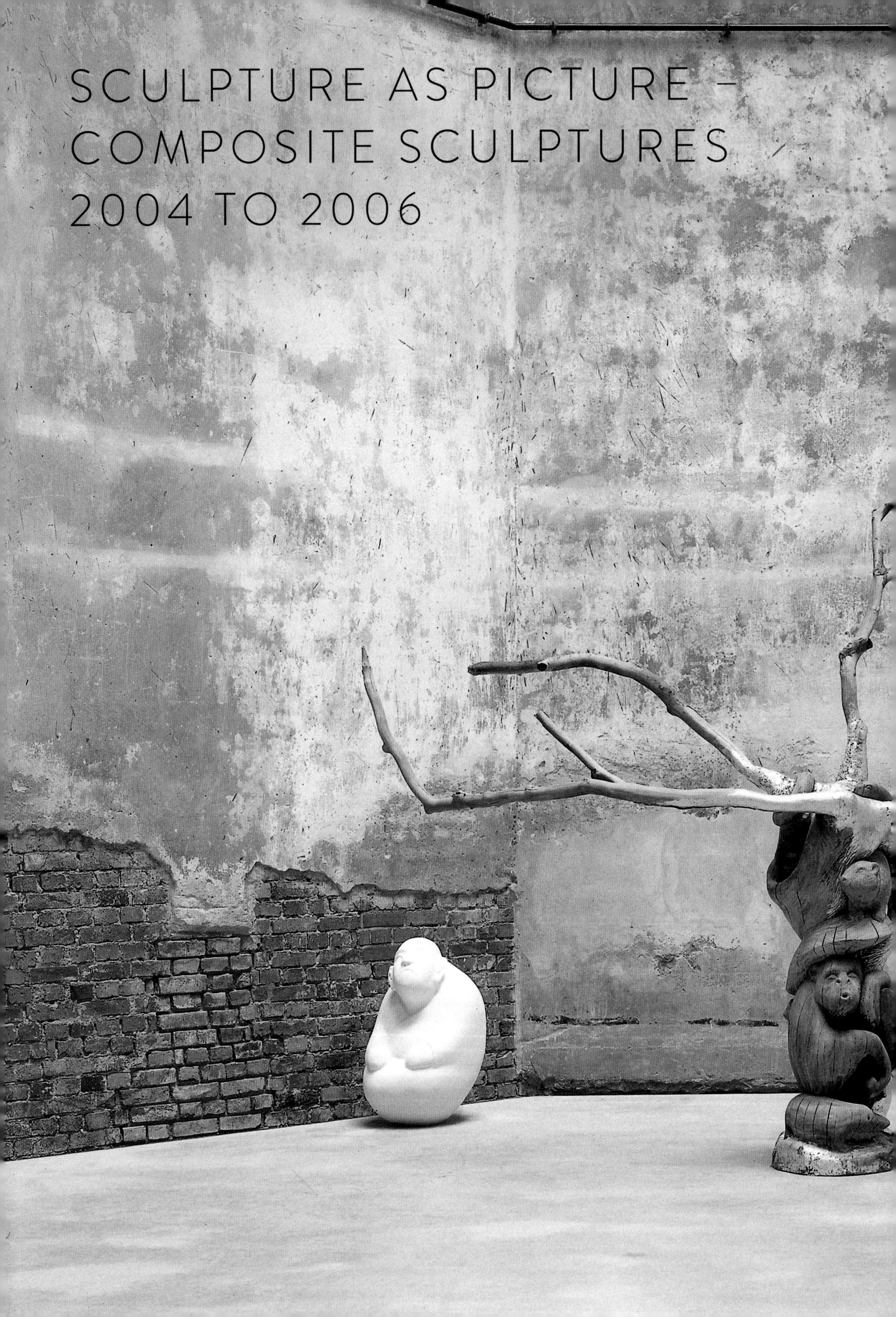

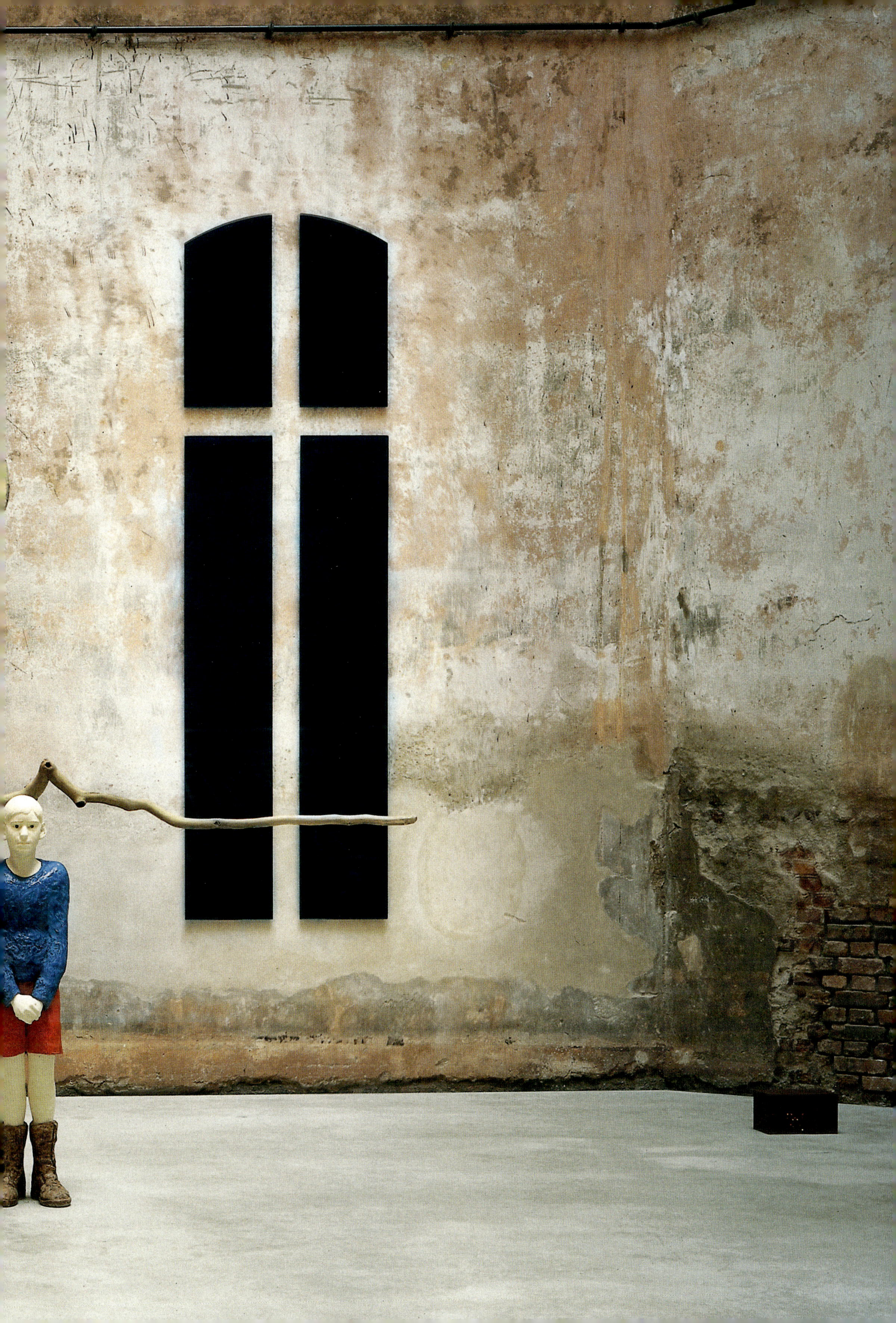

The sculptural ensemble *Alexander*, presented in the framework of the graduate exhibition at Dresden's Hochschule für bildende Künste in 2004, serves as an exemplary introduction to the sculptural work of Stella Hamberg. With its variety of techniques, it illustrates the broad range of expressive forms available to the young artist even then – from the virtuosic carving of expansive wood sculpture to various casting techniques with different materials, surface modelling and colours and degrees of abstraction, to the creation of a large stage set using these highly varied elements. To the unsuspecting visitor to the exhibition in the school's Oktogon on the Brühl Terrace, it was perhaps readily apparent that the sculptural installation had been produced by a student of Martin Honert. The somewhat sheepish boy standing in short pants in the centre recalls similar seemingly isolated figures of Honert's on the theme of childhood and childhood memories, for example *Foto* (Photo) from 1993 or *Mutprobe (Fliegendes Klassenzimmer)* (Test of Courage [Flying Classroom]) from 1999. The practice of constructing a "picture" out of several sculptures also has parallels in Honert's work, which also encompasses figural groupings, occasionally composed of people and animals with individual theatrical props, for example *Ein szenisches Modell des Fliegenden Klassenzimmers* (A Scenic Model of the Flying Classroom) from 1995. The symbol-laden combination of Alexander – a candelabrum, a Buddhist pupil, a window, a chest, and a small, grotesque figural carousel hidden in the tree-shaped candelabrum – could tempt one to interpret this and later works by the young artist mainly on the basis of their motifs. But this is only one aspect, among others of equal importance, of later works by Stella Hamberg as well, which are more or less clearly focused on the human figure or creatures of nature.

Among these other aspects is the fact that one's perception of the individual sculptures changes depending on whether they are considered alone or as an ensemble, that is, when the focus of one's gaze changes – here in *Alexander* just as in the later bronze groupings *Berserkers* or *ghost light*. Relatedness and estrangement, merging and isolation, are balanced in various ways, though in the early works like *Alexander* the heterogeneous and composite are more obvious than in the later bronzes. Around the boy's figure are grouped symbols of worldviews which on a formal level function as commentaries on the most varied sculptural traditions – from the classical marble statue to the *objet trouvé* or Conceptual art. The boy is equally tense and immobile in posture and gaze. The sculptor has clothed this figure made of artificial marble in thick, garish garments, a sweater, short pants, and tall boots; the concept of the idealising marble figure has been pursued ad absurdum, yet there is an echo of it in the smooth, light flesh tone. Such contrasts between figures and their thick, sometimes grotesque costumes are seen in single sculptures and groupings from the following years, for example in *Abel* (2005), *with or without you* (2006), *Lawrence – end of time* (2006), or *Malik* (2006); this sense of a figure being peeled out of its casing still plays a role even in the three monumental bronze *Berserkers* (2007).

The Buddhist pupil, made of styrofoam, assumes a reassuring egg shape, but he is obviously frustrated in his search for wisdom. At the other end of the sculptural ensemble stands a small wooden chest. Light from within shining through tiny holes in the side make it sparkle like a miniature starry sky. With the boy's private chest the artist was expressly not alluding to Martin Honert's *Laterne* (2000) – a cube lighted from within, which from different perspectives shows a man who from his sickbed observes Earth from space on television, while the starry sky above him forms the ceiling of his sickroom. One should also not interpret the Buddhist pupil as a deliberate take-off of the egg shape in Constantin Brancusi. Yet already in *Alexander* there are qualities in the work of Stella Hamberg, in her dealing both with meanings on the level of motifs and with earlier conceptions of sculpture, that can easily be overlooked in view of the passion that appears with such vehemence in the bronzes of the *Berserkers*, namely intellectual reflection, wit, and a sense of the grotesque.

Alexander's world is not yet exhausted, however, for it also includes the dimension of Christian tradition. The cross appears in the work in two ways: in sober, Protestant form in the mullions of the tall Gothic "window" of dark-blue acrylic, and in a sensual Catholic form in the twisted figure of the "candelabrum" with its branches extending out into space like outsize deer antlers. Like a medieval sculpture originally gilt, this element exhibits gilding that has seemingly largely flaked off over the course of the centuries – and with it the theme of time and the history of ideas. The question *Quo vadis?* (Where are you going?) is asked not only of the boy, who stands rooted in the centre of the arrangement between various offered paths to wisdom and truth, but obviously also of the sculptor.

Although later works distance themselves from the programmatic work of this graduate exhibition and reveal completely different possibilities, many core elements of the artist's subsequent oeuvre are already present in *Alexander*. Thematically, these include the ambitious claim of dealing in her work with fundamental questions of human existence. From the beginning, she has examined existential issues, the situation of the individual in his/her surroundings, the observer's subjective internal and external views, questions of philosophical reasoning and religion, and not least the relationship between human and creature and the friction between mind and body.

The desire to give convincing form to the interaction of mind and body is to some extent the fundamental theme of Stella Hamberg's work in sculpture, with which – and this is more clearly apparent in retrospect than it was in 2004 – she distinctly set herself apart from patterns in the work of her teacher Martin Honert even in her thesis project. In his works from the turn of the millennium, which frequently suggest enlarged toy figures, he concentrates above all on the artist's psychic self-awareness, and possibly that of the viewer as well, who shares with him similar experiences and memories. By contrast, from the beginning Hamberg brings into play a wholly new intensity of physical form and immediacy of configuration. This is most clearly evident in the central sculpture, the cross-shaped "candelabrum," a seemingly ancient, knaggy spiral-shaped tree, whose leafless branches quietly flail about in much the same way as the large bronze statues the *Berserkers* would three years later in a wholly different form. This tree is densely inhabited by numerous exotic animals, from duck-billed platypus to whale, from serpent to ape. At the same time, the well-fed creatures appear to call into question the existence of the tree, which is obviously their home. In medieval art we occasionally see rodents at the foot of a tree as symbols of the transient and of earthly time as opposed to eternity, as in the story of the carefree man nibbling honey from the medieval legend *Barlaam and Josaphat*. In Hamberg, the creatures form a symbiosis with the twisted tree that shelters them – all this in sculptural forms of extraordinary intensity, expansive force, and sensuality. Here the tree of life with its barren branches to some extent wrestles with the creatures that lived off it and brought about its disintegration – the duality of growth and decay continues to be an important theme in the artist's later oeuvre. The "pictures" made up of several sculptures that followed *Alexander* are in their own way testament to the love of experimentation in Stella Hamberg's way of working. At first glance, they document the seemingly simple choice of the figure as the subject of sculpture. But on second glance, they initiate the sculptural formulation of contradictions that will become in the later works an ever more sophisticated method. Part of this – as already in *Alexander* – is the composition of figures in different materials.

Abel (2005) is one of the works whose motif derives from the artist's extended stay in Greenland in the year 2000. In contrast to the slippery creature that accompanies him, the shiny blue *Dämon II*, the boy Abel, with feet formed out of roughly carved limestone block, stands rooted to the ground. His legs and torso are made of a white plastic, while his archaic, traditional fur-trimmed trousers contrast with his sporty knitted jacket closed with a zipper. The world of natural man encounters modern industrial society, and vice versa. His head, in turn, is finely carved marble with coloured eyes. The immobility of his feet contradicts the pose of his hands, his left having already stripped off the fur glove from his right.

Abel's seal-like companion *Dämon II*, made of transparent blue plastic (polyurethane casting resin) literally dazzles; it exhibits a dynamic power similar to that of *Dämon I* (2004), the figure lumbering forward on its big paws. The latter resembles a piece of designer wooden furniture, but it too is made of plastic (polyester). Both figures are filled with animal passion and humour in equal measure. They were inspired in part by Inuit fetishes and amulets.

Among the major inspirations Stella Hamberg herself cites is Chris Marker's film *Sans Soleil* (1983), to which we will repeatedly refer. In a complex and suggestive sequence of documentary and electronically manipulated picture sequences, the film contrasts everyday and ritual life in Japan, poverty in Guinea-Bissau, and the fragile idyll in Iceland and France. Different conceptions and observations of time and place, of civilisation and nature, loosely confront each other, but not without connections between them. Among them are the death of a giraffe shot while running free, video games and mangas, rituals at a cat temple in Tokyo, the poplar-ringed tomb monument of Jean-Jacques Rousseau, the stream of seemingly dozing people on ferries and in suburban trains, a village in Iceland largely buried under volcanic ash, and the leitmotif of intense gazes – often as film stills from Japanese films to Hitchcock's *Vertigo* (1958).

A key moment in this film is the fraction of a second in which the cameraman manages to capture a woman in Guinea-Bissau gazing directly at the camera, an extremely brief, direct contact between subject and viewer. The gaze, as a motif either mediating between inner and outer world or not, plays an important role especially in Hamberg's early figures, but also in the *Berserkers* and other later works as well – much as one might see the way figures are being peeled out of enclosing layers of material as a contemporary variant of Michelangelo's notion of freeing the figure from its surrounding block of marble.

Variations on the motif of the gaze are numerous. They range from the piercing gaze from *Alexander*'s button eyes to the closed eyes of *Quinten* (2005). Wide open, but at the same time protected by mask-like makeup and depersonalised, are the eyes of *Tatú – for no reason* (2004). In most of the figures from this phase, the eyes are wide open and visible, with sharply outlined lids, as also in *Abel* (2005), yet they signal the difficulty these people have entering into contact with the viewer – and vice versa. One can understand this iconographically, on the level of motif. The theme of the caught, missed, or absent-mindedly not even sought-after gaze also defines the relationship between artwork and viewer, creating room for associations.

A transition in her other works is provided by *over and out* (2007), produced for the Hans Joachim Sander Collection, Hamberg's first large-format sculptural ensemble in bronze. The apocalyptic scene takes up elements of the previous ensembles of multiple figures and motifs: a rugged young man, standing between petrol cans, and a dying steer lying on the ground (a motif included in Chris Marker's film *Sans Soleil*), next to which a young girl is kneeling. As though in the last scene of a tragic play, the group of figures exhibits a distinct pathos. What is new is a greater uniformity in the overall sculptural form, achieved by the choice of bronze as a material, which in part eliminates, for example, the distinction in motif between the figures and their clothing. Quite apart from the subject matter, the combination of a standing, a kneeling, and a recumbent figure is interesting as a three-dimensional assignment, and the modelling of the steer in crude lumps of clay combines more strongly than in the earlier works the evocation of an object with the sculptural form speaking for itself.

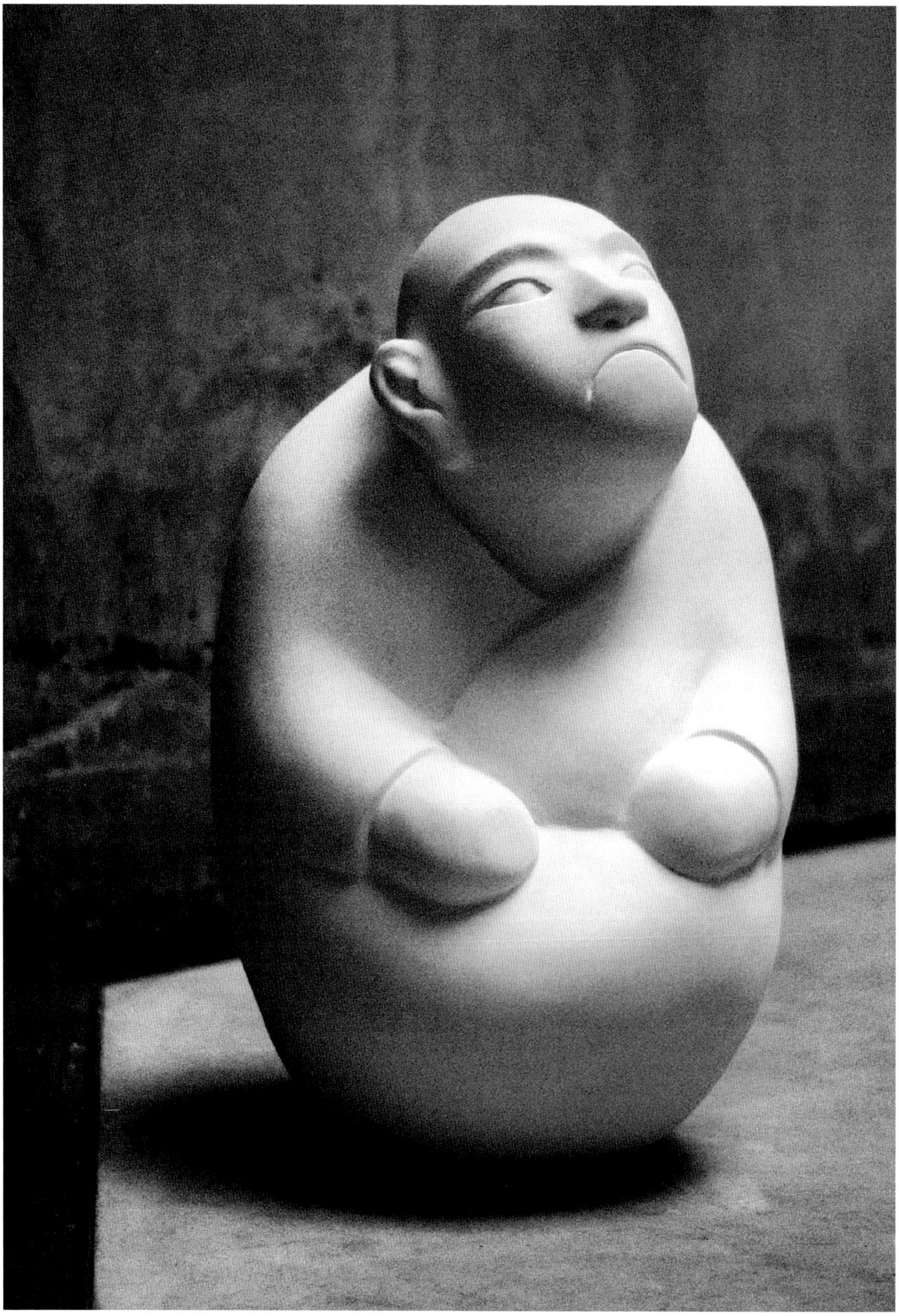

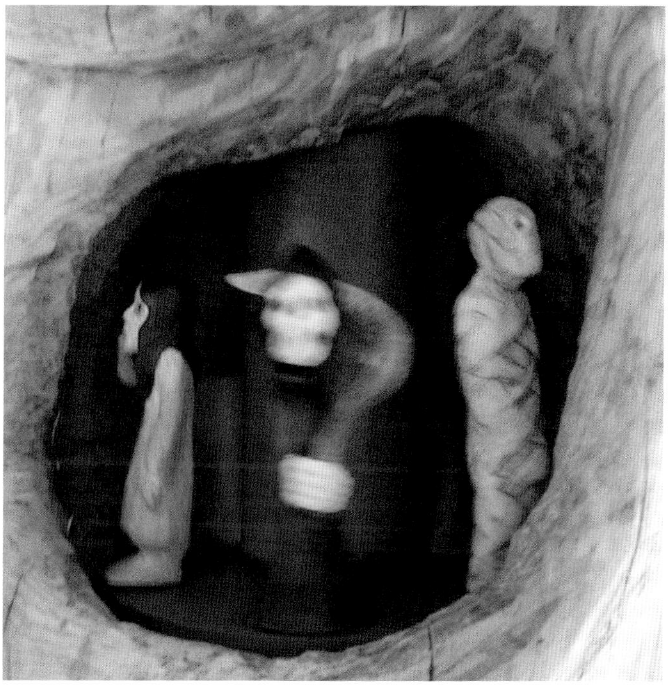

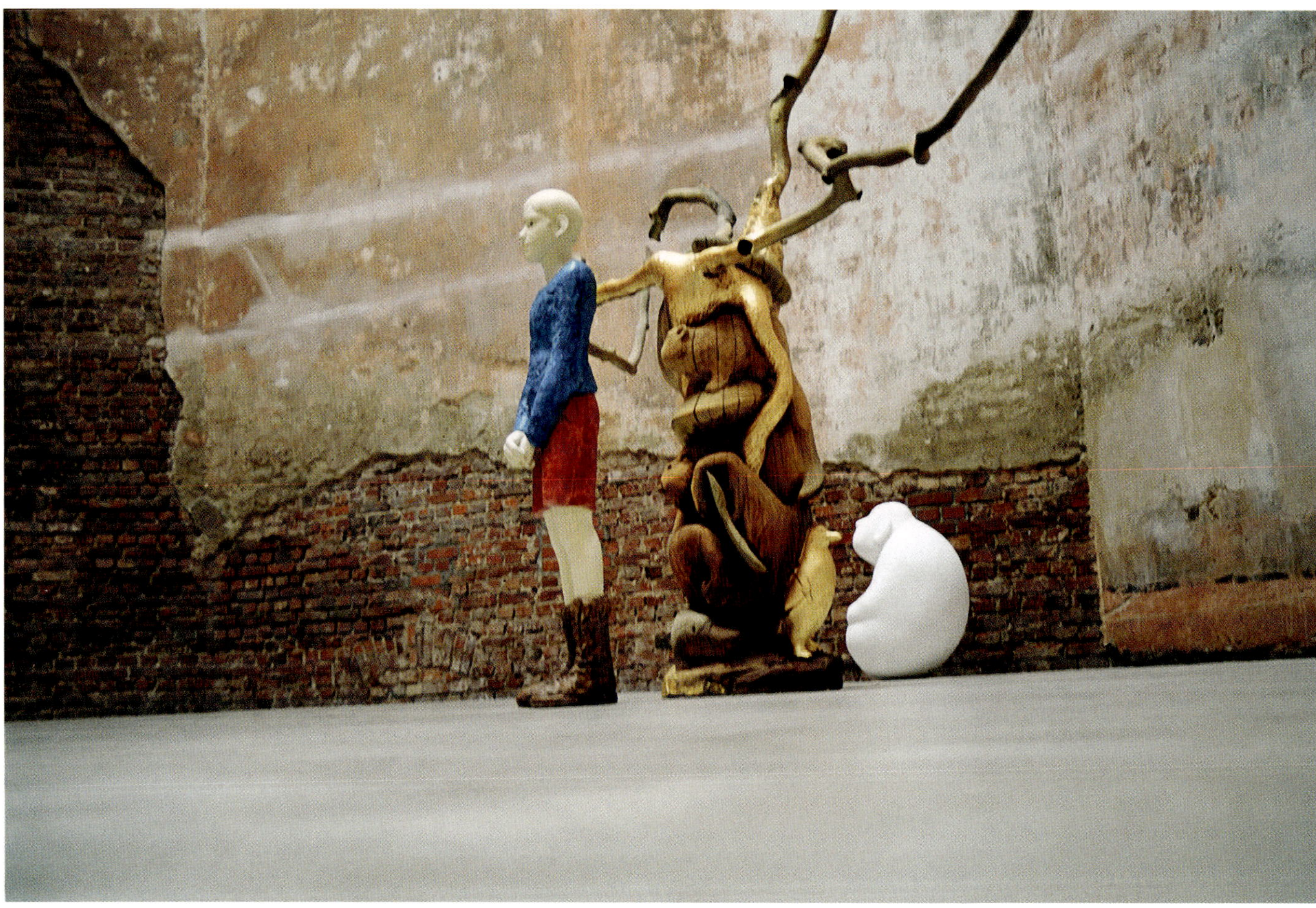

Maria 2005

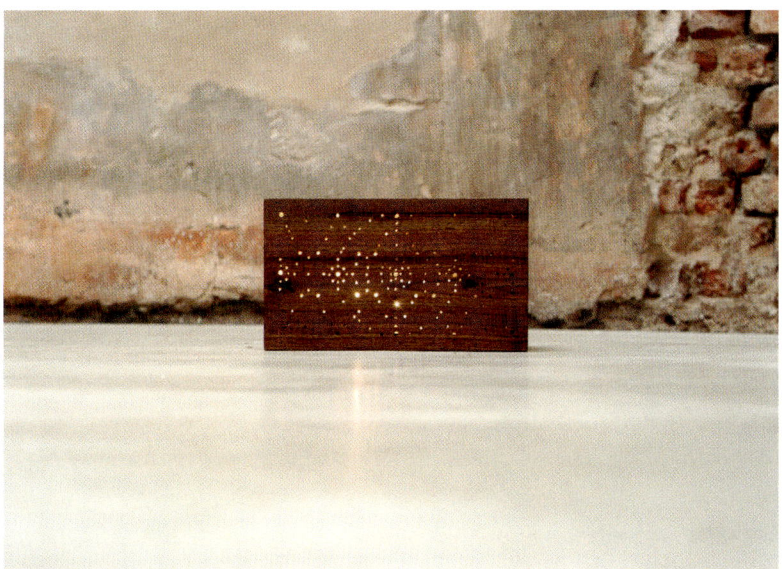

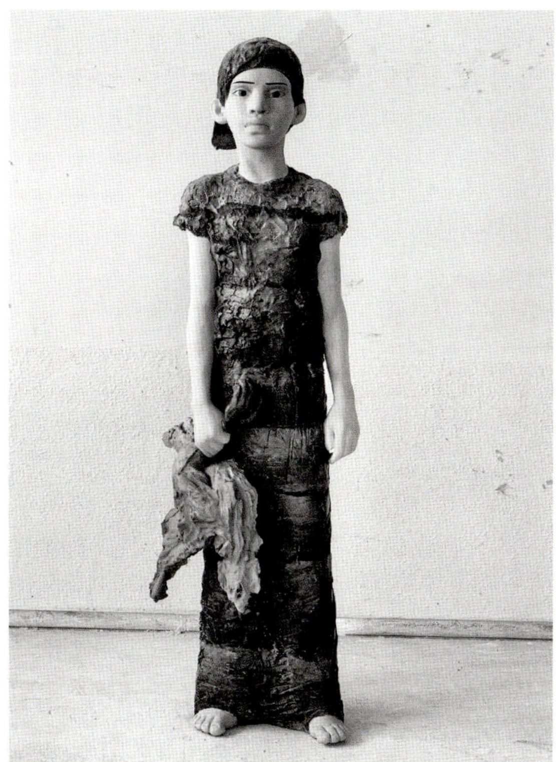

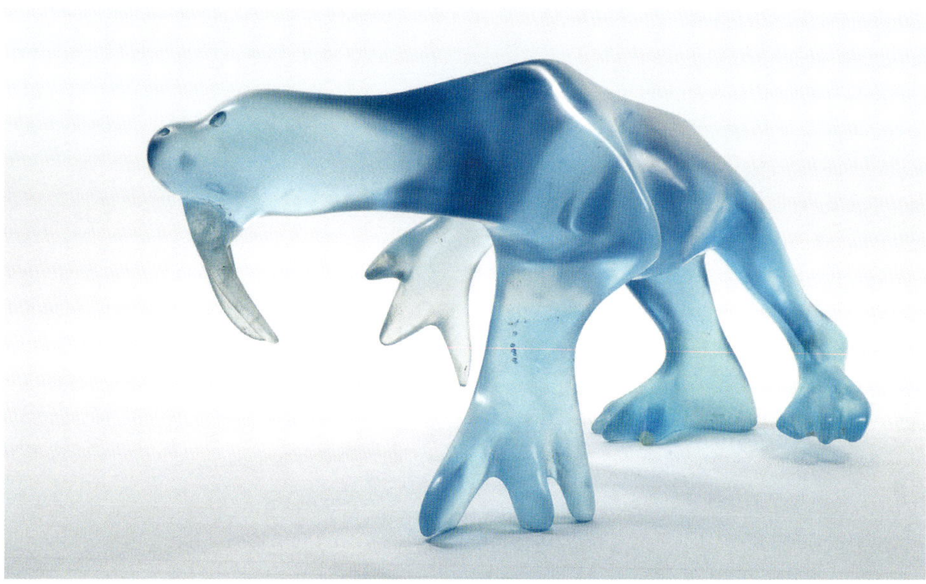

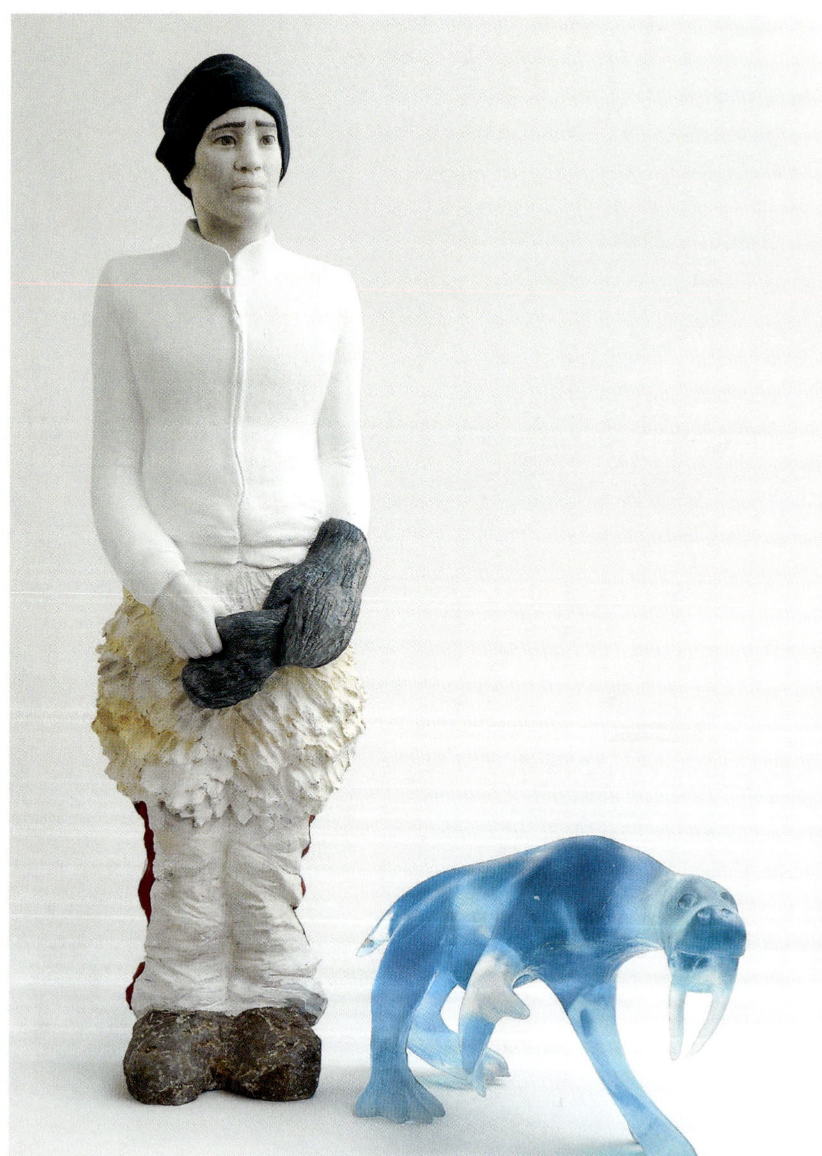

Dämon – the simplicity of a ghost-like beast 2004

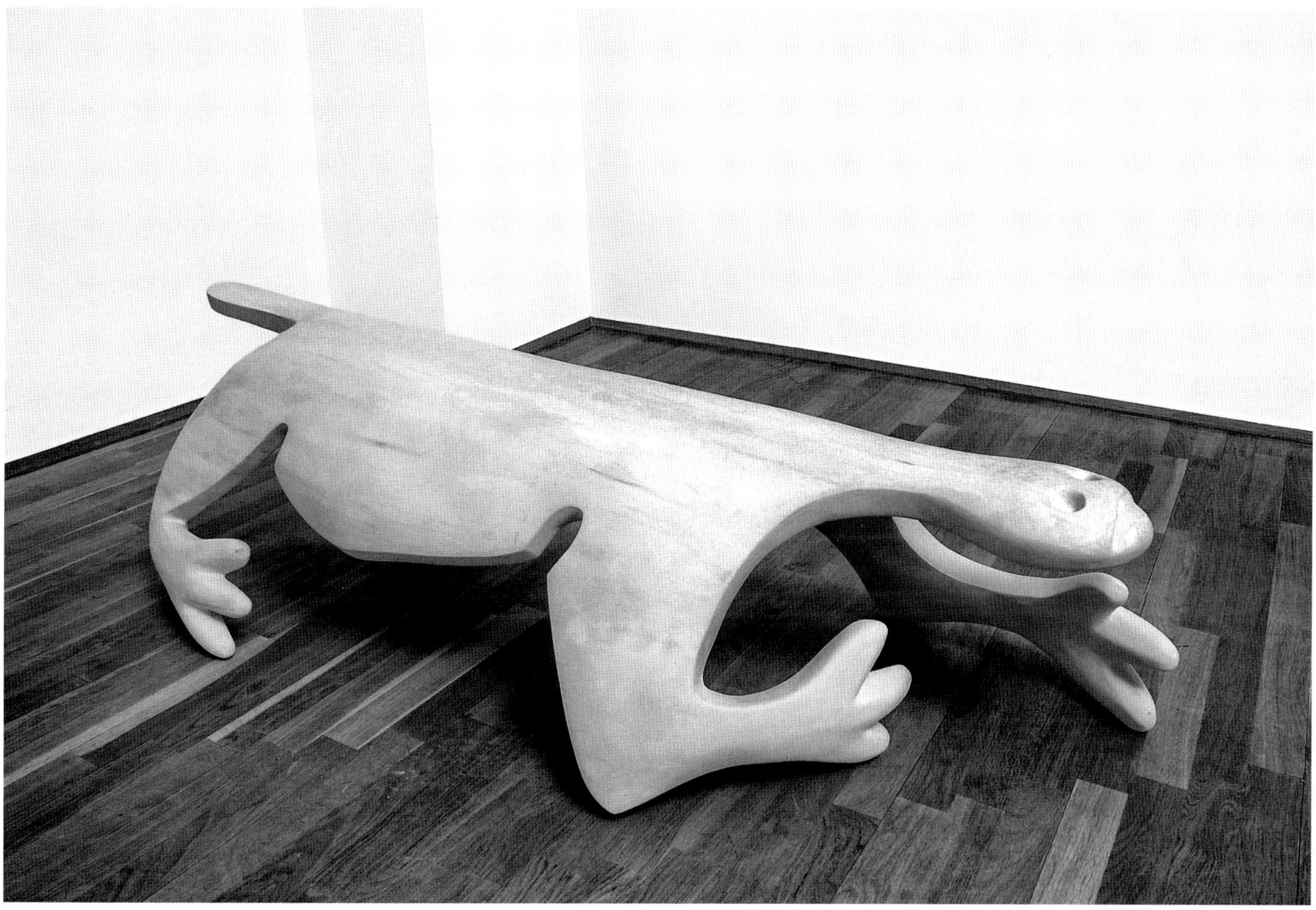

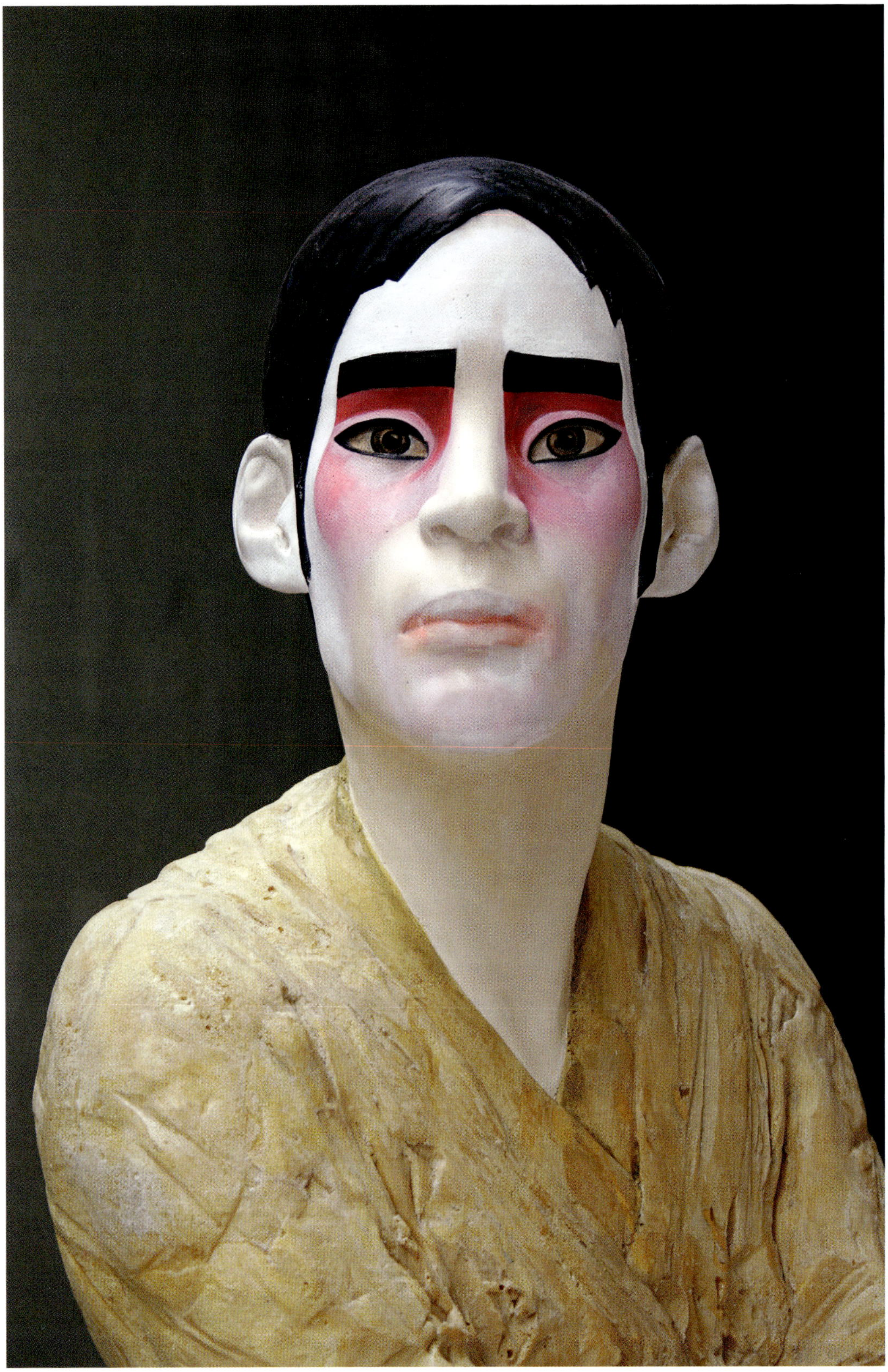

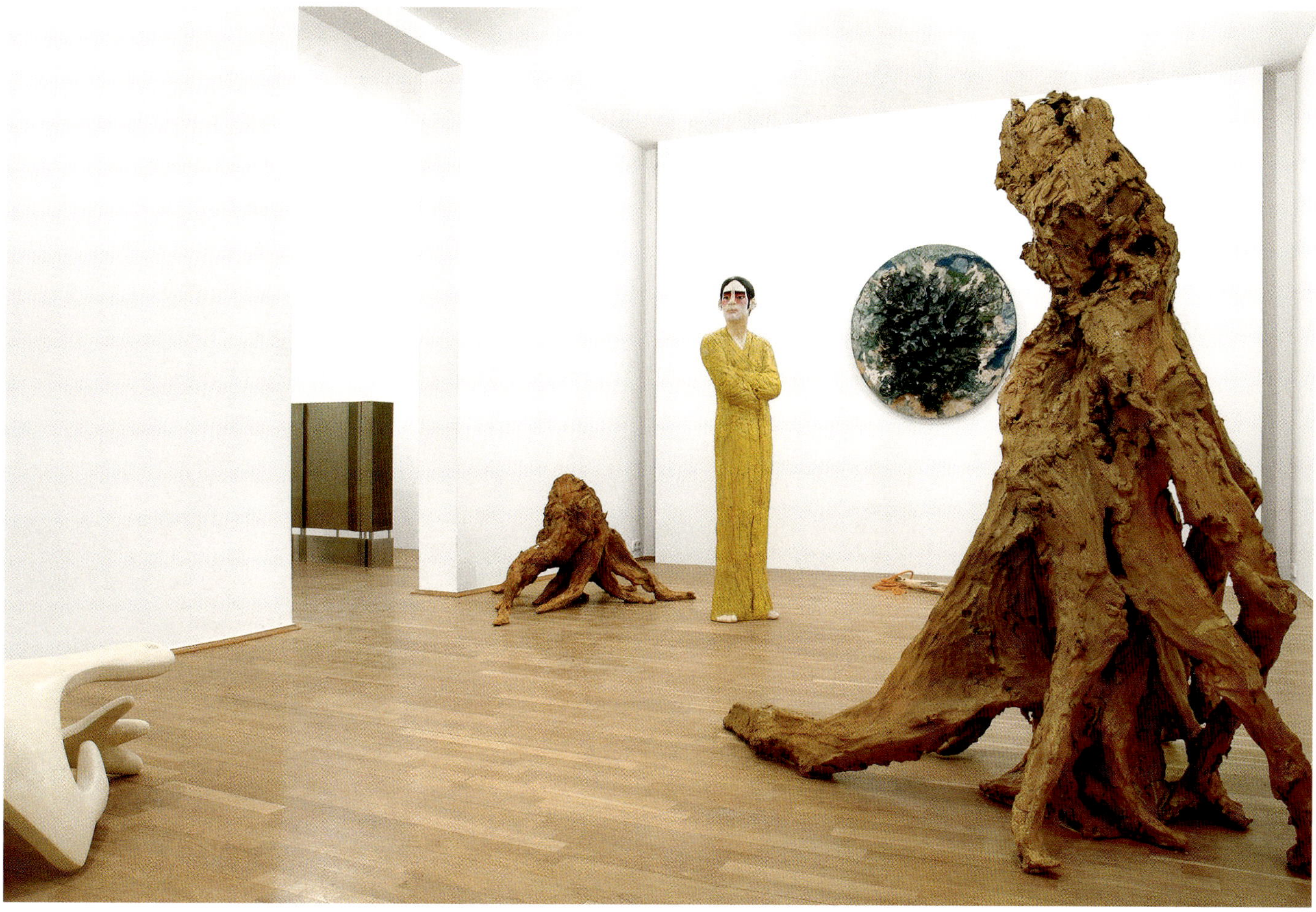

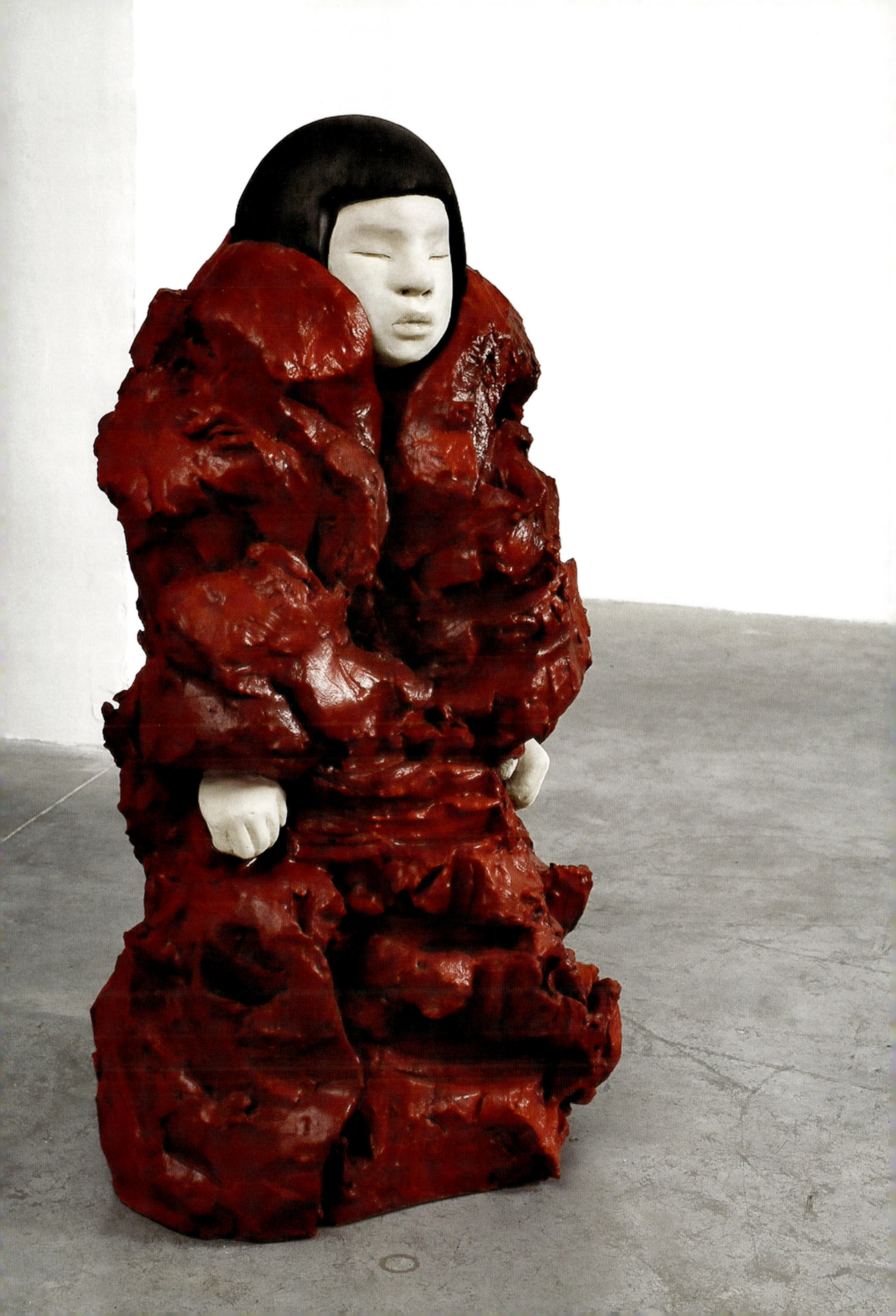

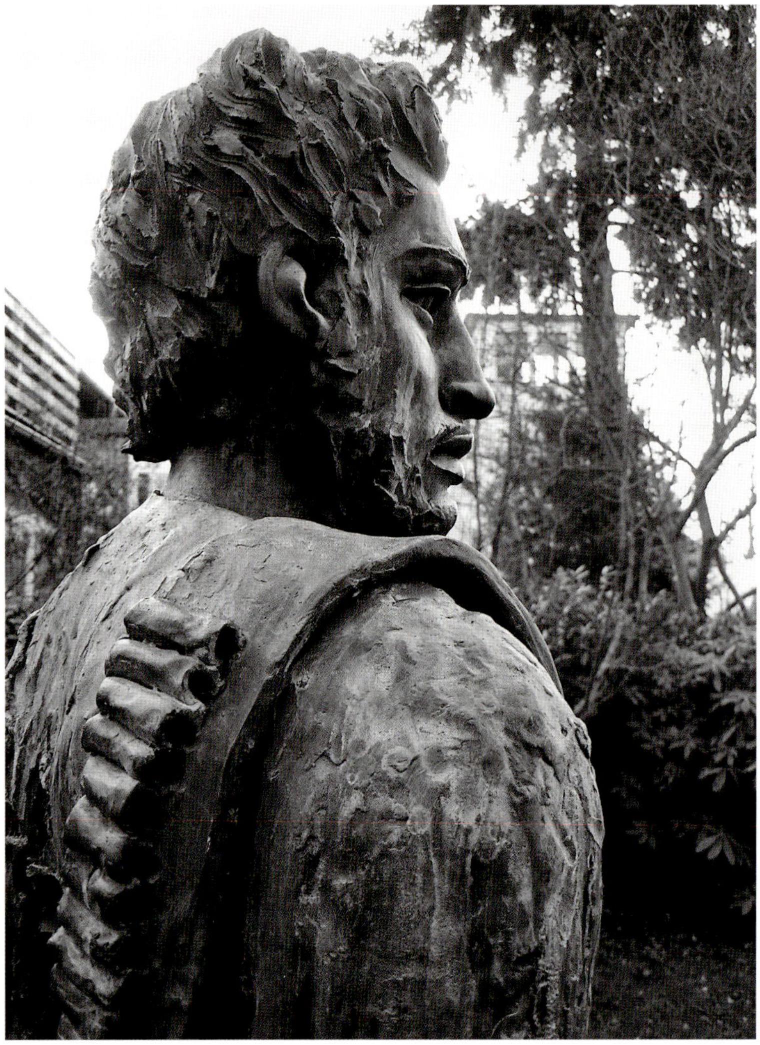

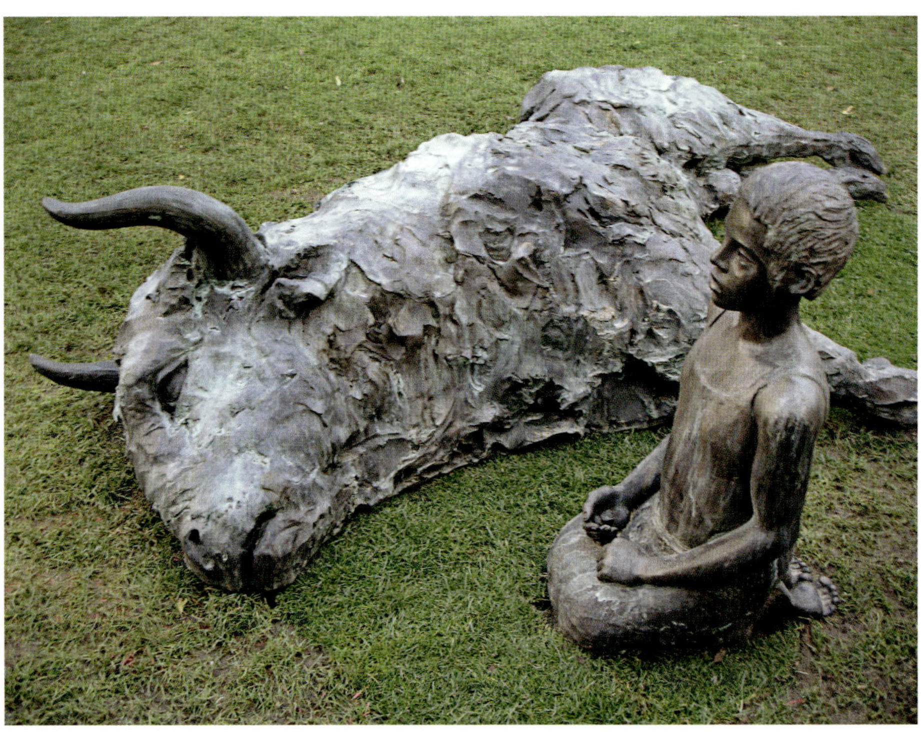

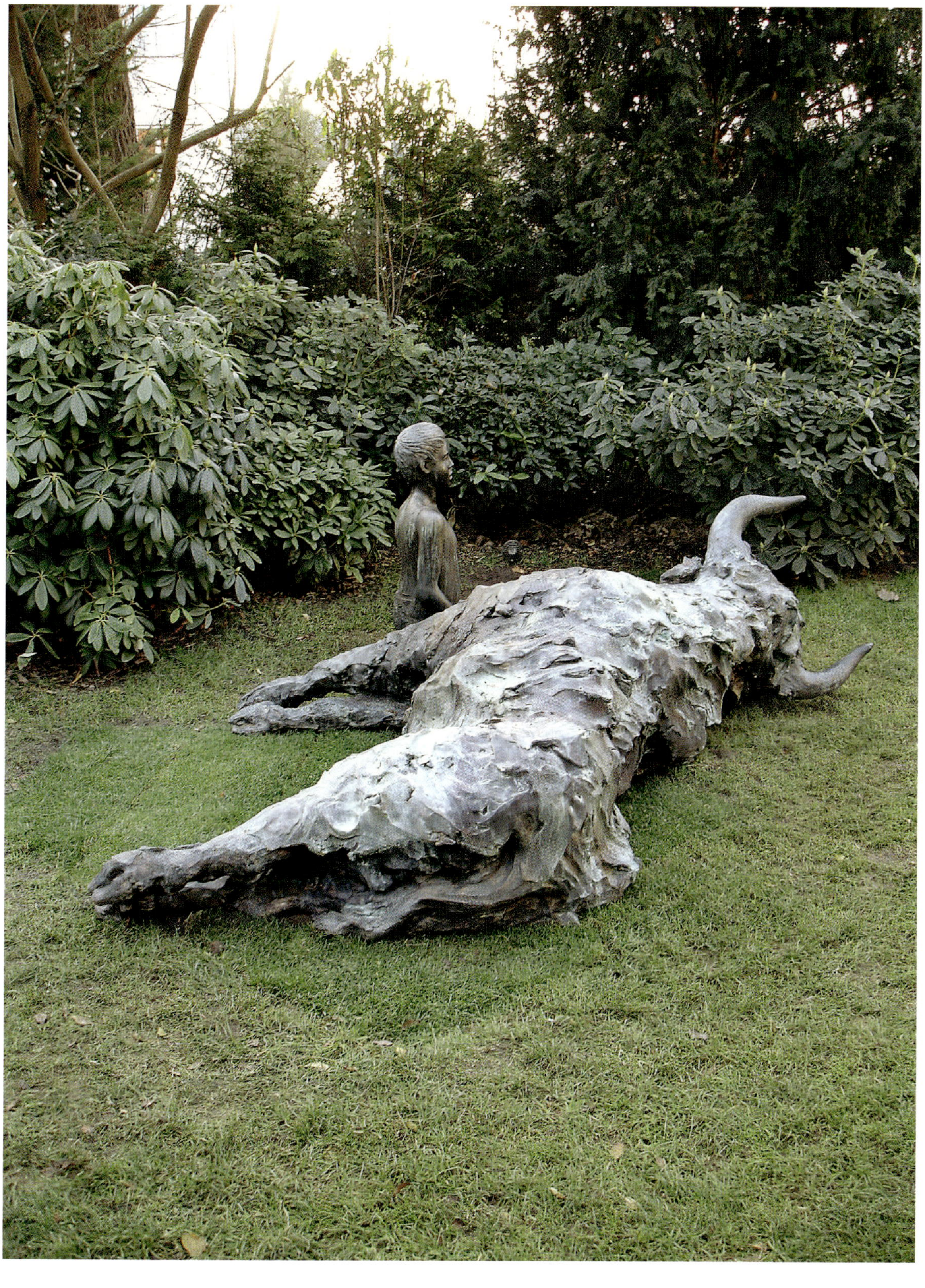

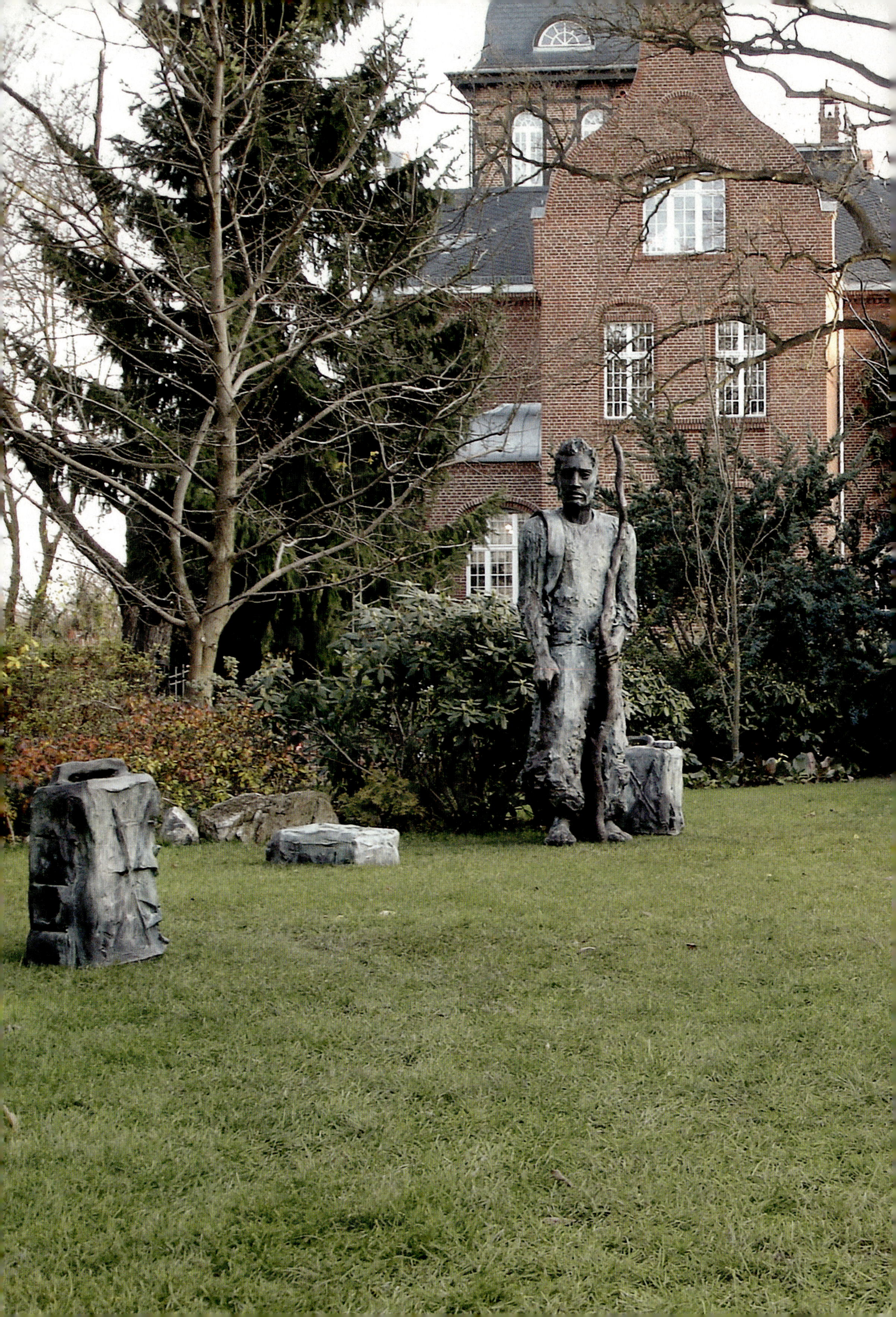

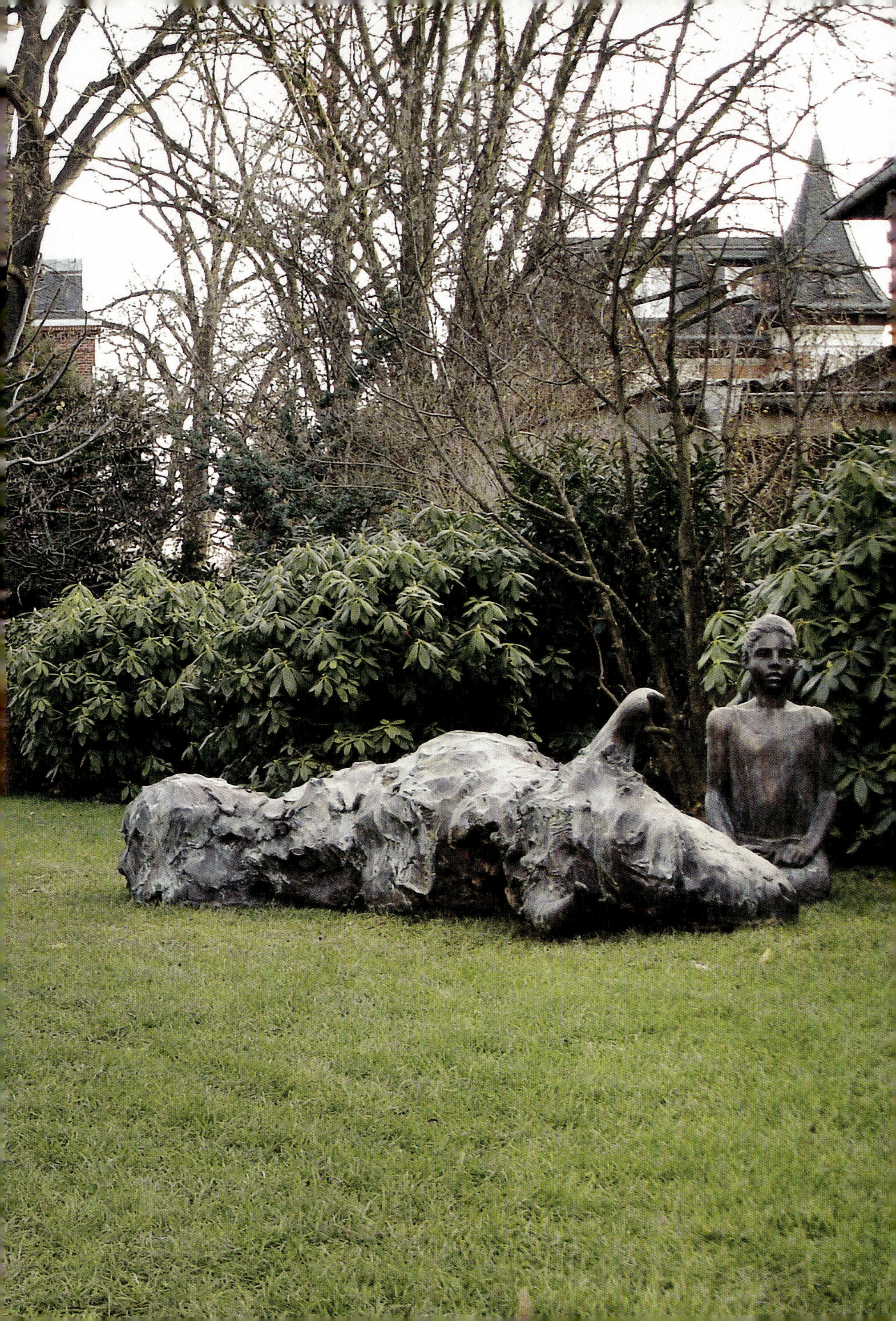

MOVEMENT AND STASIS, METAMORPHOSIS AS THE ESSENCE OF SHAPE

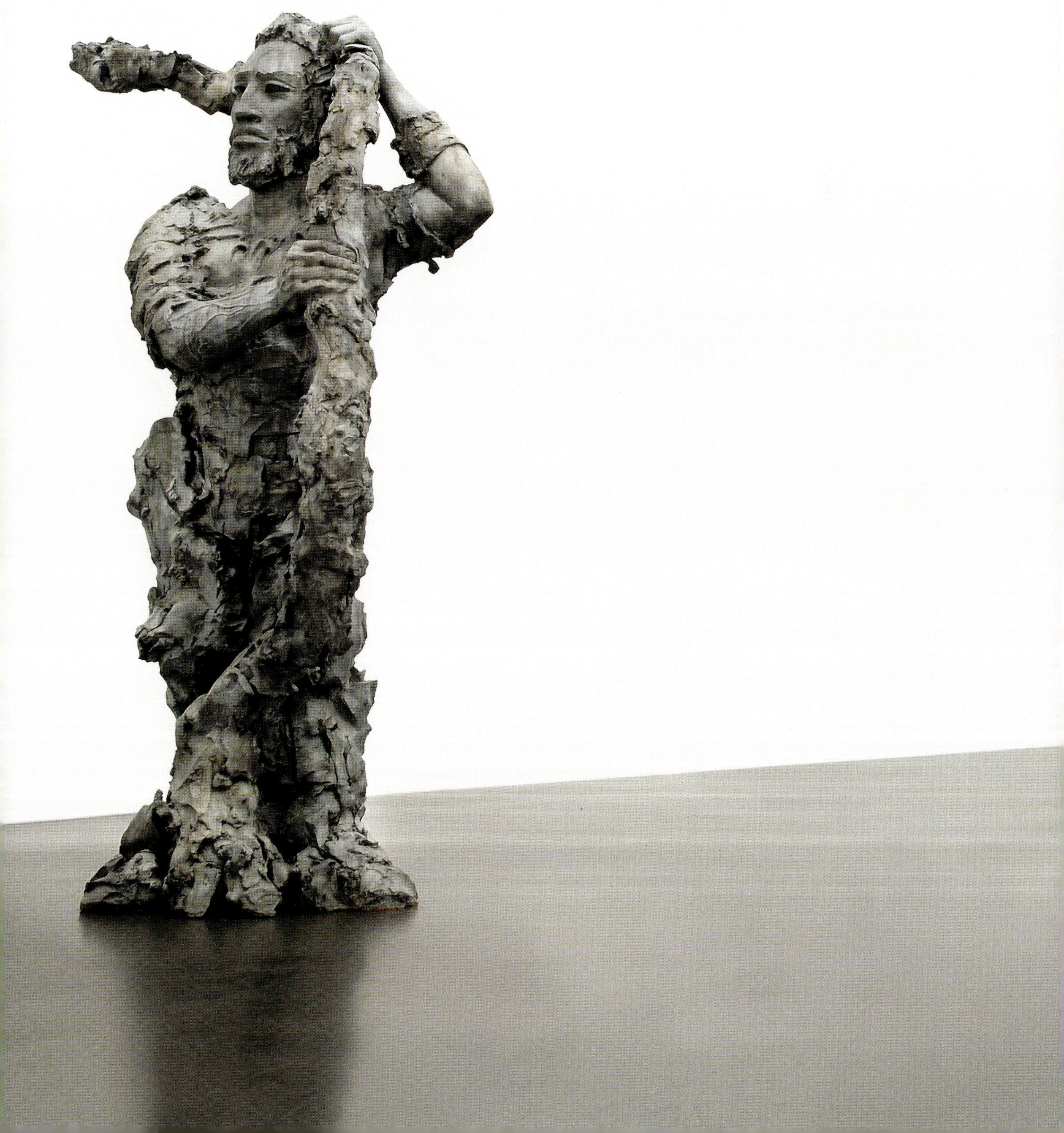

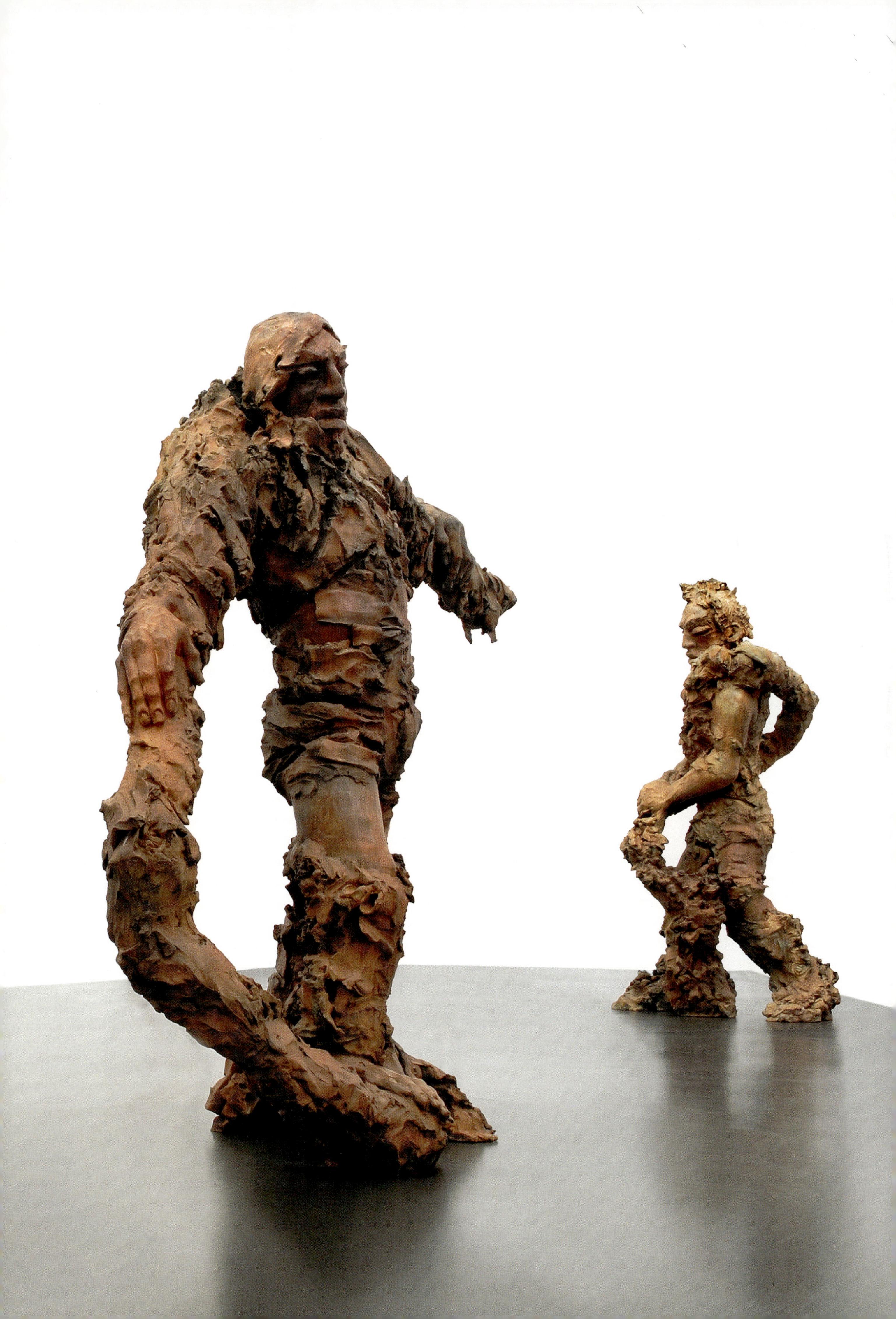

The group of powerful, larger-than-life *Berserkers* (2007/08) marks a new stage in Hamberg's work. Approaching them in person, one can hardly escape the impression of strength and of vigorous movement reflective of a troubled spirit. They appear to be muscular, to some extent continuously peeling themselves out of a mud-like substance and brandishing huge branches or serpents. It is unclear whether they are trying to free themselves from them or to flail about with them. The ambiguity of their actions, and with it an undefined aspect of their inner being, are essential features of the narrative.

When viewed as a trio, their jerky movements merge as though to the rhythm of a ritual dance. Each figure reveals still other individual rhythms as one walks around it. None of the *Berserkers* directly relates to another, their moments being performed as though in a trance. The theme of the figure's isolation and its relationship to outsiders – whether the two other *Berserkers* or the viewer – here attains a new intensity. Depending on one's point of view, the figures also suddenly stand still, only to take up the interrupted movement once again as one continues to look at them.

It is not a matter of course that one can indeed view the *Berserkers* from the most varied perspectives and in doing so appreciate different qualities and characteristics of the figures. In most phases of its history, sculpture was designed to be seen from a view point, or only a few, even when placed freely in space. Late Renaissance sculptors like Giambologna and Adriaen de Vries developed sculptures that could be admired from all sides, mainly as a demonstration of their artistic virtuosity in competition with painting. Whether with a spiral-shaped single figure, or *figura serpentinata*, or intertwined groups of multiple figures as in the theme of the Rape of the Sabine Women, it was a matter of developing sculptures that were equally interesting from every angle, without necessarily making different thematic statements. With the motif of the bent branch or vine brandished by the *Berserkers*, Hamberg employs a trick much like the sculptors of Mannerism as a way of creating a sculpture interesting from every viewpoint. But unlike those of the Mannerists, her figures have a slightly different character from each new perspective, seem more dynamic or more lethargic, more introverted or more extroverted. They are constantly changing, yet in another way always the same, as one might expect of a bronze statue. Part of the fascination of these figures and of their meaning surely derives from this alternation between animated metamorphosis and constancy.

With her move to working in bronze, features such as the fashionable or clunky pieces of clothing, accessories, tattoos, etc. that immediately attracted the viewer's attention in the earlier figures fall away in favour of the overall three-dimensional form. The sculptor's decision to create three monumental bronzes was both courageous and ambitious. Bronze was sculpture's first artificial material, produced in the smelting process out of copper and tin, and because it was created through fire out of other materials, since antiquity it has been considered an expression of eternity. It was the radiance and energy of the material that led Stella Hamberg to choose it. At the same time, it was a practical, formal decision, for no other material can reproduce the finest modelling, even a fingerprint, as sharply and precisely through the processes of creating a mould from the clay model, producing a wax positive, and then making the final casting. With their material and dimensions alone, Hamberg places these aggressive yet self-defeating figures in the great tradition of bronze statues associated since antiquity with representations of gods, rulers, saints, and intellectual heroes, and also, since Auguste Rodin's *Thinker* or his *Burghers of Calais*, with allegorical interpretations of human existence. One might relate the *Berserkers* to these latter works. As in her naming of other pieces, here the sculptures are not to be understood as illustrations of a theme supposedly indicated in the title; the title has simply been attached to the works the way one names a person. If one thinks of them as ancient Nordic warriors in bearskins, then the foreignness modern civilisation would see in them is also illustrated – a theme already touched upon with the Old Testament name *Abel* – or, conversely, the fundamental constructive and destructive potential still inherent in man in his domesticated way of life, as a glance at the daily news confirms.

Rodin's *Thinker*, the isolated, larger-than-life central figure in the tympanum of the sculptor's *Gates of Hell*, was in its time a response to Michelangelo's world judge in the Sistine Chapel's *Last Judgement*. Whereas Michelangelo's Christ still had the power to raise up the blessed and cast down the damned, the hunkering *Thinker*, with his right elbow propped on his left knee, has no opportunity to employ his enormous muscular strength to any fruitful purpose. He still belongs to the type of monument exalting the Christian promise of salvation, yet is characterised by disappointment over his loss of faith in it – Ghiberti's *Gates of Paradise* have become the *Gates of Hell*, the resurrected figure a fallen and broken one.

These and other Rodin figures that so greatly influenced figural sculpture in the 20th century, especially in Germany, would be followed by two world wars, the Holocaust, and other horrors unimaginable to every rational and feeling person. If one considers the *Berserkers* as a monument to the man of our own time against this expansive background, they seem astonishingly optimistic, simply owing to their primal vitality and presence. It is checked by various motifs and formal features, yet unbroken by such constraints.

Even though Hamberg was not making an explicit reference to Rodin with the *Berserkers*, from an art-historical perspective they are related to the work of the great Frenchmen in another respect. If one leaves aside the *non finito* in Michelangelo, Rodin was the first sculptor to expressly make the sculptor's creative process his subject matter, the modelling of forms as well as the cutting away and reduction in his works. This is also seen in Hamberg, perhaps even in a more elementary form than in Rodin, for all the innovation associated with his introduction of the torso alone as a fully valid sculpture, his figures, despite their animated surfaces, are incomparably more finished than those of the deeply fissured *Berserkers*.

One's perception of the *Berserkers* varies, depending on whether one contemplates them from a distance or up close. While from afar their surface is perhaps still reminiscent of an animal-hide garment, seen up close it is an impulsively animated and lacerated relief, one in which it is not always possible to distinguish between the body and the clothing. What one sees goes far beyond mere traces of expressively gestural modelling. To some extent the seething dynamism of the material causes permanent metamorphosis to become the figures' vital essence. The intellectual content of these figures is thus expressed in their heightened and highly differentiated materiality. In this they differ fundamentally from the mirroring surfaces that belie the physicality of Thomas Schütte's *Large Spirits* (2000), compared to which the *Berserkers* seem like an antithesis that vehemently demands the unity of physicality and spirit. Seen up close, especially *Berserker III* (2008), the metamorphosis of forms combines, in addition to wholly abstract elements, changes from anthropomorphic to vegetal shapes, and thus stands as a metaphor for the unity of Creation. This has been achieved only very rarely in the history of sculpture; one could cite the Parlers' console busts turning into foliage in Cologne's Schnütgen Museum and in Ulm Cathedral (14th century), or Gian Lorenzo Bernini's figural group *Apollo and Daphne* (1622–1625) in the Galleria Borghese in Rome.

Berserker II 2007

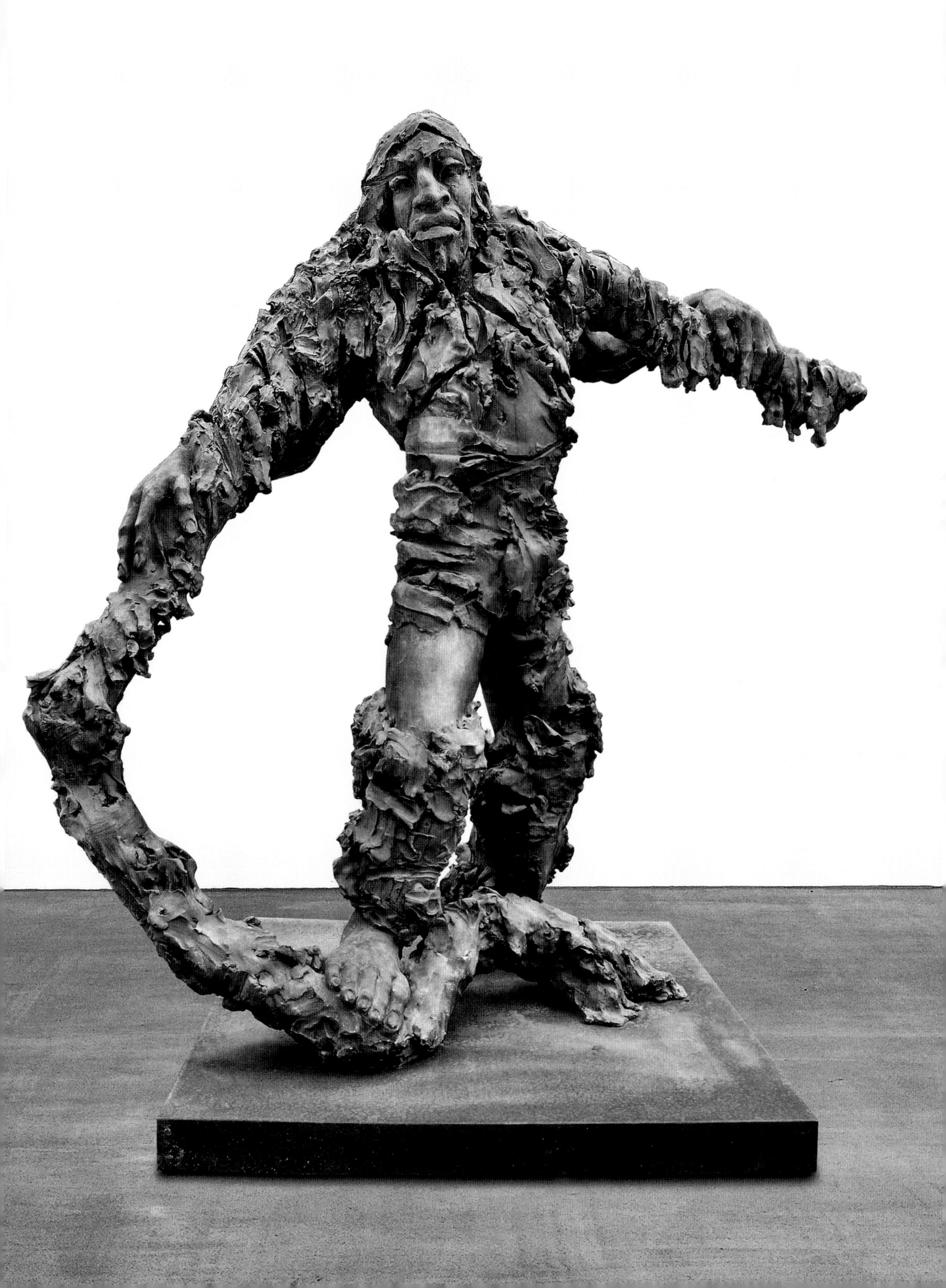

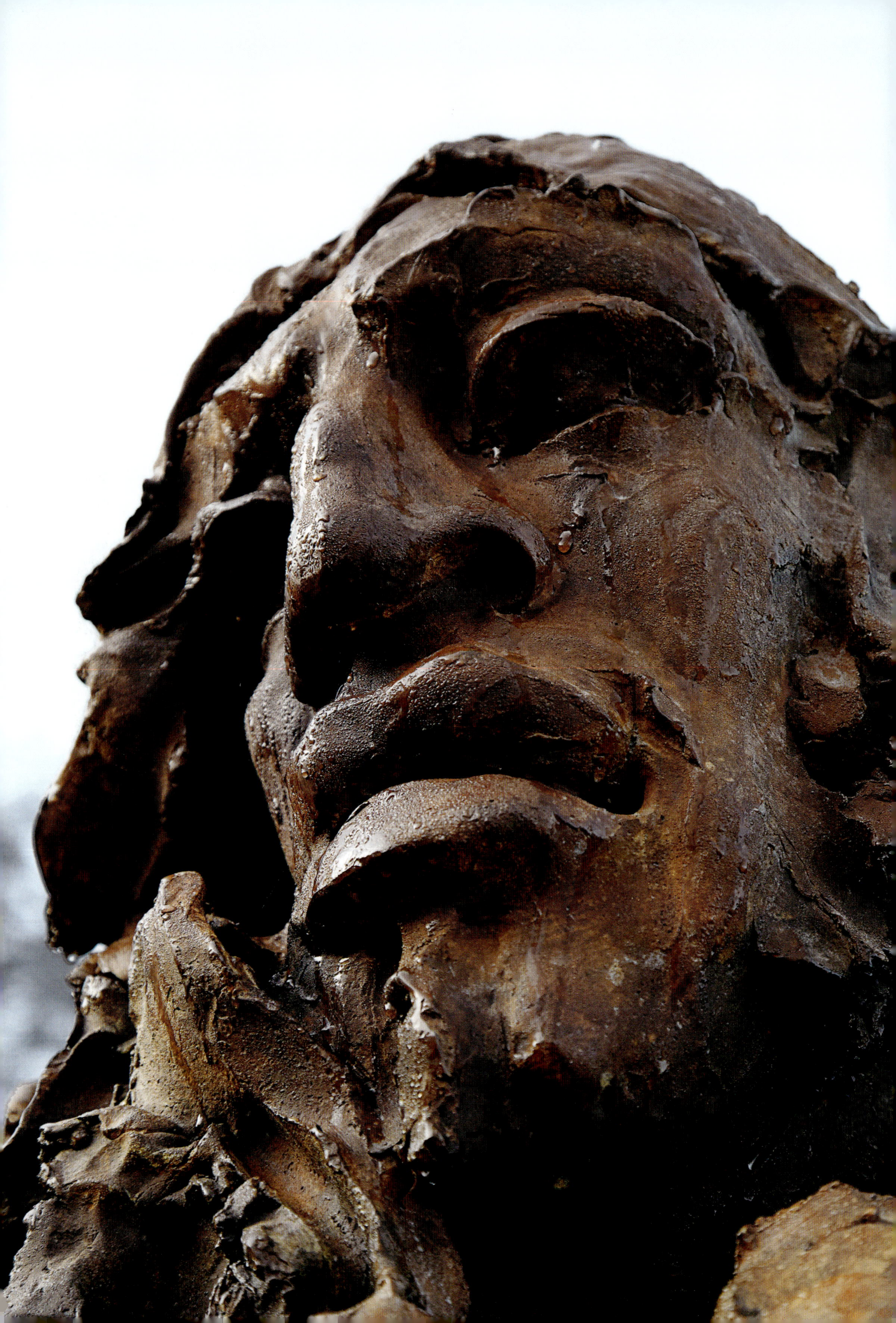

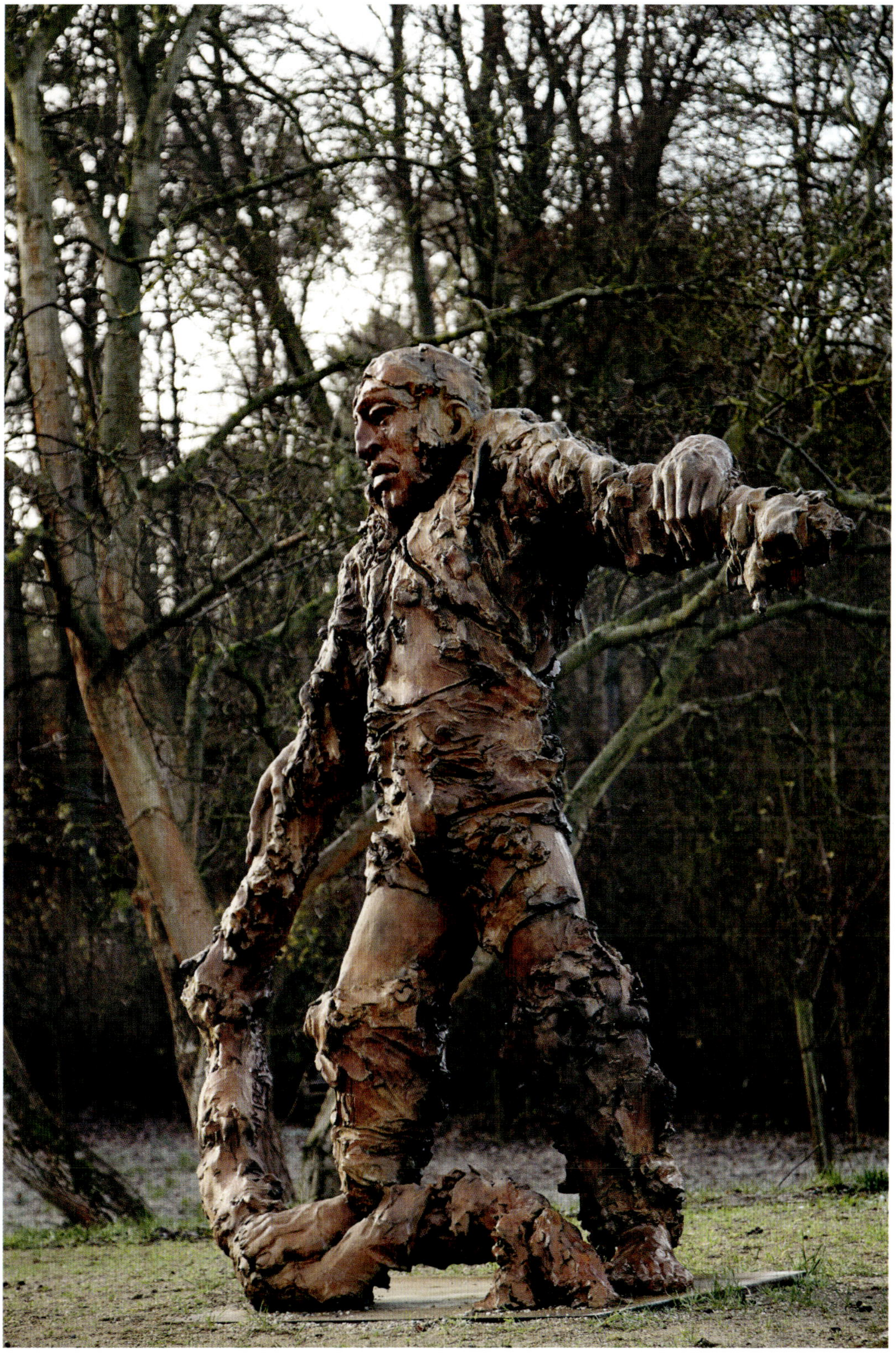

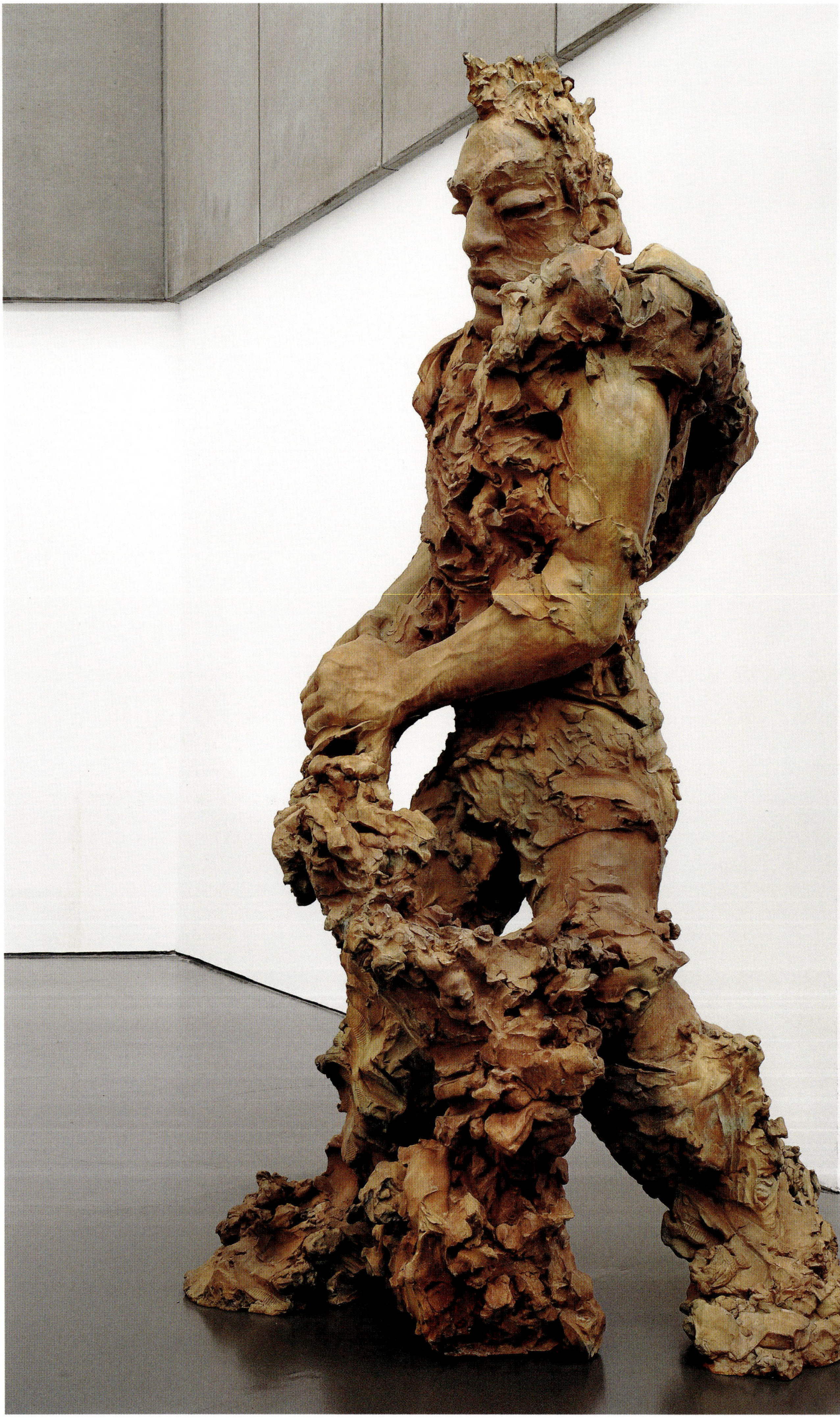

Berserker III 2008

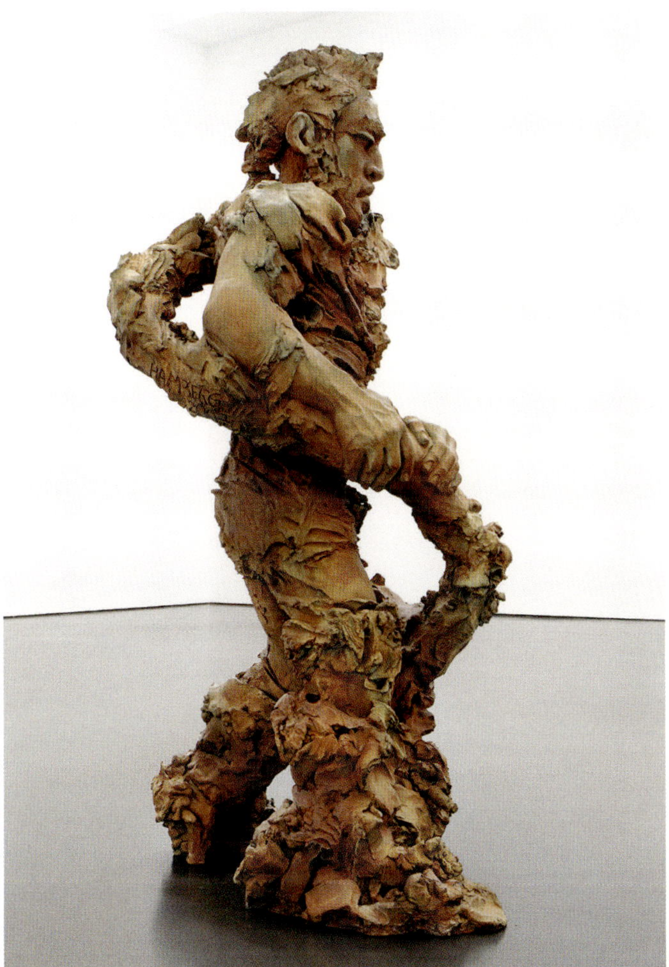

Berserker II 2007

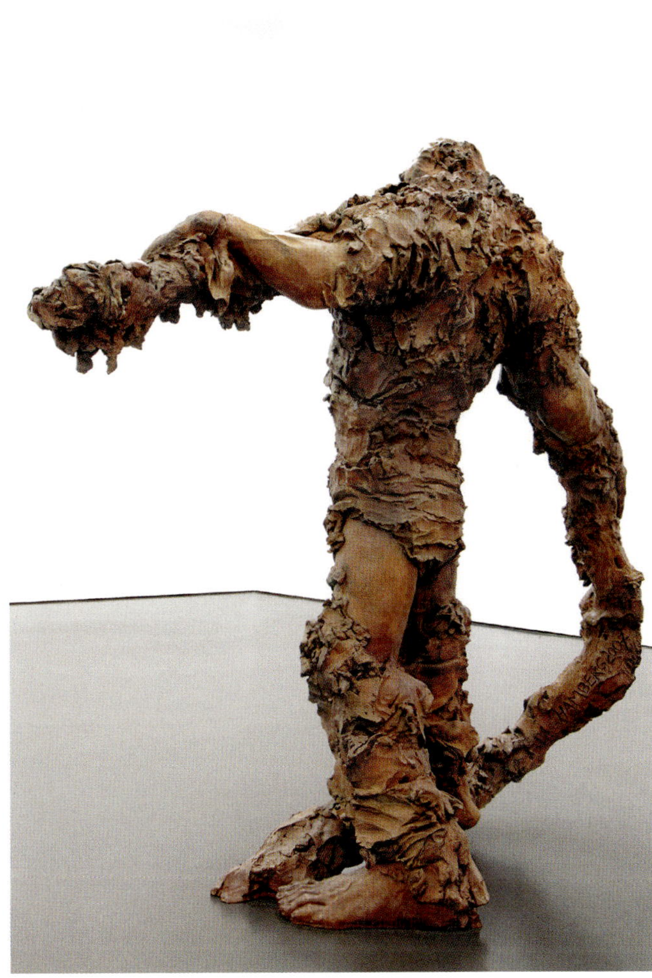

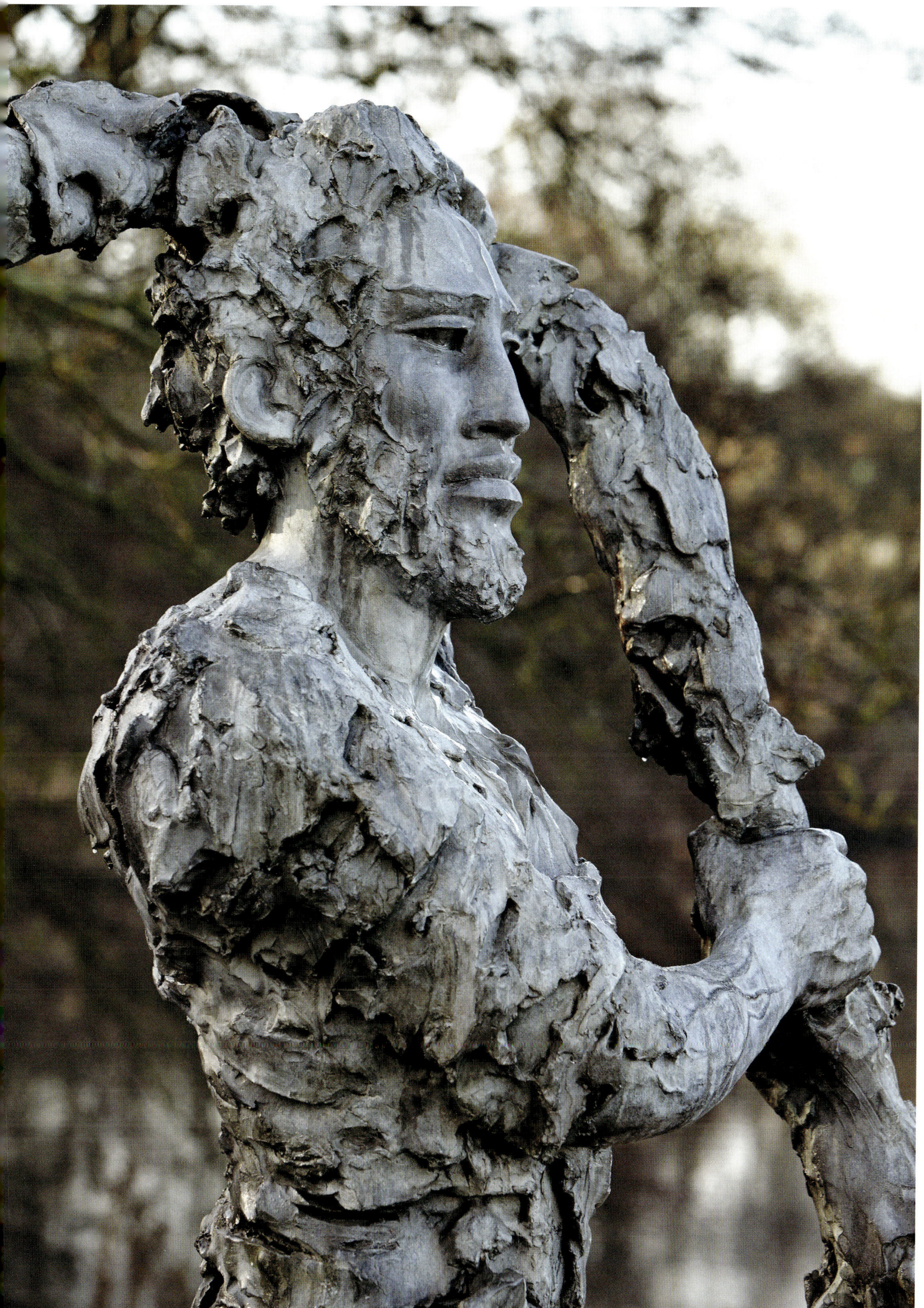

THE EMERGENCE AND DISAPPEARANCE OF FORM OUT OF AND IN MATTER

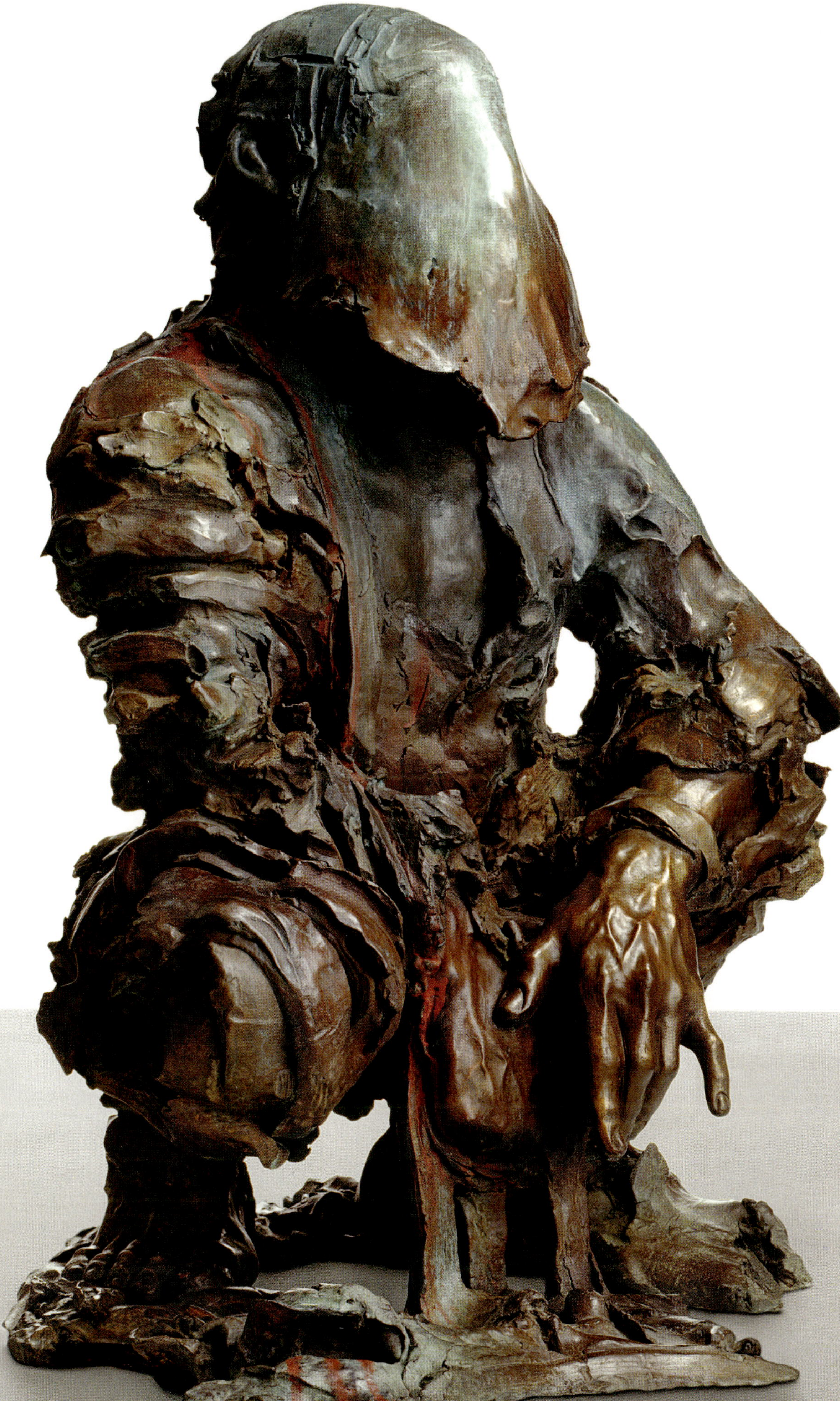

The great biblical chaos that preceded the seven days of Creation appears in the circular relief *sieben100millionen* (Seven100million; 2008), which at first seems like a glimpse into the formless primal matter out of which came the separation of water and earth, man and animals. One thinks of the tondo, the round format popular in the Italian Renaissance for depictions of the Virgin or as a frame for portraits, as a clearly structured genre, but here one is immediately astonished by the turmoil of forms. Are we looking down into a muddy morass threaded by streams of water, or from a cave at the root systems of trees? From above, one first recognises the spine of a large fish in the left half of the circle; upper right, one identifies a leg, an arm, then a foot, and another hand of a crouching figure. Is it the Creator himself or the first human being? In any case, it is not outside the circle of Creation, but is itself a part of its material dynamism. Leaving aside the idea that the relief is an illustration of the Creation, one cannot even be altogether certain whether one is here witnessing a coalescence of forms out of a shapeless mass or rather their dissolution and absorption into it. The work's impact cannot be appreciated from an illustration in a book; this is largely owing to its immense size – 320 cm (10.5 feet) in diameter. Viewers are immersed in a cosmic deluge that has no beginning and no end.

Hamberg had employed the circular relief as the setting for a contest between form and chaos several times before, as in *prayer* (2006), where suddenly, out of the impenetrable material, a lion appears and attacks a gnu from behind, sinking its fangs into its neck. But as a symbolic and graphic illustration of the relationship between form and material, *sieben100millionen* goes far beyond that work. The relief is an important milestone in the artist's sculptural work in that it directs one's gaze to three-dimensional formal details on a monumental scale, combining the creation of a single large form with the analytical view of the excerpt.

Despite its virtually opposing subject matter, a comparable work of elemental force yet filigree delicacy is the two-part bronze sculpture *vom Verrecken und der absoluten Unmöglichkeit zu sterben* (On Death and the Absolute Impossibility of Dying; 2008). It comprises the wall relief *das Tabu* (The Taboo) and the crouching figure *der Gefährte* (The Companion). Both elements, different in form and motif yet related, deal with a person's dying. In the relief it is even more difficult to identify motifs than in *sieben100-millionen*, and ultimately it is perhaps of little importance whether the central motif was developed out of a cart stuck in mud, a splintered branch or bone, since the metaphor of the image lies mainly in the detail of the sculptural form. With its irregular outline, the relief seems as though torn out of a larger context. It opens up three-dimensionally like a wound, the splintered bone jutting out of it. In this case, the uneven patina, ranging from brown to blood-red to various muted and garish shades of green, is largely responsible for the effect. *der Gefährte* is a heavy, crouching figure that is neither about to straighten up nor sit down, but persists in this intermediate position. It is difficult to tell whether it is a man or a woman. Its head is turned slightly to the left, as though gazing at something, but its face is veiled, covered with a cloth, so one cannot see its eyes. Its pose is actually stable, yet the figure appears to melt and flow onto the floor. Telling details are the right foot and, especially, the delicate left hand that frees itself from the largely amorphous structures that form the rugged, heavily churned up surface. Where the surface appears to divide into separate layers that distinguish the figure's body from its clothing, a hand appears in front of the bared breast. It is sensitive but inactive, its little finger pointing into emptiness. The patina is expressive here as well, corresponding to the three-dimensional structures penetrating each other in a painterly way.

As Christian art began to develop ways of depicting empathy and emotion in the 12th century, the combined themes of death and mourning were primarily found in images of the Crucifixion, the Descent from the Cross, and the Lamentation. One picture type that emerged out of this thematic complex in the 14th century was the pietà, Mary mourning her dead son lying across her lap. Yet this Christian pictorial tradition is never solely about death and sadness, but to some extent – as in the title of Hamberg's two-part sculpture – the "impossibility of dying" as well. Implicit in depictions of the crucified Christ, especially, there was always faith in the resurrection, or to put it more precisely: artists managed to find a sculptural form for a paradoxical message, namely they had to depict a man on the cross as dead yet filled with vital energy. The pietà is also not only about lamentation for the dead, as a rule, but combines with it elements of the elevation and rescue of the deceased deity.

In dealing with the theme of dying, it was obvious that Hamberg would consider interpretations of it in the art of antiquity, as well as two iconic depictions from this great Christian tradition: Michelangelo's early *Pietà* (1497–1499) in St. Peter's in Rome, and Matthias Grünewald's *Isenheim Altar* (1512–1516). Although she did not adopt any of the motifs of these very different monuments, she did incorporate her study of specific elements, for example Christ's tattered loincloth in Grünewald and the flowing masses of fabric that cushion the recumbent figure in Michelangelo. Moreover, the colouring of the figure of the crucified Christ on the *Isenheim Altar* played an especially important role in the differing patination of the two bronzes.

sieben100millionen 2008

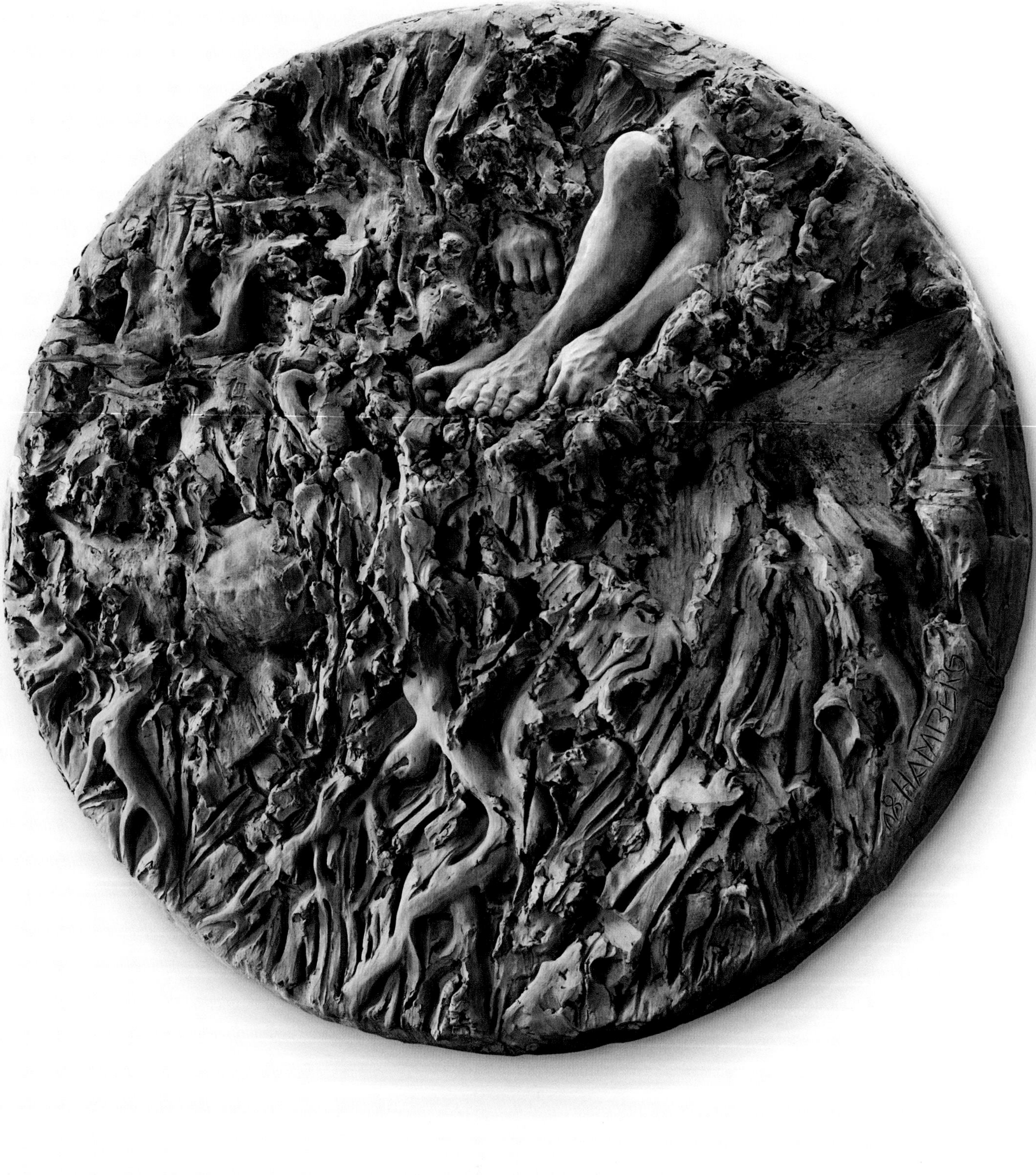

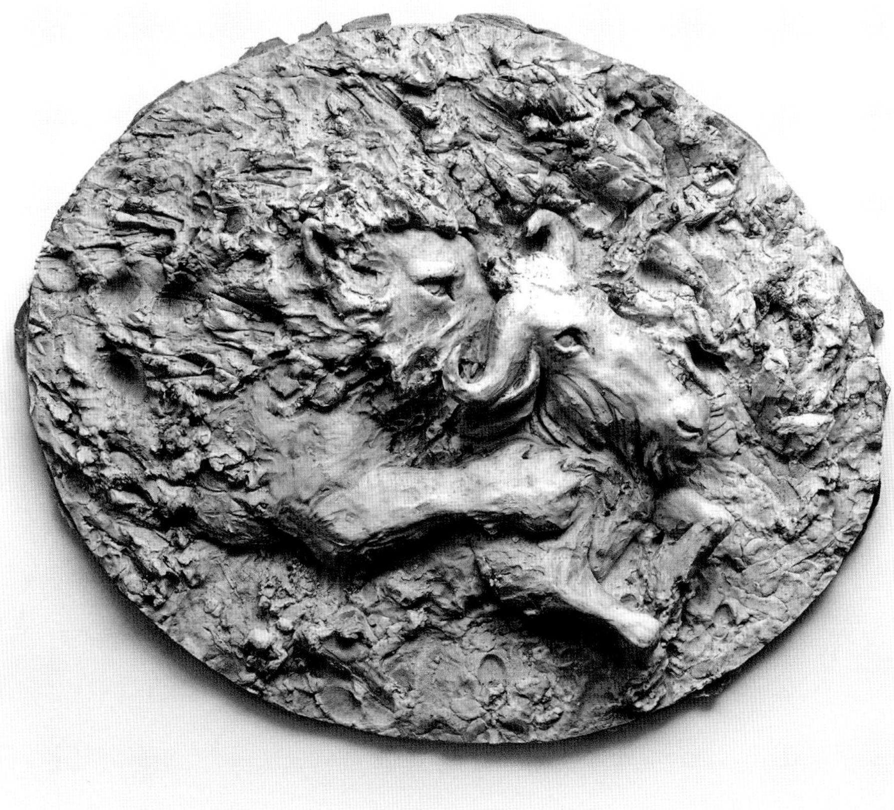

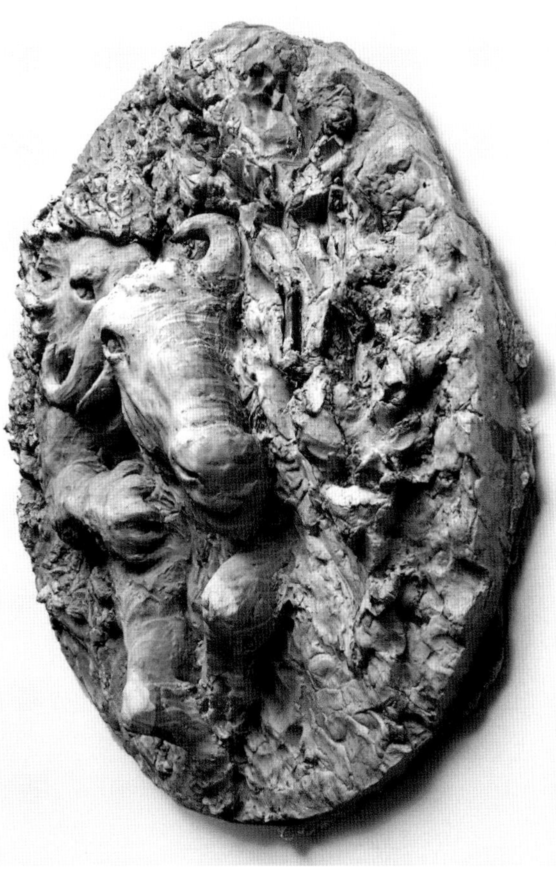

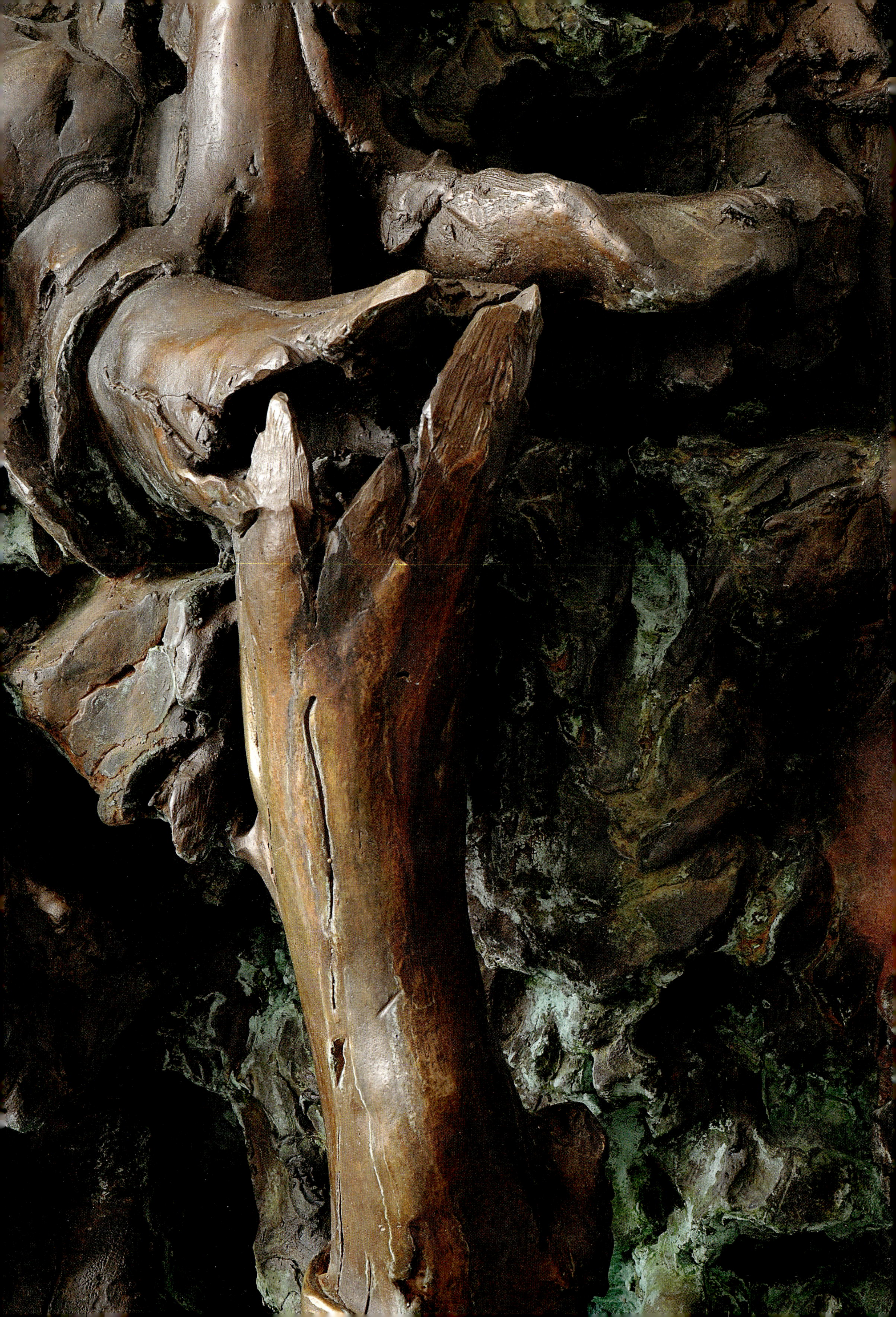

vom Verrecken und
der absoluten Unmöglichkeit
zu sterben 1 –
das Tabu 2008 (detail)

über Land 2009

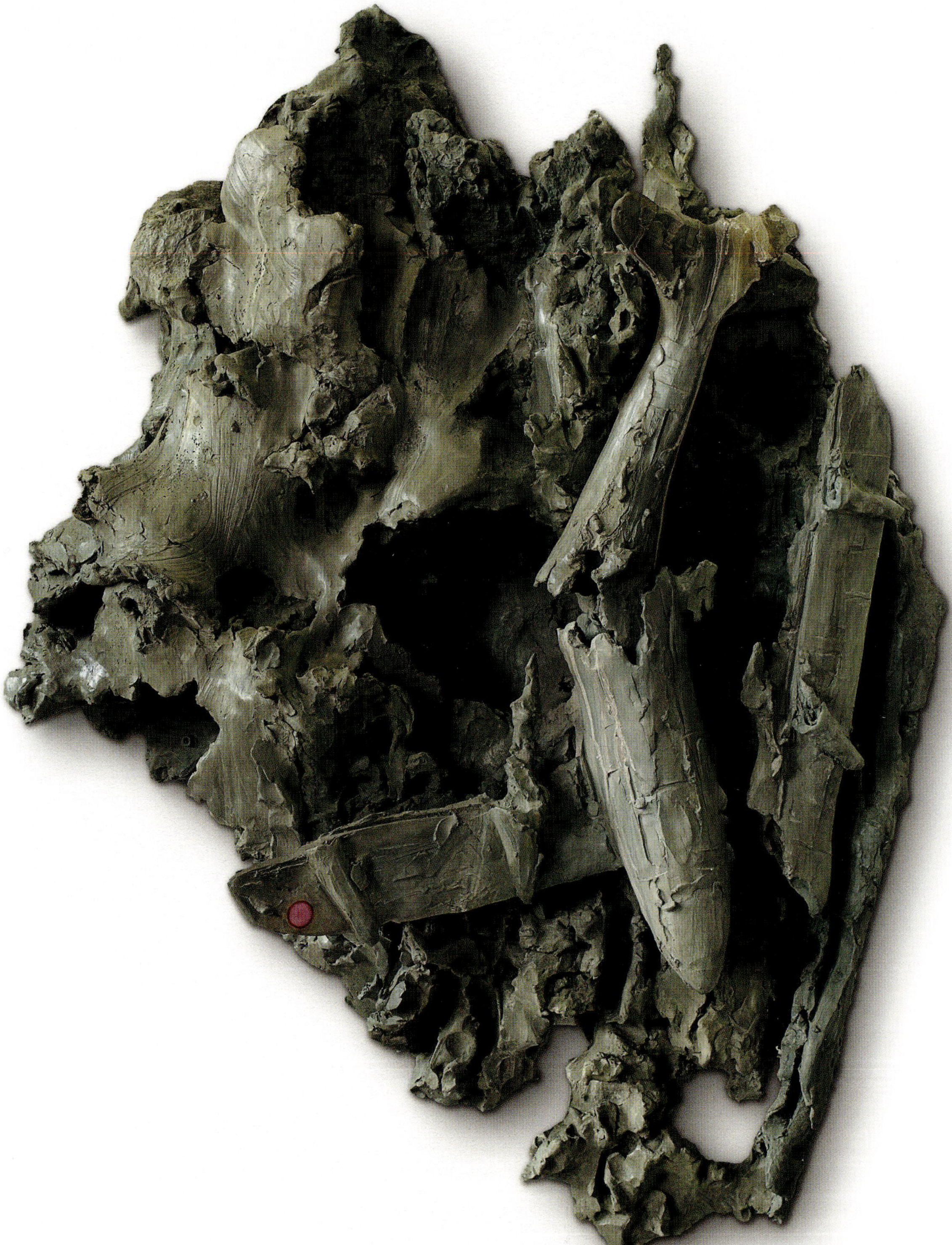

vom Verrecken und
der absoluten Unmöglichkeit
zu sterben 1 –
das Tabu 2008

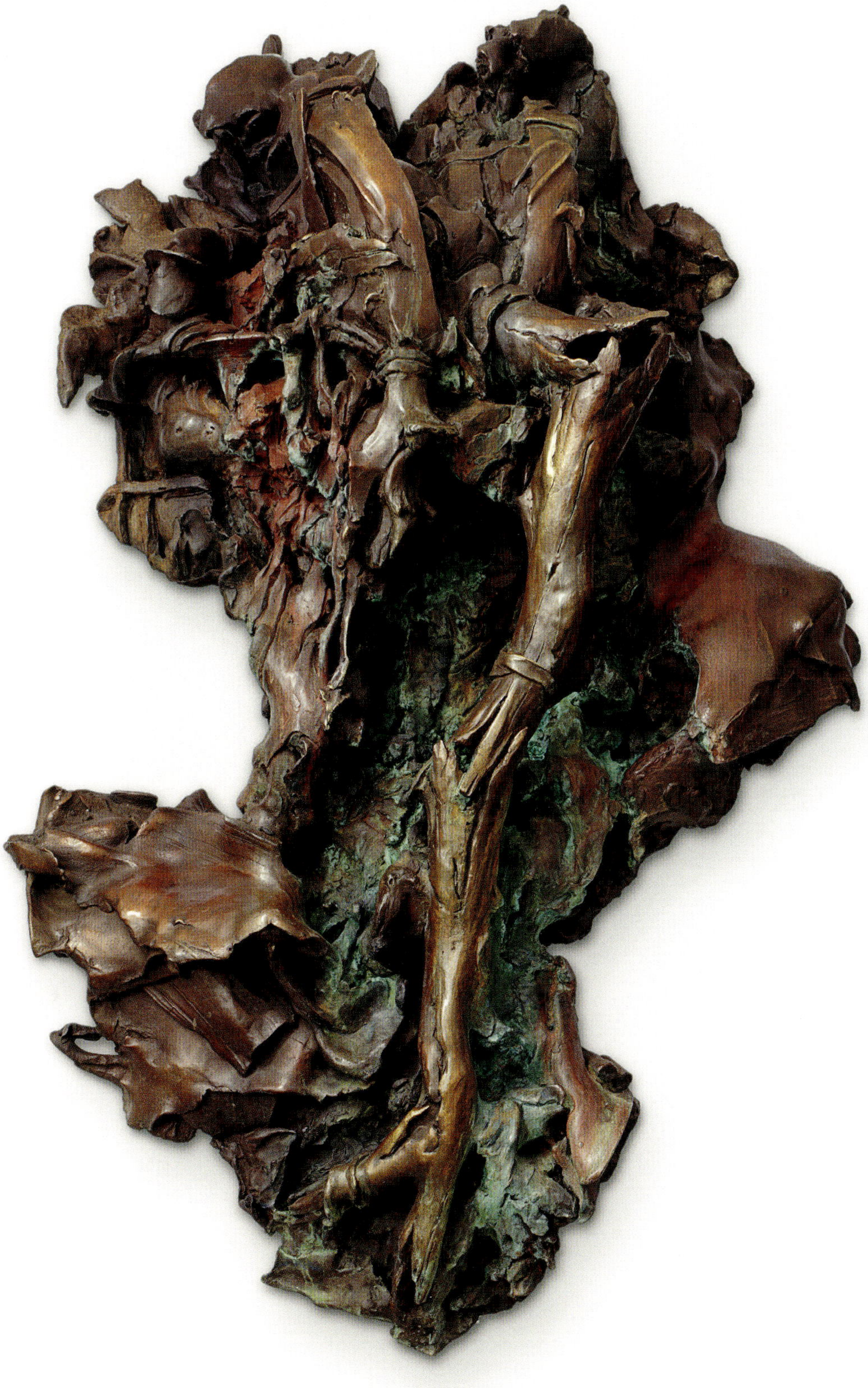

vom Verrecken und
der absoluten Unmöglichkeit
zu sterben 2 –
der Gefährte 2008

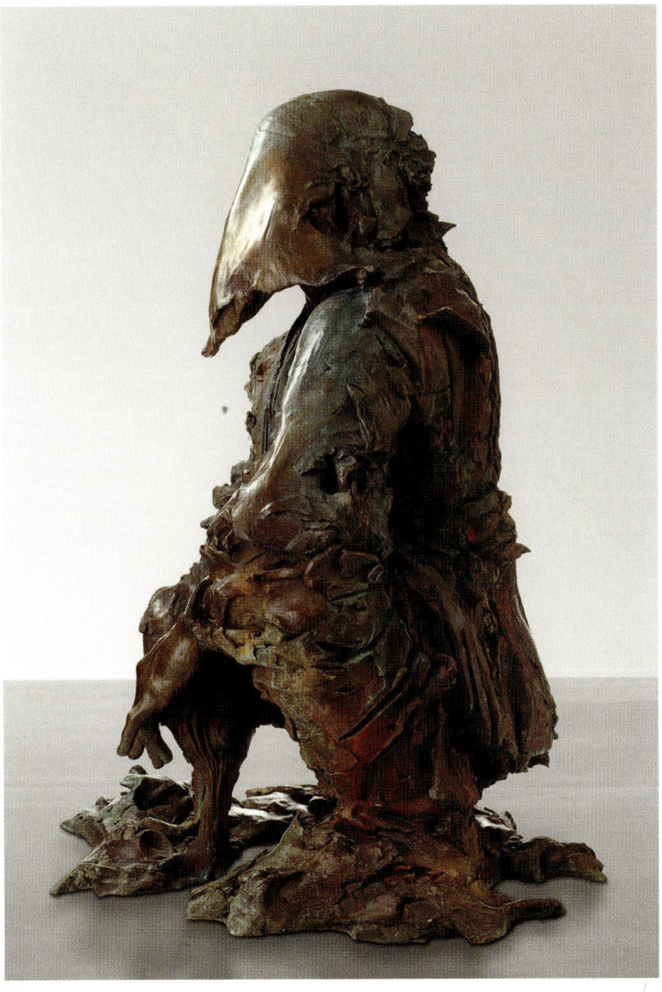

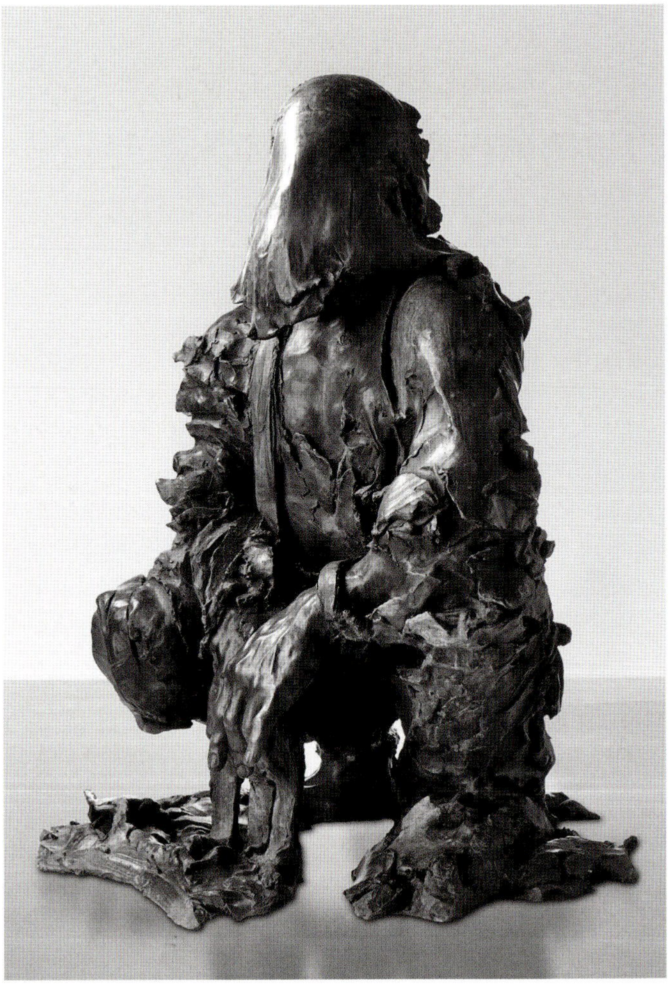

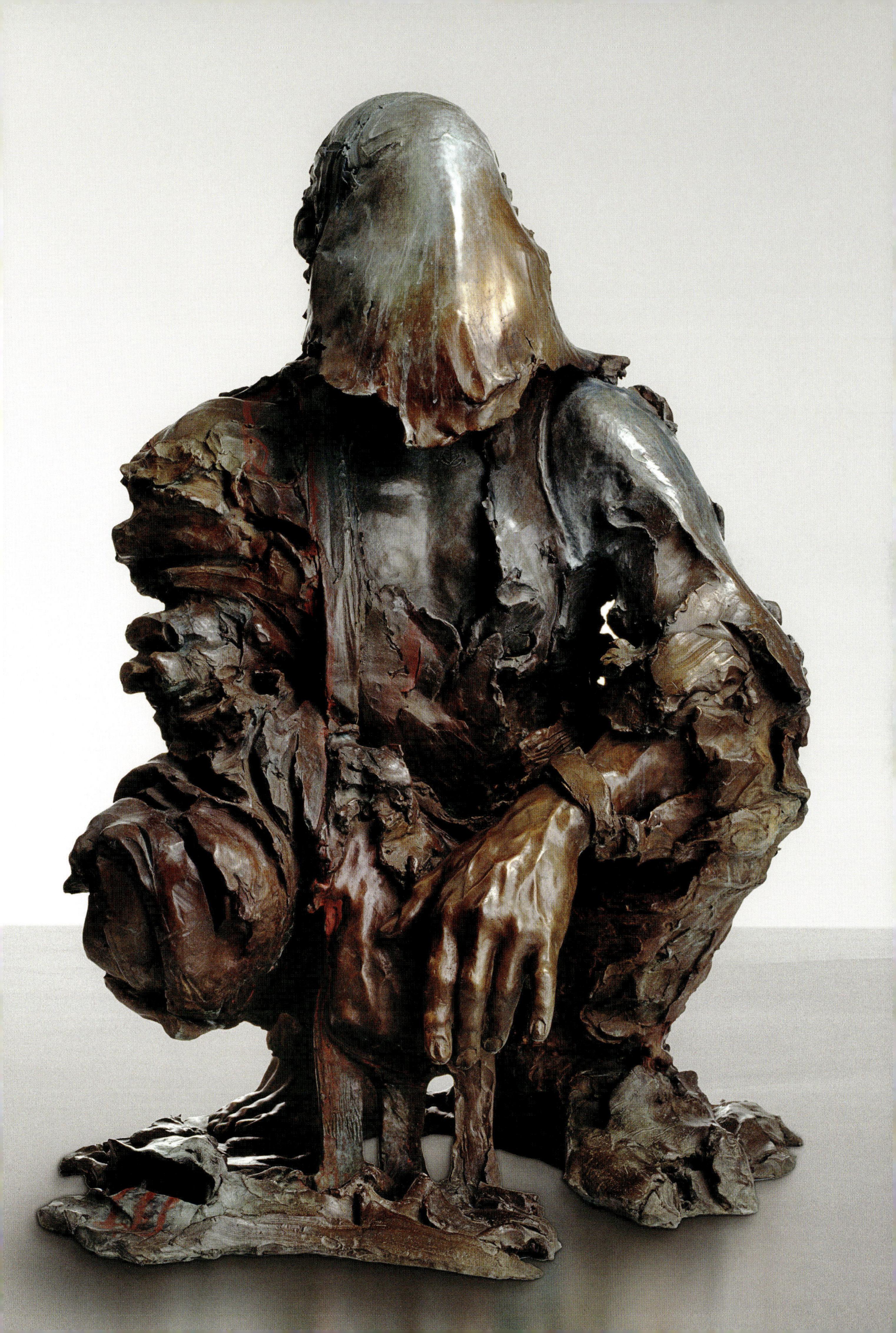

RESET – THE IMPOSSIBLE ZERO POINT

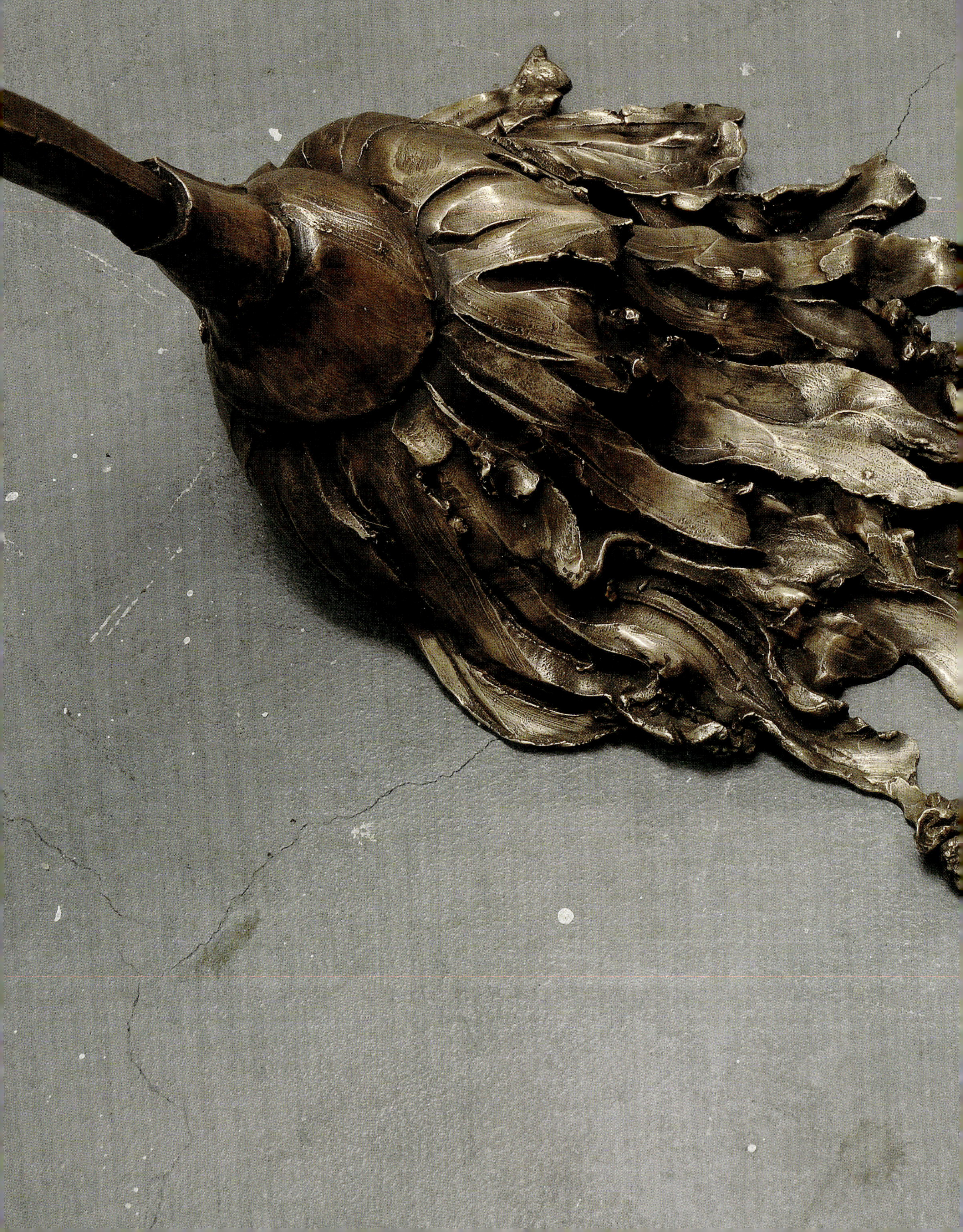

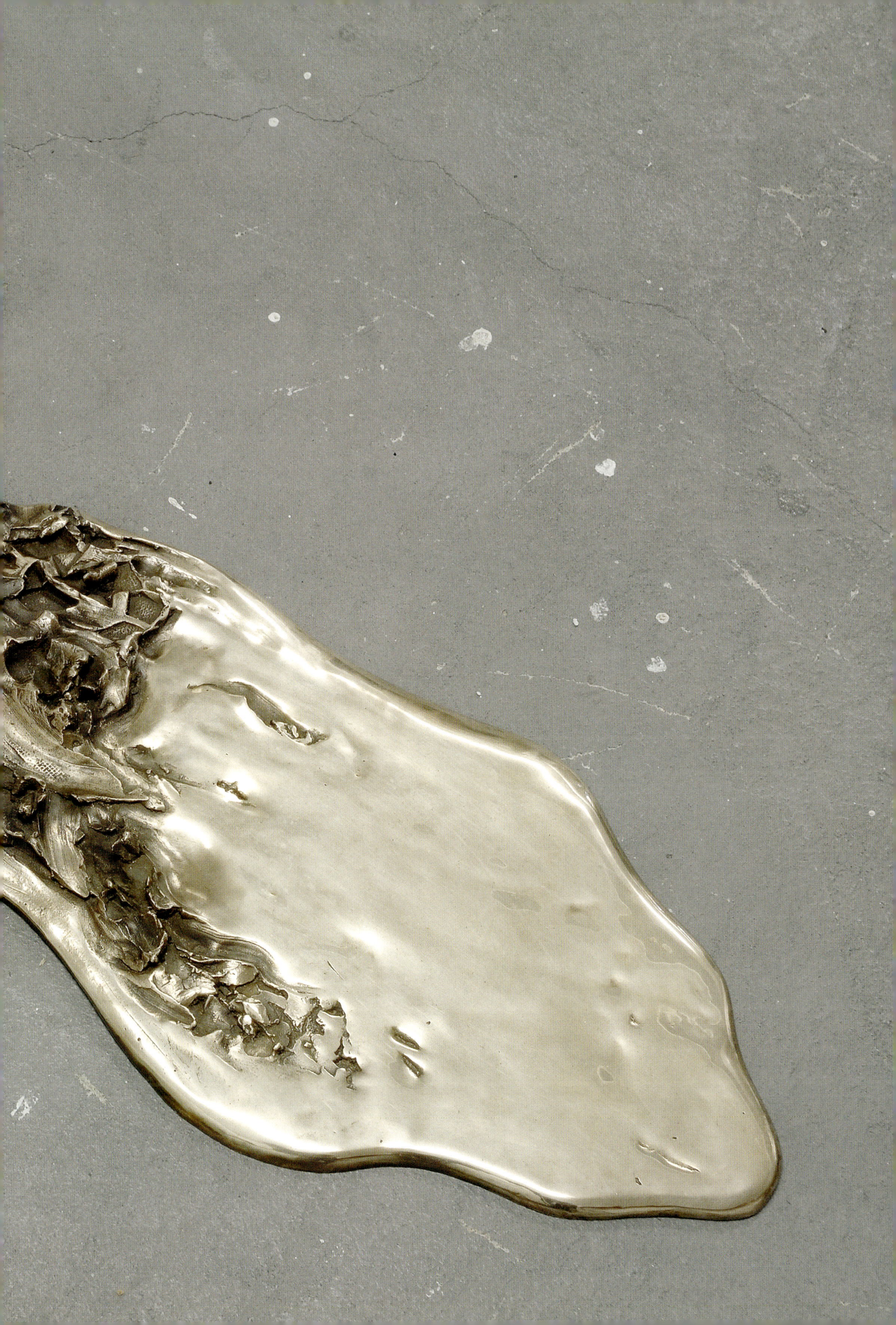

Is it possible to briefly forget everything, to take a completely impartial look at the world, and to some extent start anew on a blank page? In connection with the theme of the gaze in her early sculptures, and also proceeding from the central importance of the eyes in the film *Sans Soleil*, Hamberg has dealt in depth with the problem of the blind spot. The image that falls on the part of the human retina where the optic nerve begins cannot be seen, for the retina is blind at this spot. But the brain always fills in the gap.

Half work of art, half lesson in art theory, the action *out of season* was documented in a series of photographs. Hamberg herself explained that they are

> the picture series from an action from March 2011. A black room, actors hidden beneath ski masks, plaster, water, black paint. A computer-operated camera took a picture every ten seconds. The action consisted of handling plaster and black paint with no aim in mind. Pictorial elements and aesthetic forms were created without conscious design, by chance, and again disappeared during the course of the action. The action presented nothing but itself, its performative character, and became an autonomous, episodic picture by way of this almost grotesque situation and lack of structure.

In this battle of materials without a public but documented in photographs, it was not a matter of somehow producing a gestural, expressive, spontaneous form, but simply of demonstrating the impossibility of failing to create form when one plays with material. If one were to search for an art-historical reference, it might be found not so much in Performance and Action Art since the 1960s as in René Magritte's *La trahison des images* (1929), the picture of a pipe with the famous inscription "Ceci n'est pas une pipe" (This is not a pipe), or later – paradoxically – in Joseph Beuys's action *Das Schweigen von Marcel Duchamp wird überbewertet* (Marcel Duchamp's Silence is Overrated; 1964).

Although the recognition that when dealing with materials one always leaves behind traces, temporal as well as personal, may seem simple and banal, it is not particularly obvious even to some in the exhibition and museum business. Again and again, those who work in the art world daily encounter statements like "this presentation of works of art (in such and such materials from Plexiglass to stainless steel) is wholly immaterial and timeless!" And what is the consequence of this for fine art, especially three-dimensional sculpture? That in order to make its spiritual content visible, it always employs a physical, material form – in contrast to music or literature, for example. It thus engages in a special way with the likewise physical and spiritual existence of man and nature and comments on it, even when its declared intention is to refrain from such comment. This by no means challenges the value and quality of other artistic approaches, which sometimes intend by a very reduced physical shape to concentrate on the iconographic symbolism or on the interaction with the viewer. But it does make it clear that this is not Stella Hamberg's way, which does not skirt around the classical unity of body and spirit assumed for figurative art from antiquity to the Middle Ages, the Enlightenment in the waning 18th century, and to some extent beyond it. Such insistence on the expressiveness of every figure is perhaps "out of season," but absolutely up to date, as shown by the illustrated reference in this book to Kim Novak's snail-shaped lock of hair focusing on the blind spot in Alfred Hitchcock's film *Vertigo* as a quote from Chris Marker's film *Sans Soleil*.

Hamberg realised another playful metaphor for this not easily digested statement in her work *reset* (2009), which depicts a mop, a brush, and a puddle of water, and clearly belongs among the humorous or grotesque facets of her work. The joke is not so much the bewilderment of the expectant gallery visitor, who instead of bronze statues finds only a bronze mop, as it is the absurdity of seeing the object meant to create a tabula rasa immortalised in cast bronze.

Among her more recent works, *vanishing sculptures – clay I* (2015), a somewhat flat, silhouette-like figure virtually fused with its own mirror image under water, takes up the paradoxical idea of a sculpture whose three-dimensional form simultaneously illustrates its dissolution.

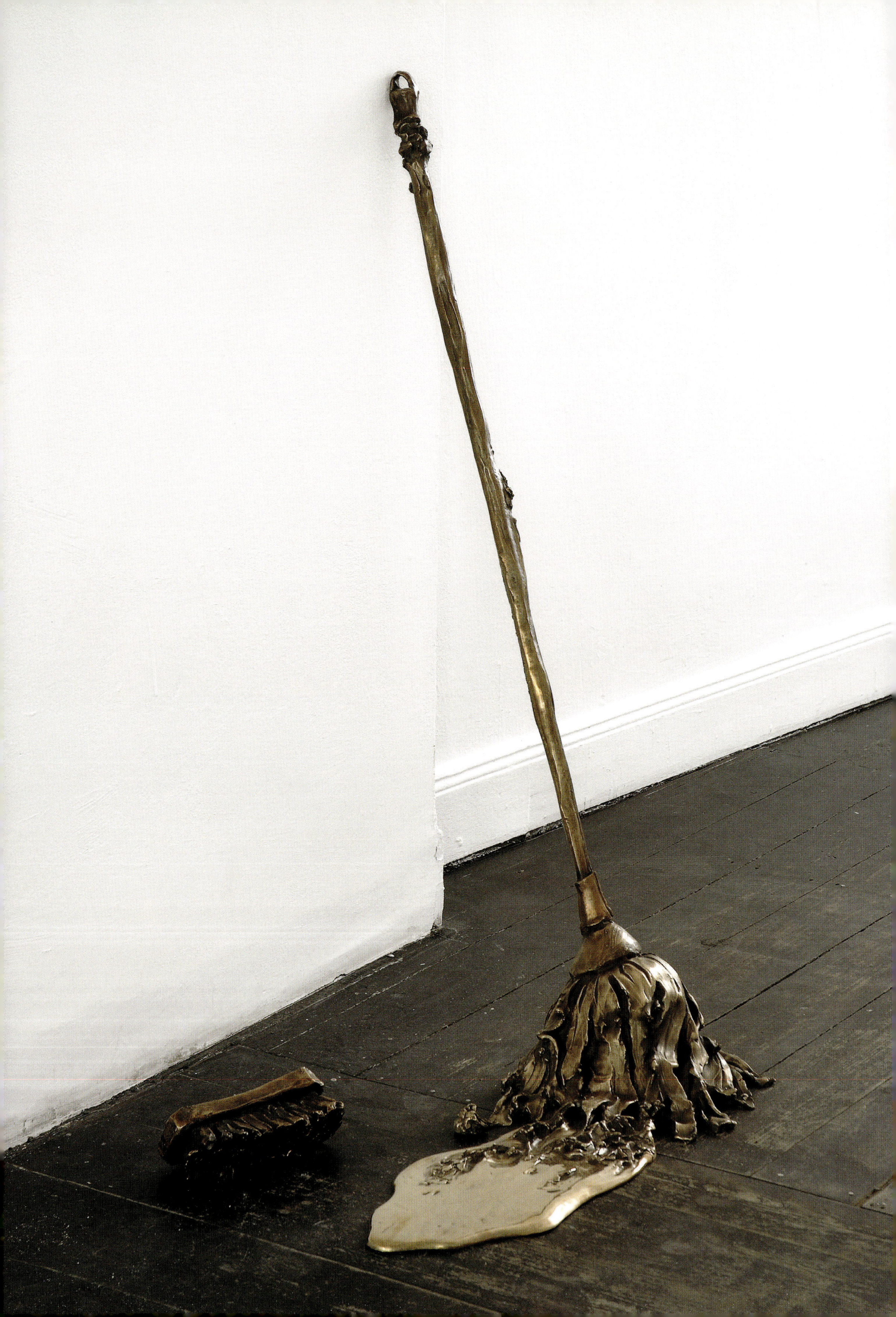

out of season 2011

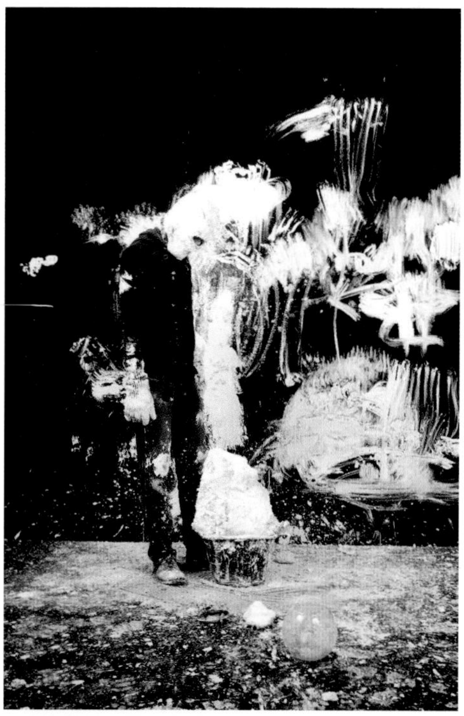
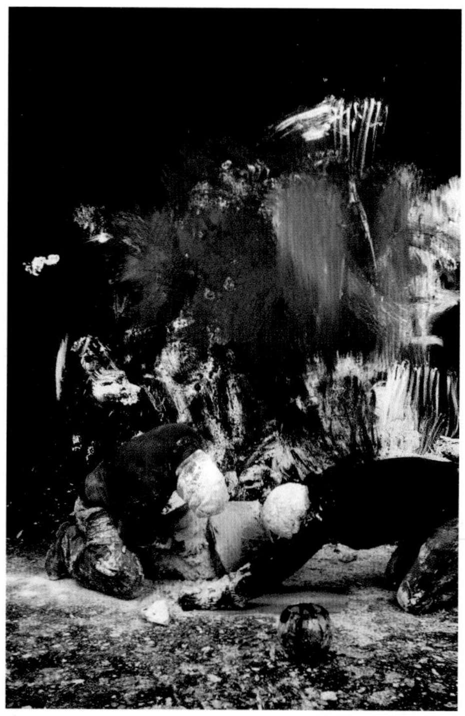
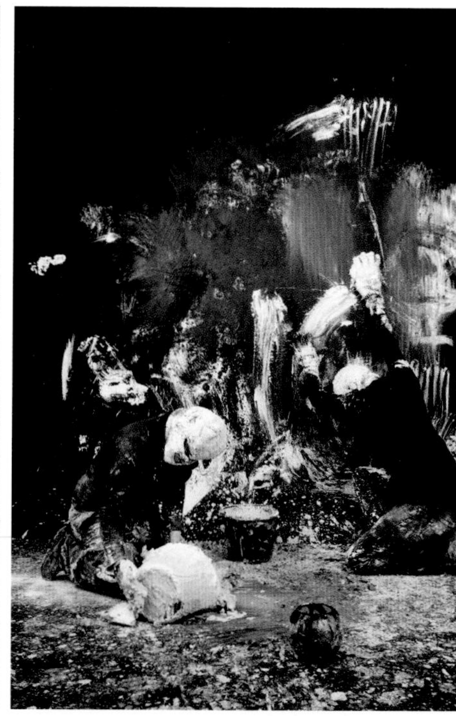
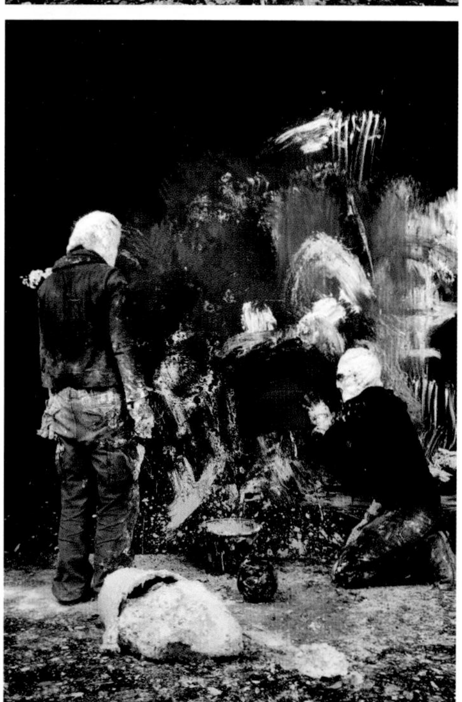
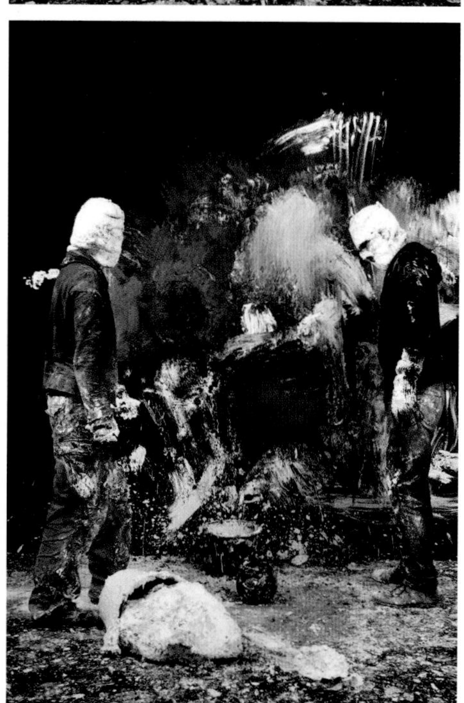
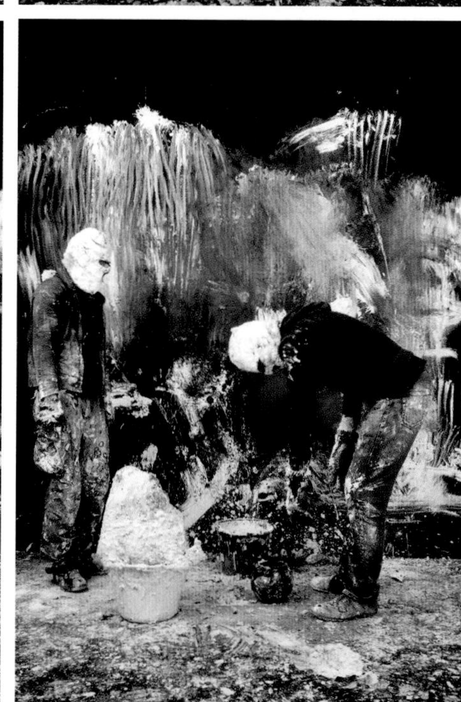

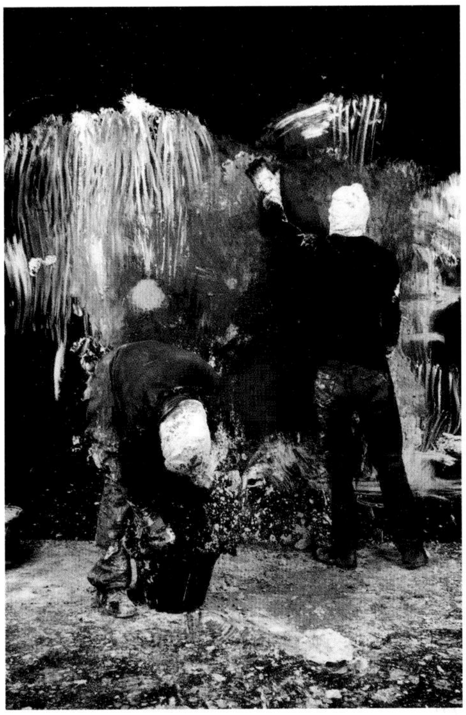
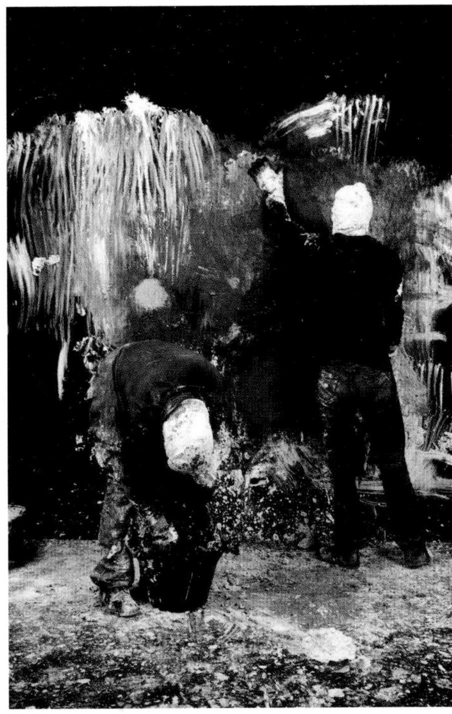
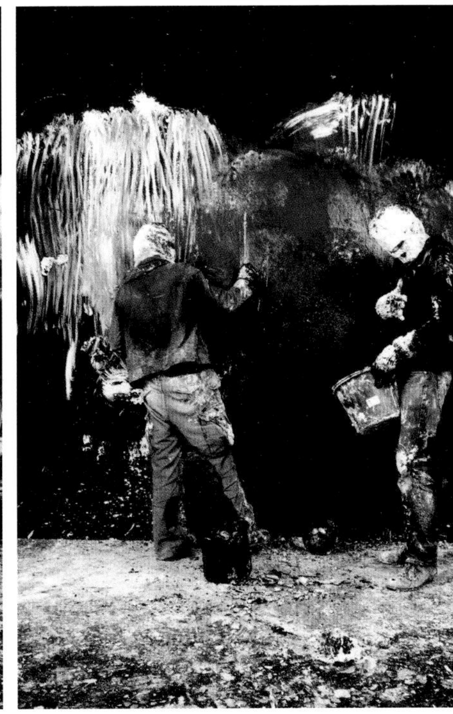
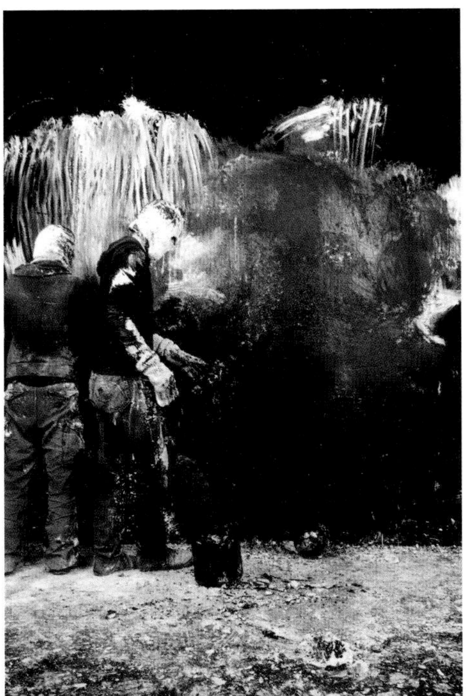
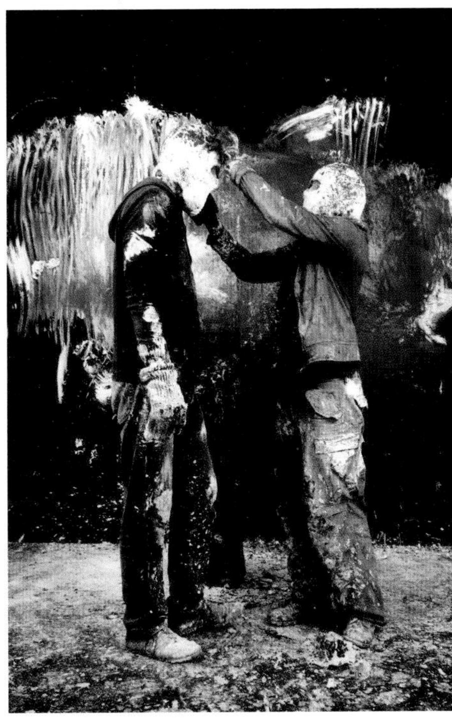
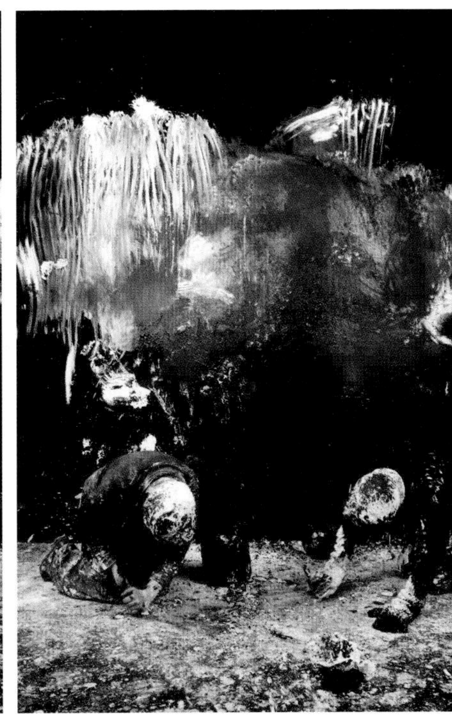
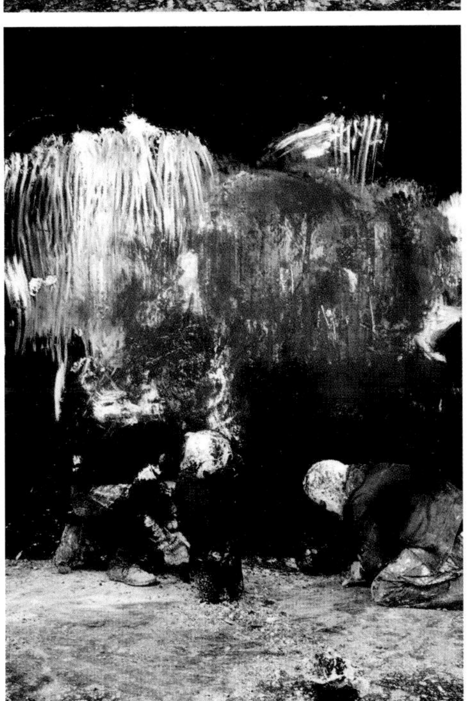
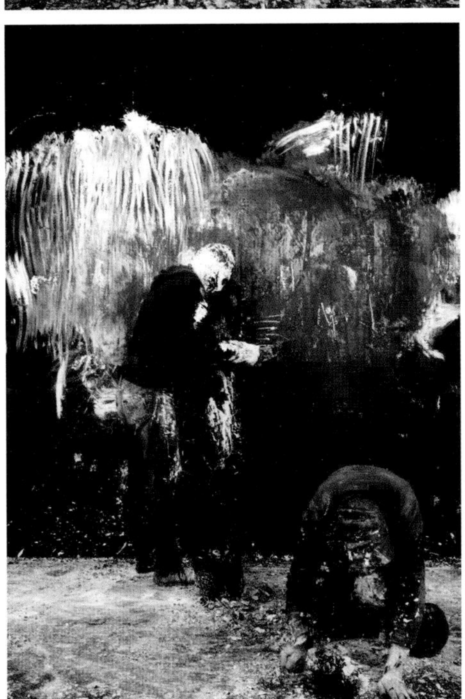
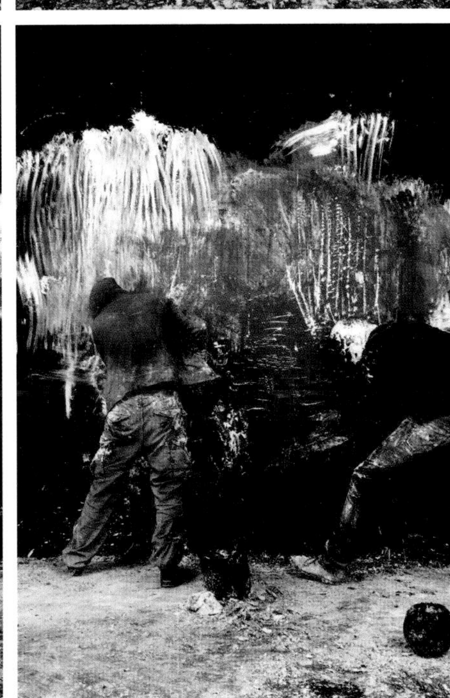

DA CAPO – FIGURAL SCULPTURES

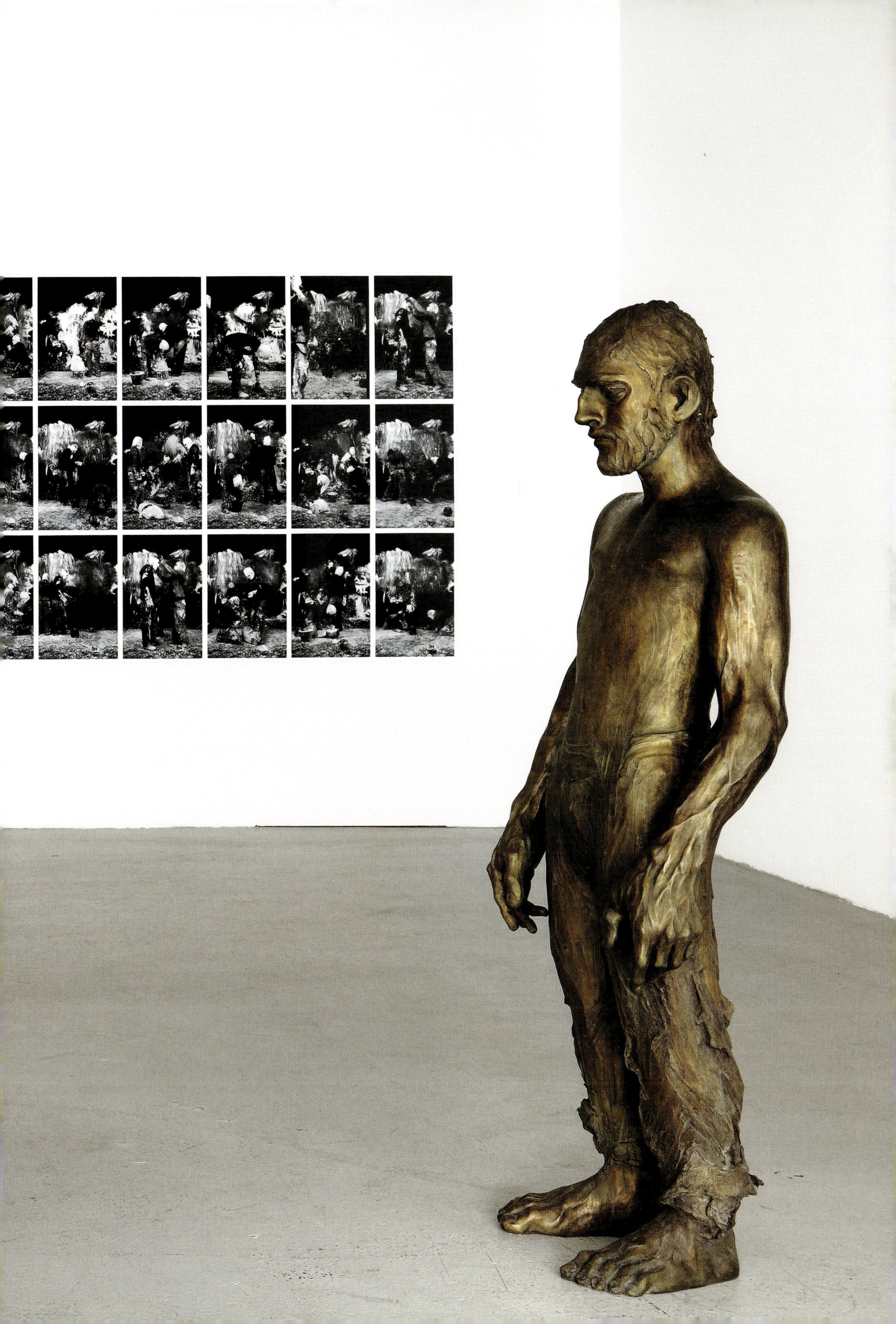

Hamberg has said that a decisive childhood experience that led her to sculpture was seeing the *Dying Gaul* in Rome's Capitoline Museums, the Roman marble copy of a Hellenistic bronze original from the 4th century BC. A further impetus, pictured among the historical sculptures in this book, was the *Barberini Faun* in Munich's Glyptothek. The two works are anything but statues of extroverted, functioning heroes; instead they depict strong, half-resting, half-active figures in a transitional state, the one between life and death, the other between sleep and dreaming. Neither of them is focused on a viewer, let alone a hereafter; they simply present themselves. The one half sitting up, at first glance not wholly recognisably bracing himself against death, the other lolling lasciviously as though waking from a dream.

In her joint exhibition, Hamberg showed under the title *ghost light* the figures *Das Mädchen*, *Der Freund* and *Der Fremde* (The Girl, The Friend, The Stranger; 2010) arranged as a trio, not in motion, but more with the potential for it or just before it. In contrast to the more allegorical *Berserkers*, these three young people are presented with bare torsos and suggestions of trousers, not superimposed as in earlier works but indicated in the overall modelling, which in this case is painterly and characterised by soft transitions. Three different poses create the basic sculptural motif: *Das Mädchen* leans expectantly against the wall, her hands buried in her trouser pockets; *Der Freund*, with long arms and oversized hands hanging at his sides, his hips thrust somewhat forward, stands upright in a provocative pose; *Der Fremde* is a muscular figure calmly seated on the floor and wearing – like the Gallic warrior – a short gold chain around his neck. Although there is no reference to Albert Camus' *L'Etranger* (1942) in the waiting, lurking figures, there is something of the charged atmosphere of the beach scene in the glare of the sun that immediately precedes the gratuitous killing in that Existentialist narrative. Thus *ghost light* joins the series of semi-theatrical pictures comprised of multiple figures in Hamberg's work, yet each figure is at the same time a fully developed character study. The gazes of all three figures, with their strikingly outlined eyelids and pupils, are not focused on anything specific, but rather indefinite, as though they are searching in vain for contact with the outside world, much like the older figure *Abel*.

The larger-than-life kneeling figure *Frau* (2013) is a tightrope walk between narrative motif and three-dimensional translation. Her slender torso is perfectly erect, and she gazes into the distance with wide-open eyes. Her face, stylised with neoclassical pathos above a tall neck, is ringed by serpentine hair, and with a trace of bitterness about her mouth the figure seems like a cross between Cassandra and Medusa. But her lower body, with its powerful thighs and fused, shapeless feet is more reminiscent of a mermaid. A spiritual being and a natural creature appear to confront each other. Her left hand lies open and relaxed on her thigh, her right is closed into a fist. Antinomies are among the essential features of Hamberg's sculptures – rarely are they so blatant as here.

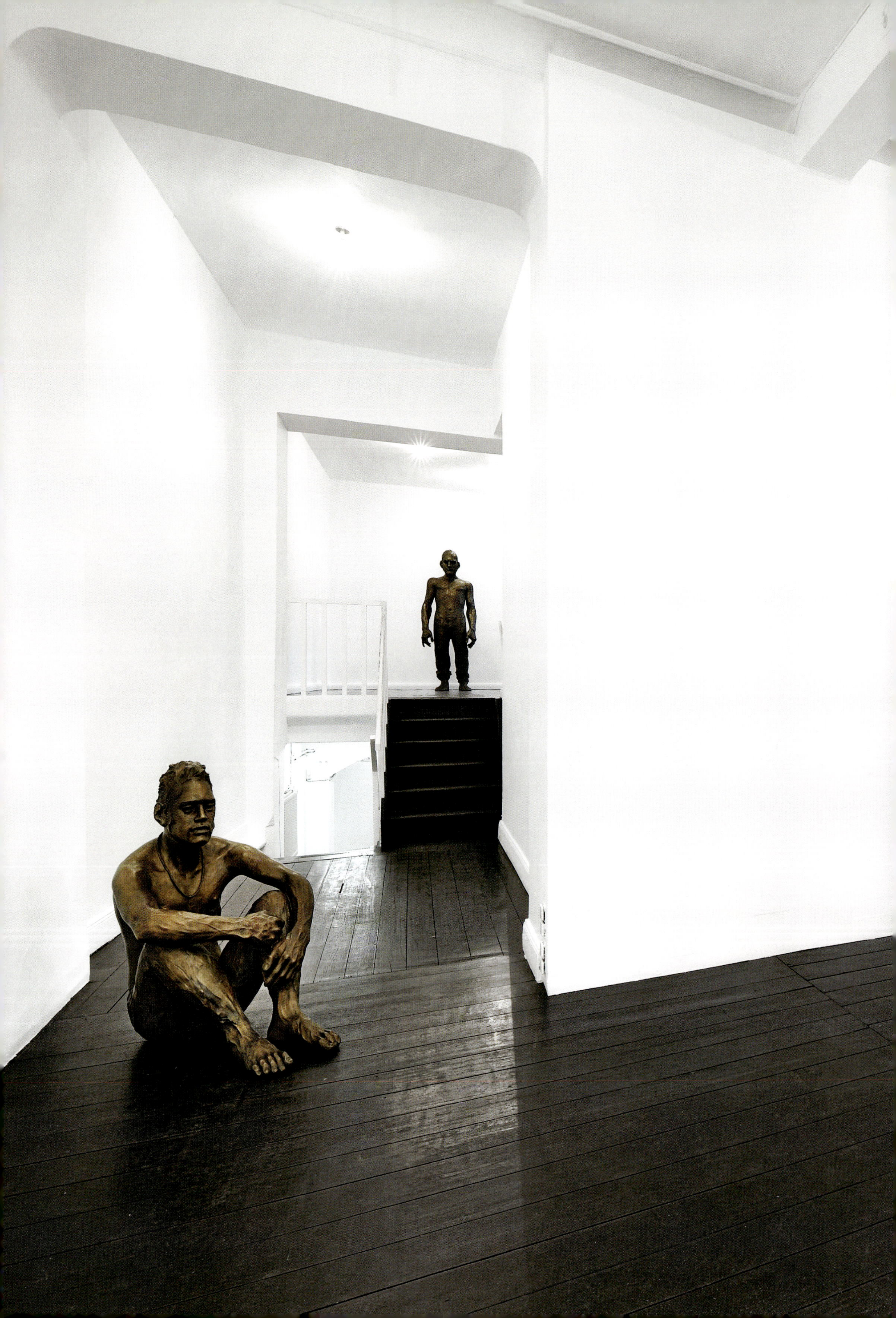

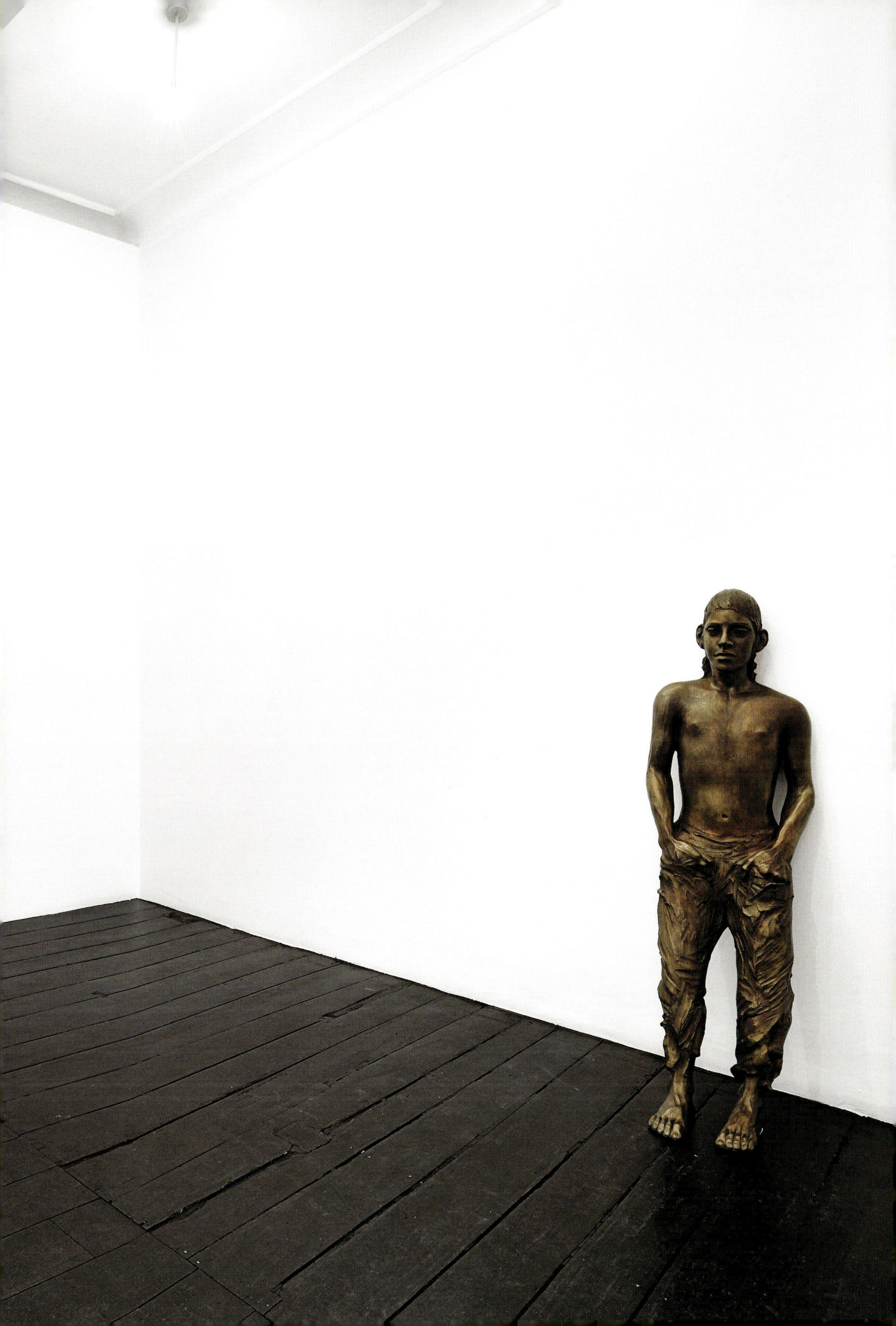

Der Freund 2010

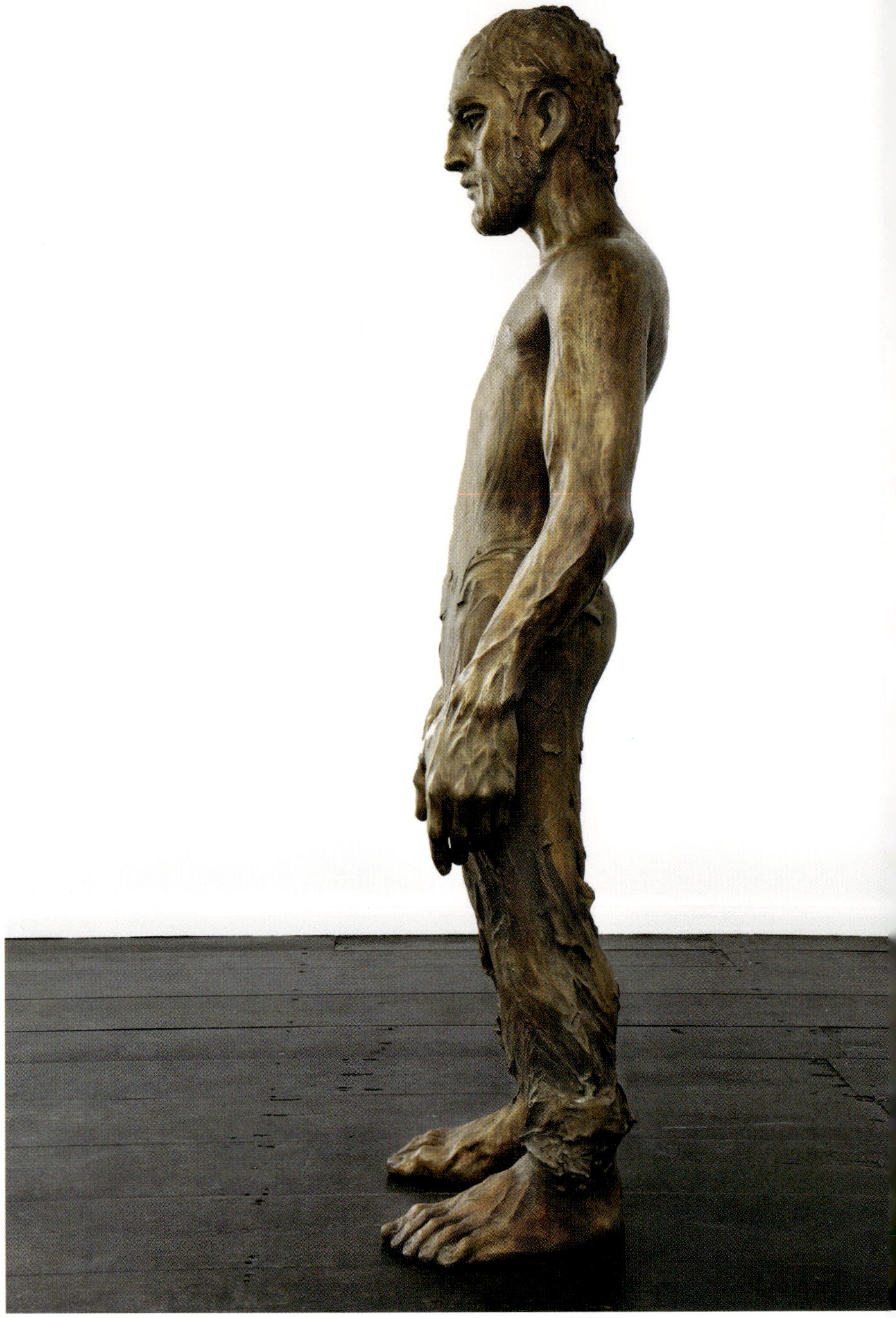

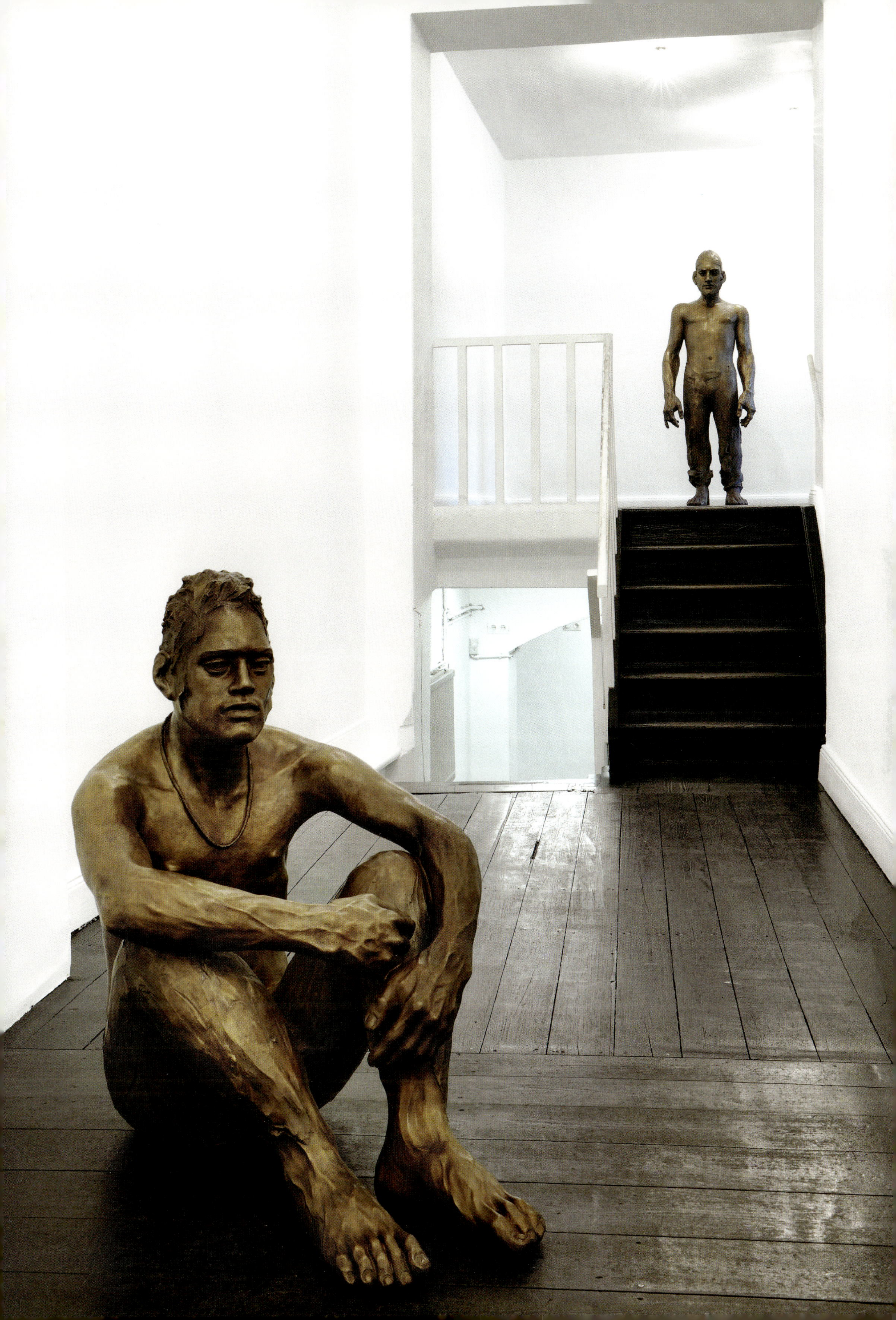

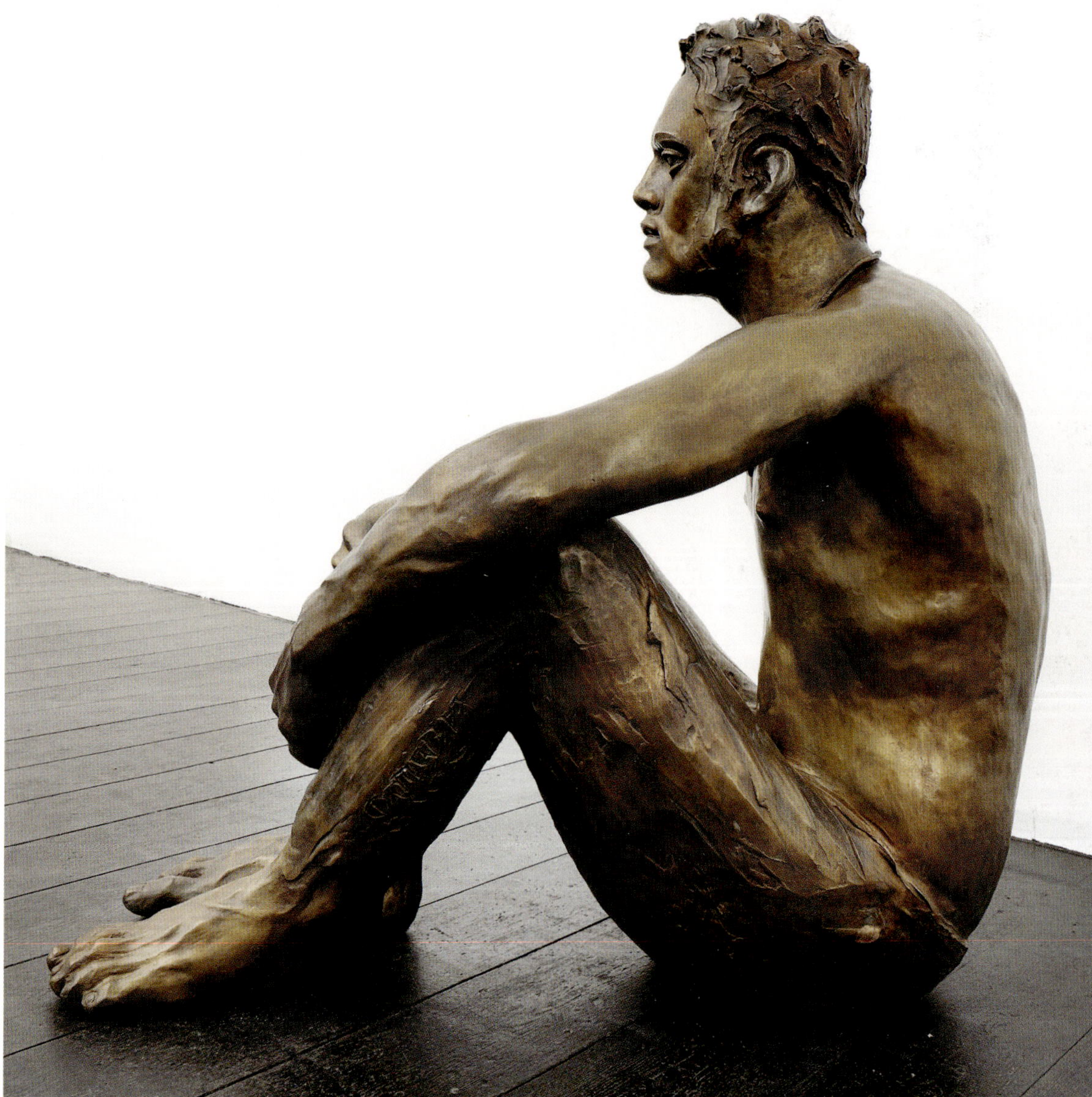

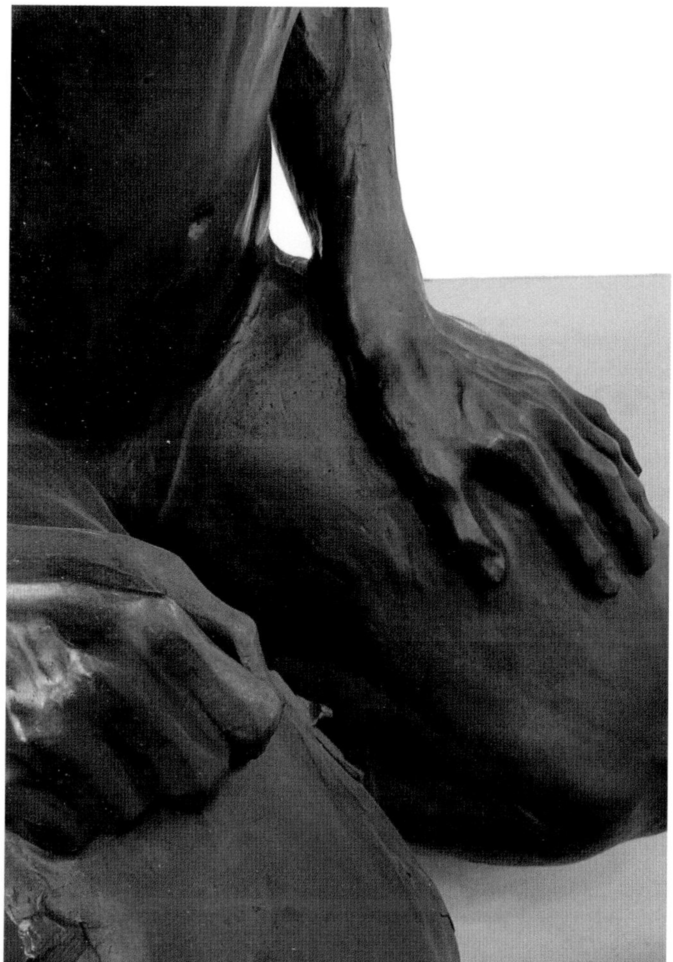

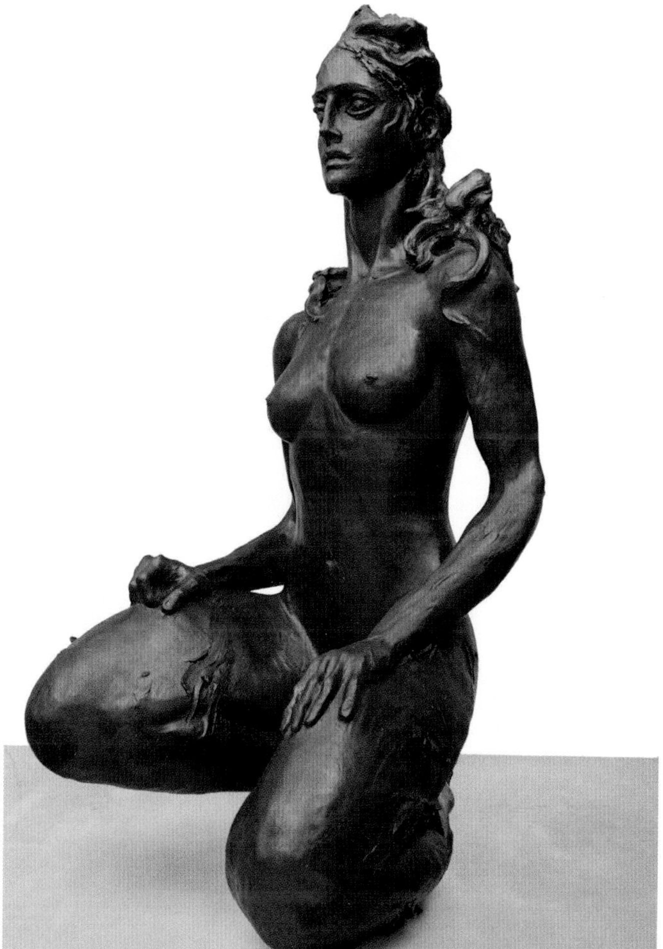

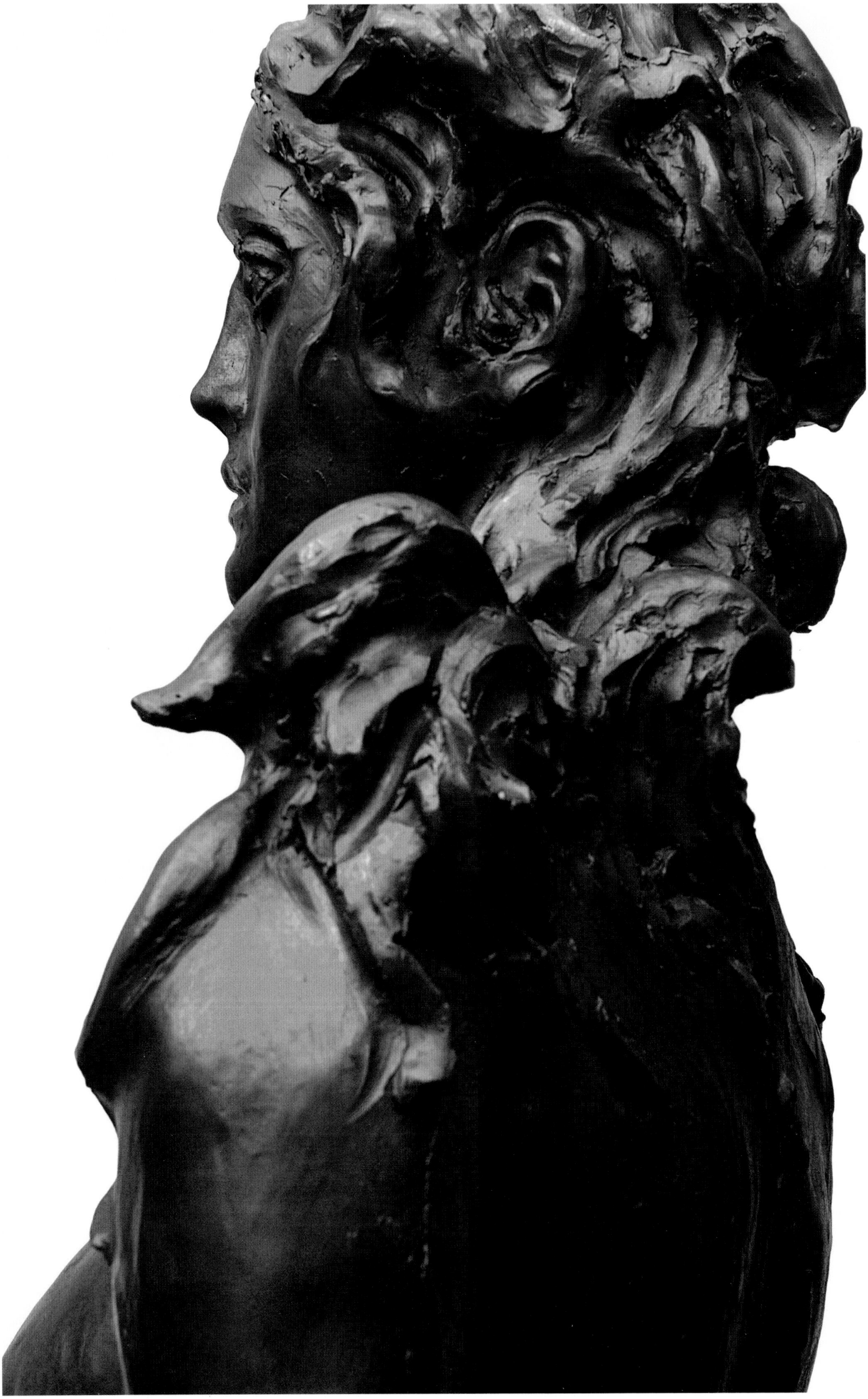

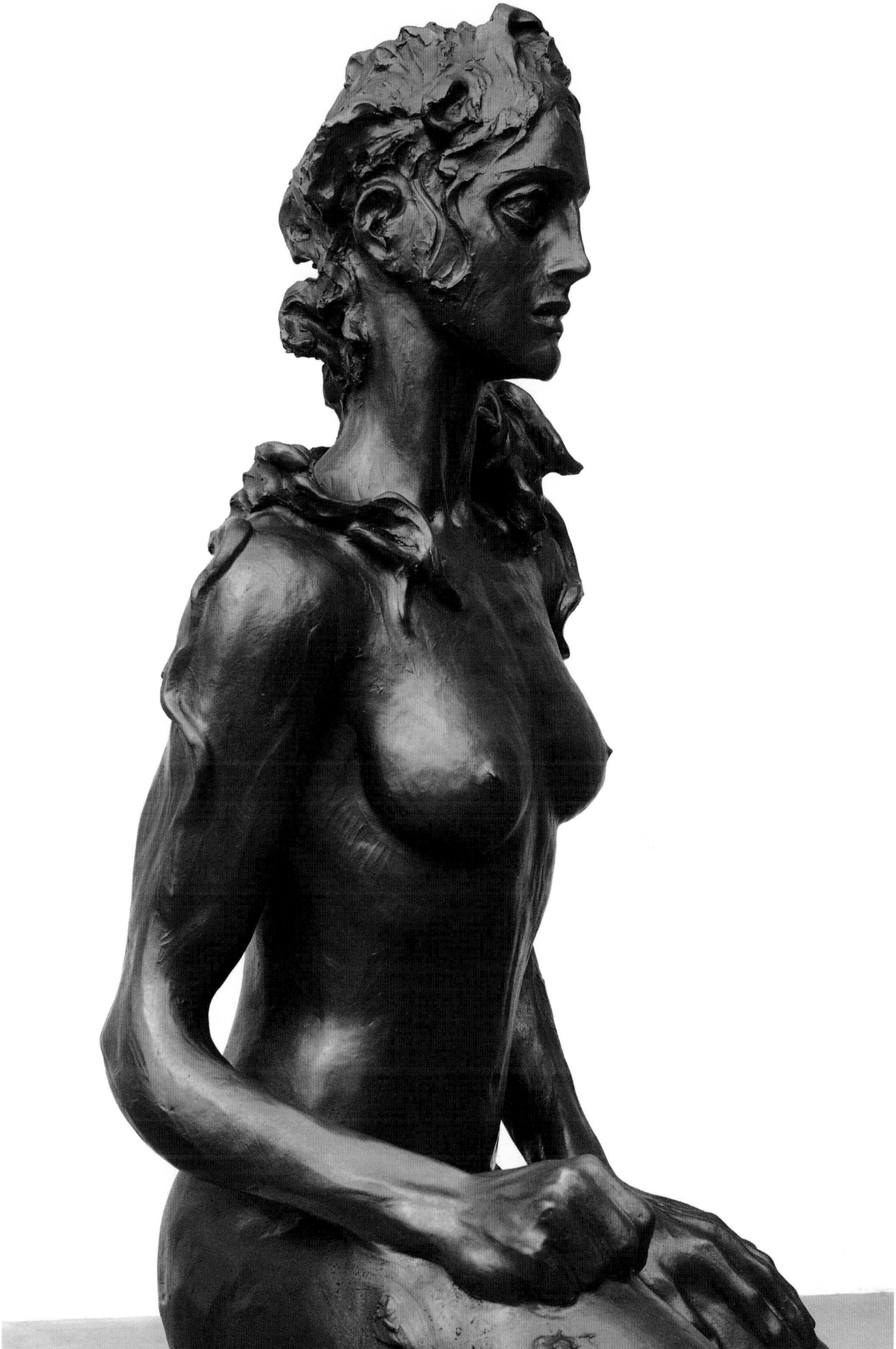

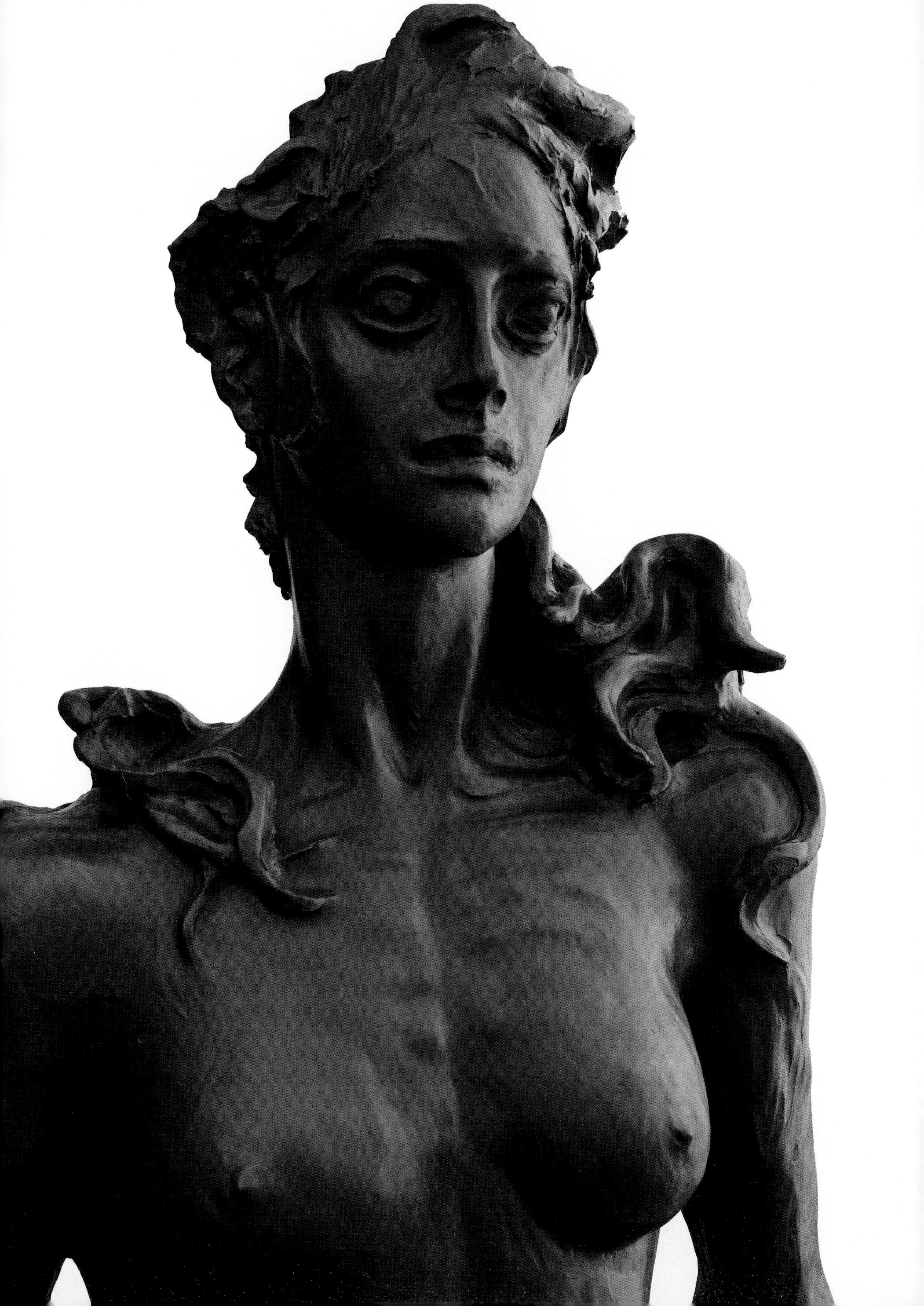

Das Mädchen 2010

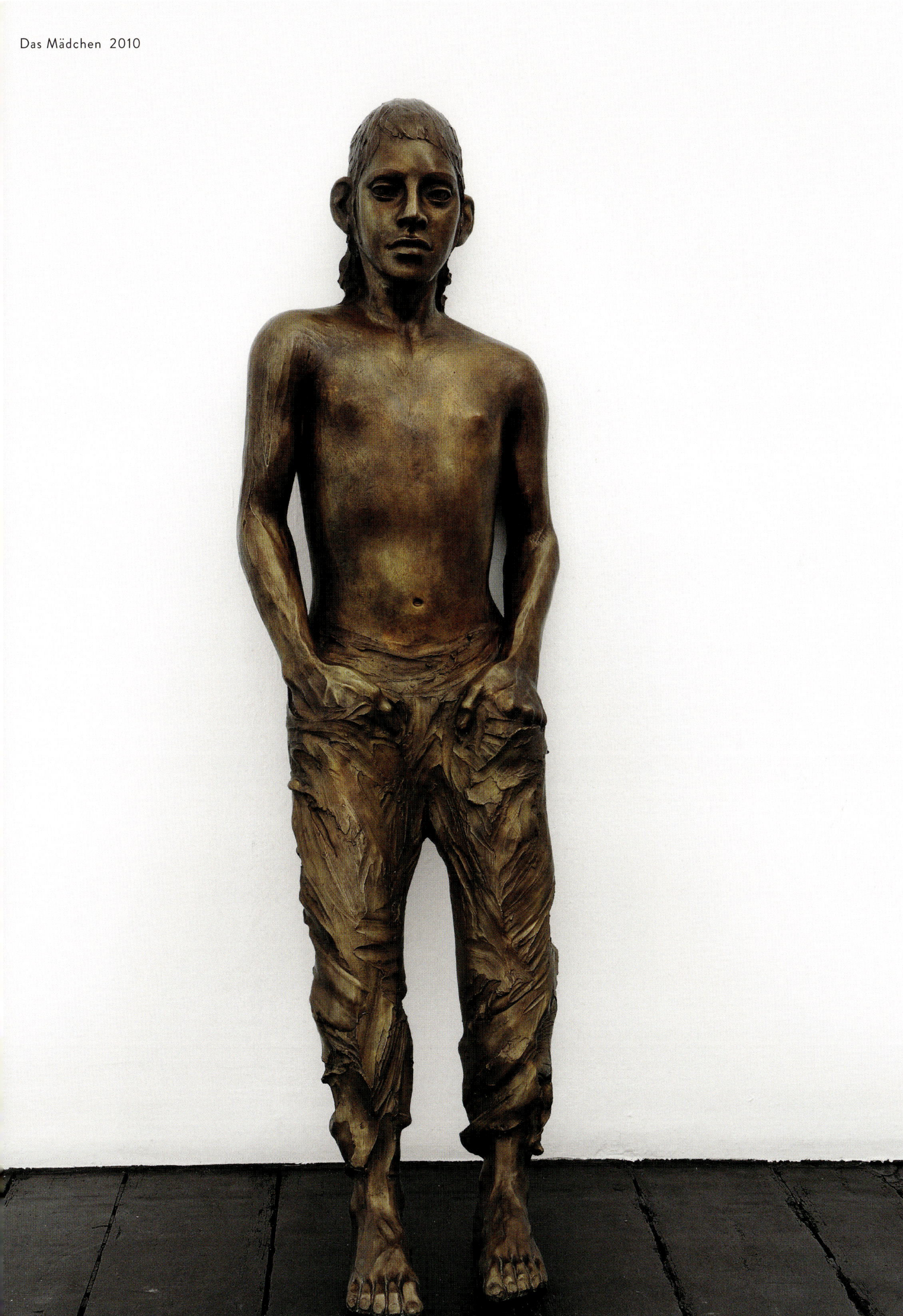

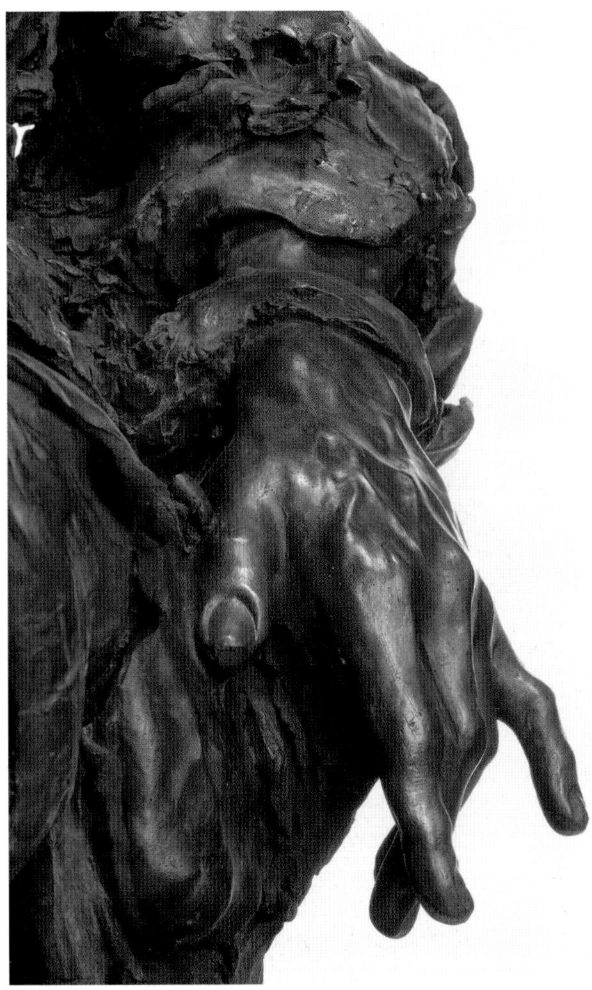

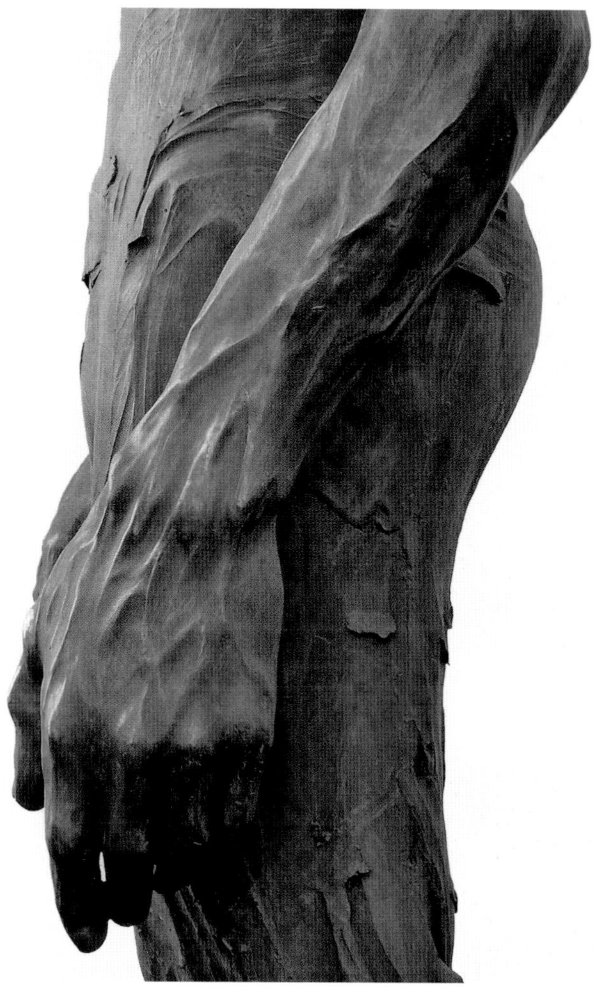

HUND – THE STEP TOWARD FOUR-DIMENSIONAL SCULPTURE

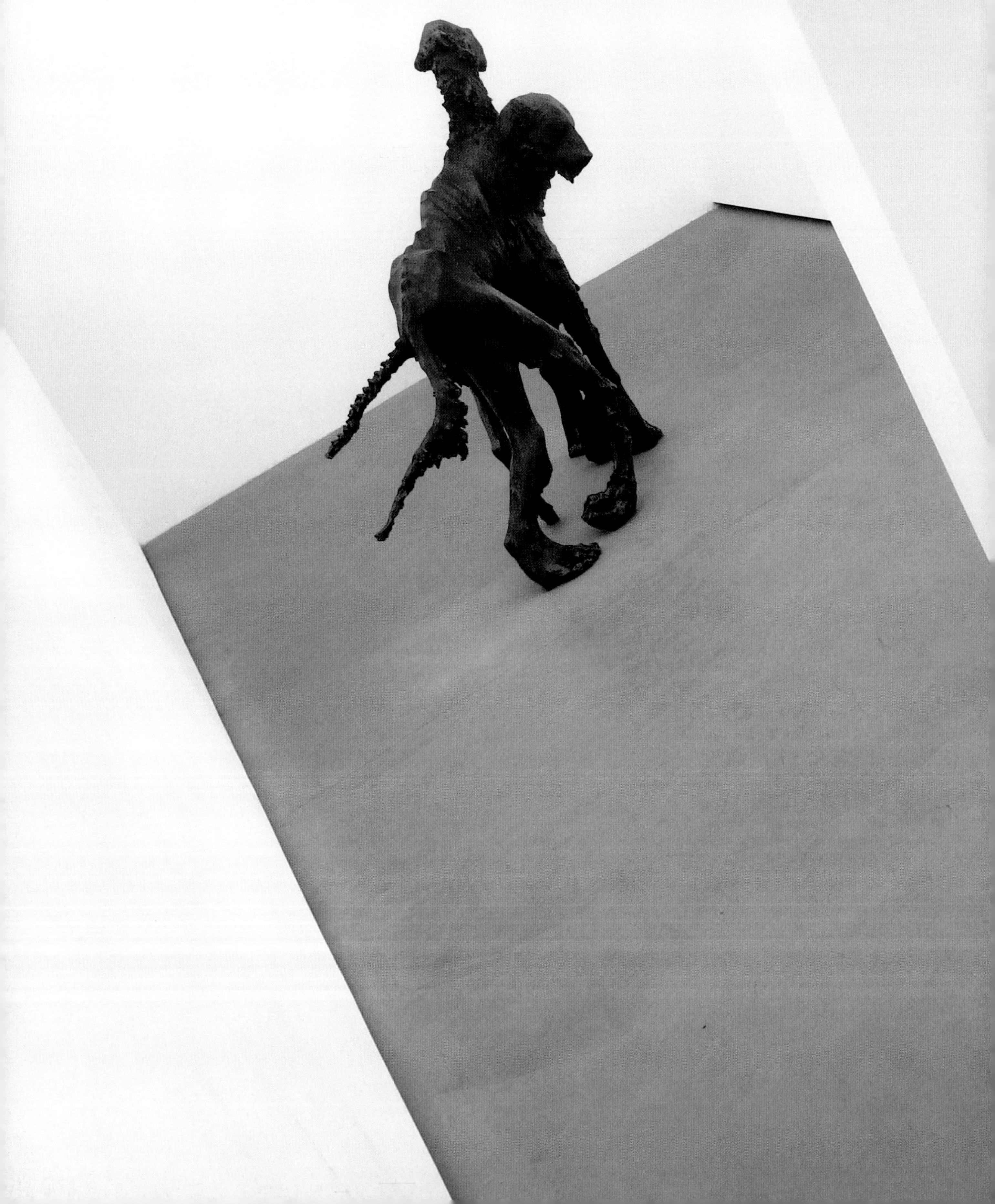

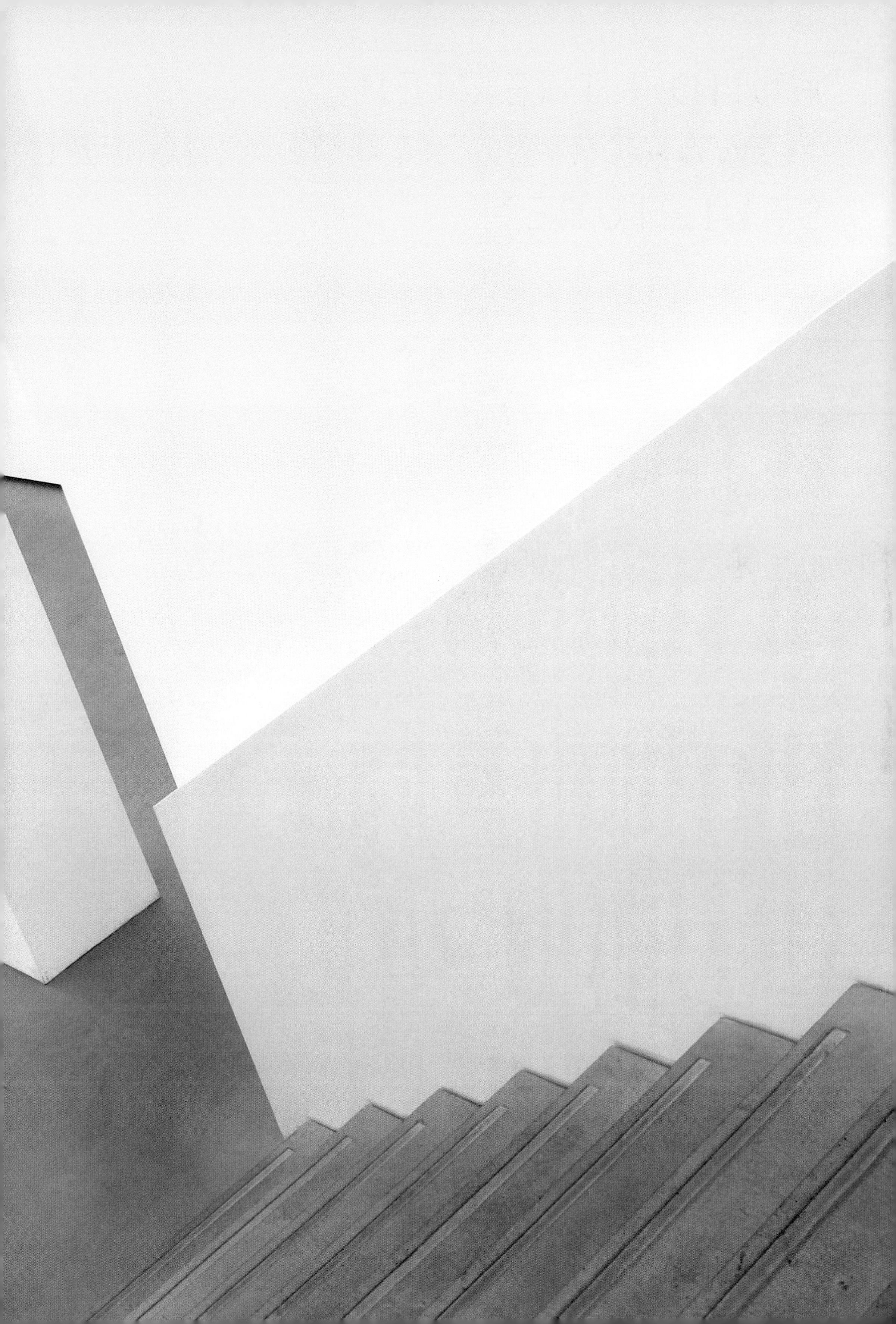

After the *Berserkers, Hund* (Hound; 2013) was a new, and with its complex three-dimensional structure, another key work in Hamberg's oeuvre. The sculpture depicts a larger-than-life animal in movement, with three heads, six legs, and two tails, which functions as a sculptural image from all possible angles. What is most astonishing is that one quickly forgets to wonder what this creature is meant to represent, monster or freak, menace or faithful companion (hound, the title tells us after all), for thanks to art it somehow seems perfectly natural.

Hamberg's well-known focus on metamorphoses since the *Berserkers* is here driven to an extreme. There, with a spiral-shaped entanglement of figural movement and attributes, the sculptor still employed a compositional technique that one might to some extent compare with the methods of the 16th-century Mannerists, though *Hund* represents a wholly novel category of figural sculpture, one in which several figures are more or less perceived as one. This single figure is seen in various physical states, from skeletal to fleshy, and moving in different rhythms and at different speeds. In this case, in addition to direct and spontaneous sculptural configuration, a high degree of planning, calculation, and decision-making appears to have gone into the system of the transitions from convex and concave modelled forms, from different surface areas, and above all from different straight, curved, or broken axes corresponding to the "hound's" virtual skeleton. Sensational studies of figures in motion and sequences in time have rarely been presented in sculpture, but those that have been are highly forceful. In this connection, one recalls such famous masterpieces of Hellenistic sculpture as the Gigantomachy on the Pergamon Altar, the *Winged Victory of Samothrace*, and the *Laocoön* group, or Leonardo da Vinci's graphic studies for never realised equestrian monuments, and diverse sculptures by Gian Lorenzo Bernini, from early figural groups like the above-mentioned *Apollo and Daphne* in the Galleria Borghese to his late *Verità* in the same collection. One might also mention the motion studies in wax by Edgar Degas, which were cast in bronze only posthumously. Another pictorial tradition, more in the nature of a motif, is the illustration of different stages of life, generally with several figures and only as an exception a single figure or one with several faces, as in Titian's *Allegory of Prudence* (ca. 1550–1565) in London's National Gallery, which combines the faces of an old, a mature, and a young man with the heads of a wolf, a lion, and a dog. Finally, one might mention the Baroque tradition of heads in ivory that present the visage of a living man backed by a death's head – an effective *memento mori*. To appreciate how Hamberg's *Hund* relates to these many different traditions, one has to analyse it more closely.

The straight-on view of the animal's left side is especially important. From this perspective, one sees only two of the three heads. The figure striding forward and the standing one overlap. The left head is eagerly extended forward, and the left foreleg is placed to the front in lockstep with the left hind leg. These motifs are combined in the outlines as well: the curved neck of the head on the left continues in the arc of the spine and on to the two-part, half skeletal tail. A curve leads from the head to the left foreleg, and from this leg another curve leads to the point where the forward-striding left hind leg and the set-back middle back leg separate. The third hind leg, being dragged along as though infirm, appears as a surprise between them. The one primary motif of a forward-striding figure is checked by the second one of a standing figure: the middle and right foreleg are almost vertical, even braced slightly to the front, on an axis with the erect neck of the middle head, which again appears partially skeletal and likewise fits into a logical overall figure back to the tail. Two rhythms, two speeds in a single figure, which behaves differently not only in space, but also in time. Varying points of view are not even required to appreciate these differences; they are not only in the eye of the subjective viewer, but in the nature of the figure itself. It thus seems appropriate to speak here of a four-dimensional sculpture, one that conducts itself variably in space and time.

In this case, the morphological variations and transitions also have a temporal dimension. They extend from body parts covered with fur, and to some extent naturally animated, to emaciated ones either covered with bare skin are partially skeletal. The latter, like the wholly fictional skeleton made visible beneath the skin, evoke the primeval dinosaur skeletons we see in natural history museums. The reptilian head of the striding figure does as well. Is this a relic from the distant past, a creature of our own time, or some apocalyptic monster? In any case, it is a highly ingenious sculpture.

It would be impossible to describe here all the other views and partial views in equal detail. If one moves around the figure toward the front from the side view described, it first appears to straighten up, and in the view of the front at an angle from the right, the heads extend outward like a bird of prey spreading its wings. The view of the right side is dominated by the animal's unkempt and matted fur and especially by the lame leg being dragged along, as in general by the very differently shaped feet of this allegorical hybrid and their placement. In views from the back, finally, an impression of the grotesque and bizarre predominates, the figure's heads and tails swinging back and forth depriving us of a comprehensive, overall view. It is precisely this back view that makes it clear that Hamberg was not concerned to create a virtuosic depiction of a chimera, but that the true theme of the sculpture is the interplay of its contradictory morphological, temporal, and psychological features animated through movement. *Hund* is a formal statement about what a sculpture can possibly communicate and at the same time an existential metaphor.

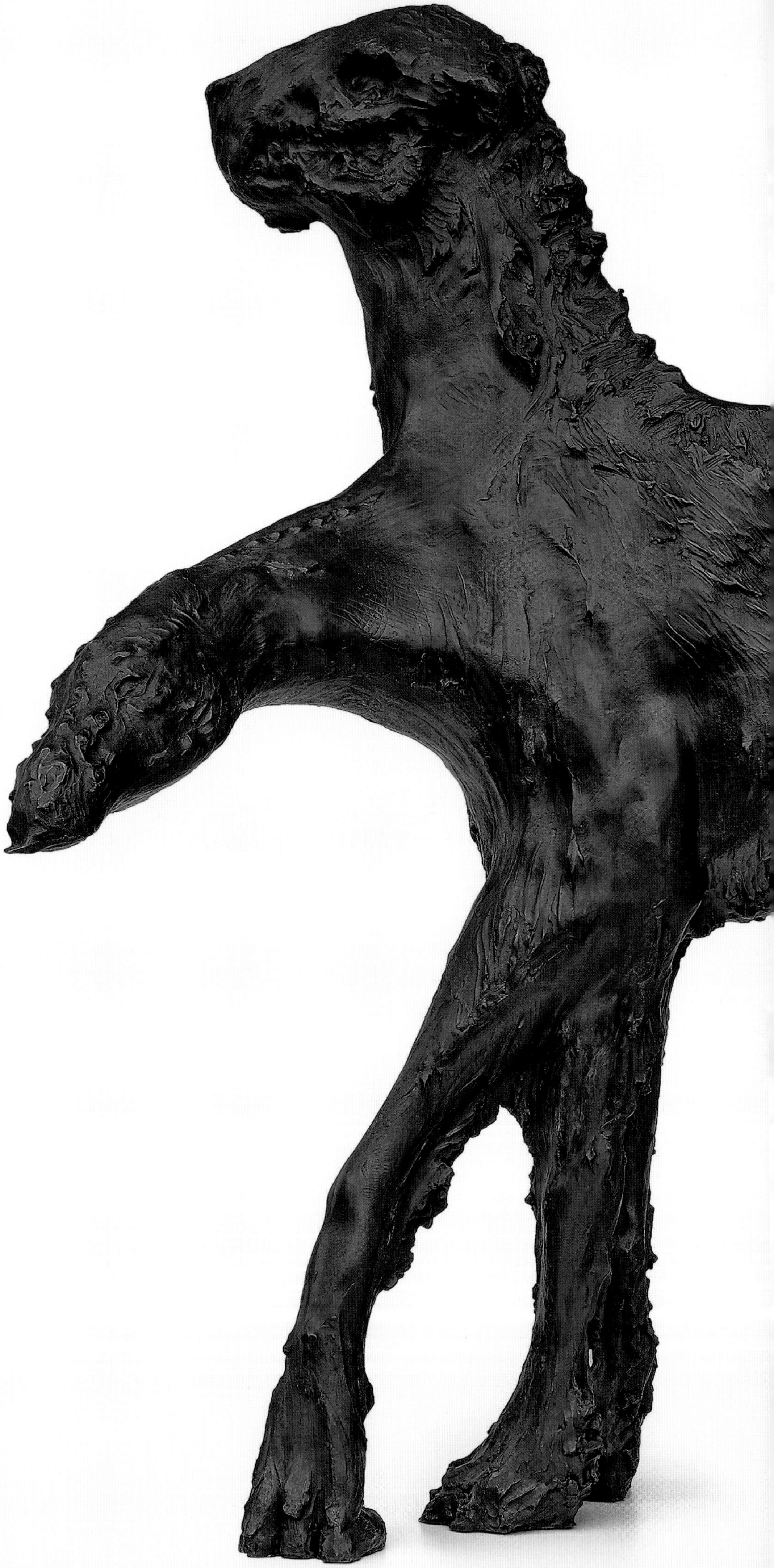

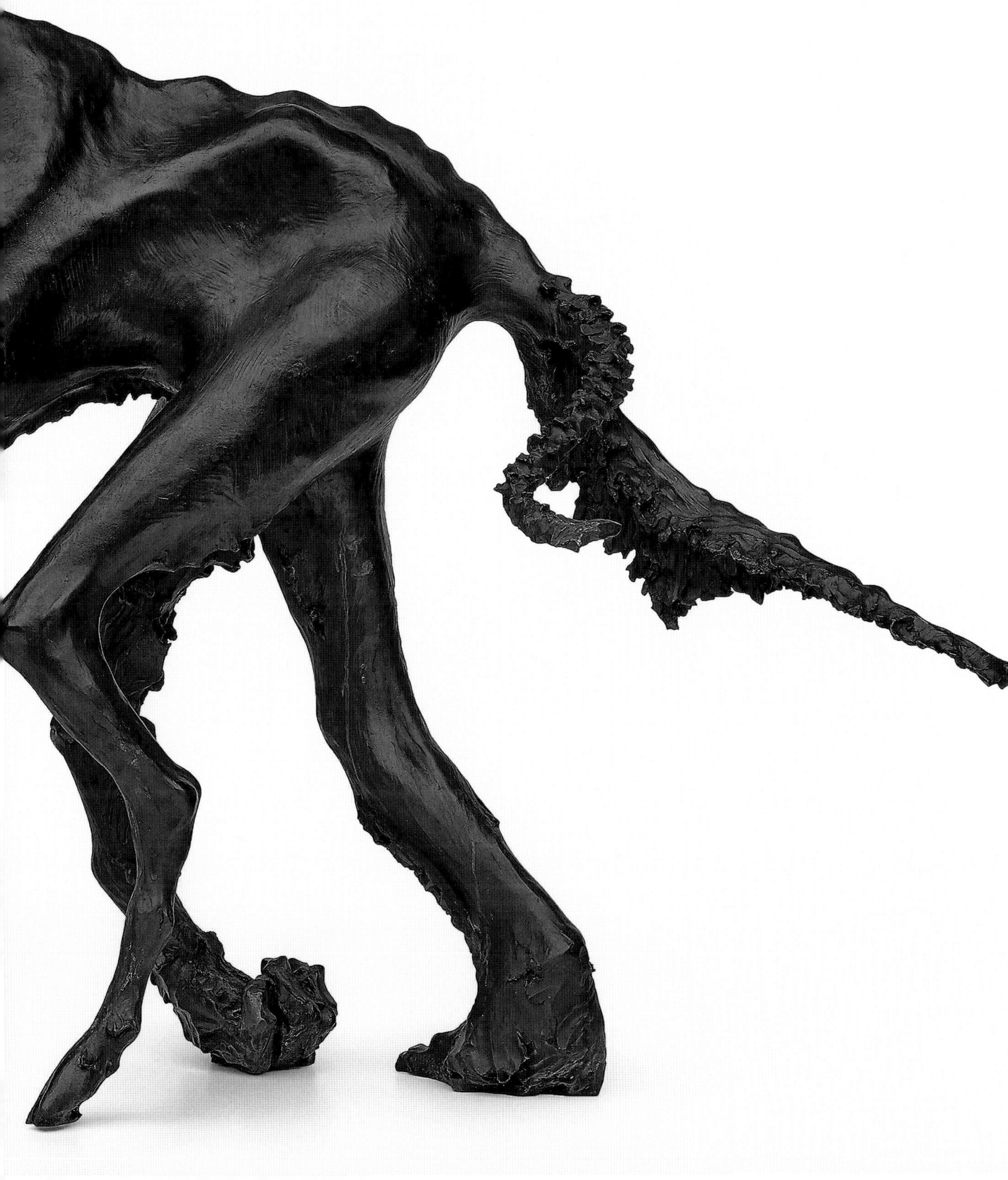

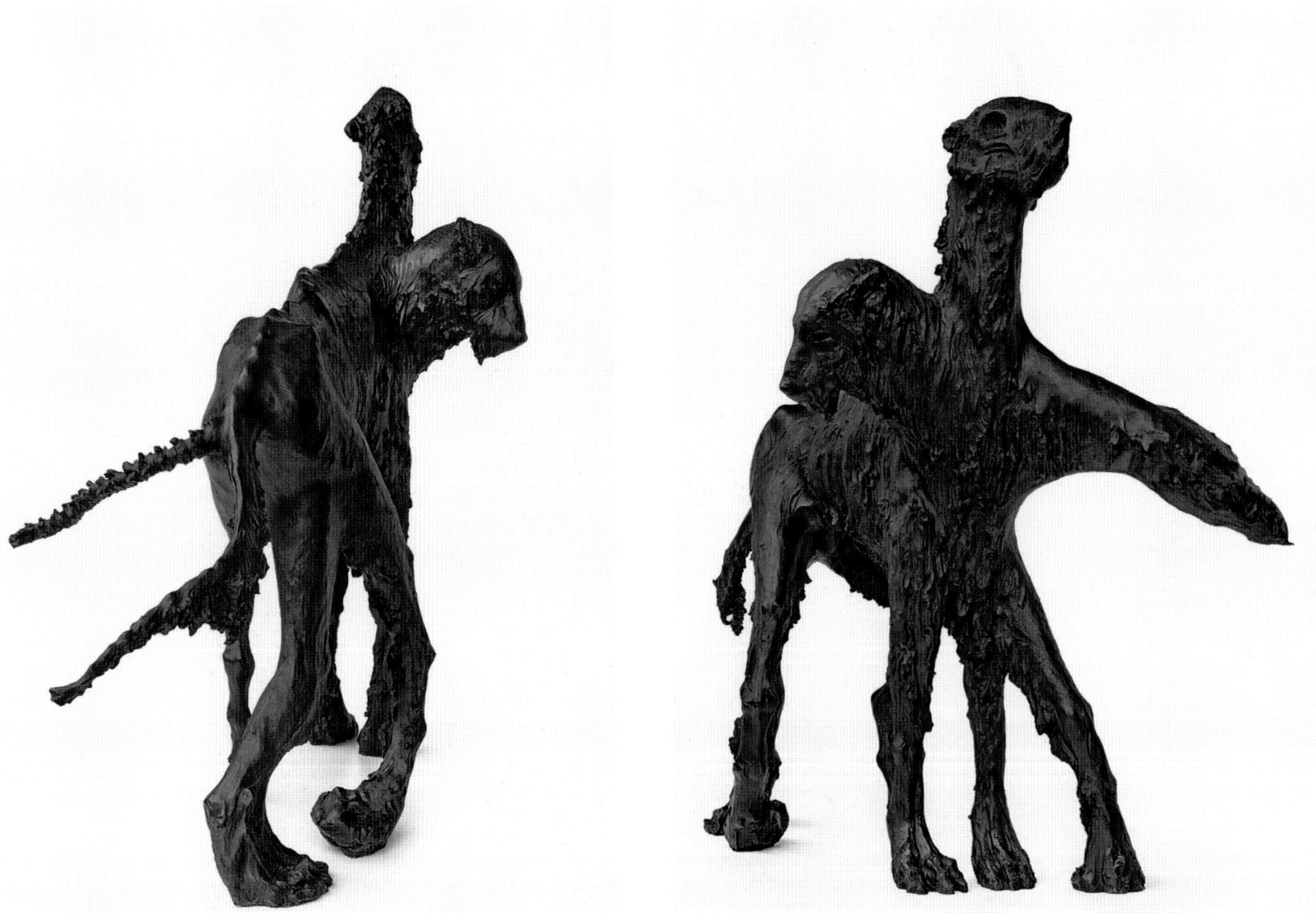

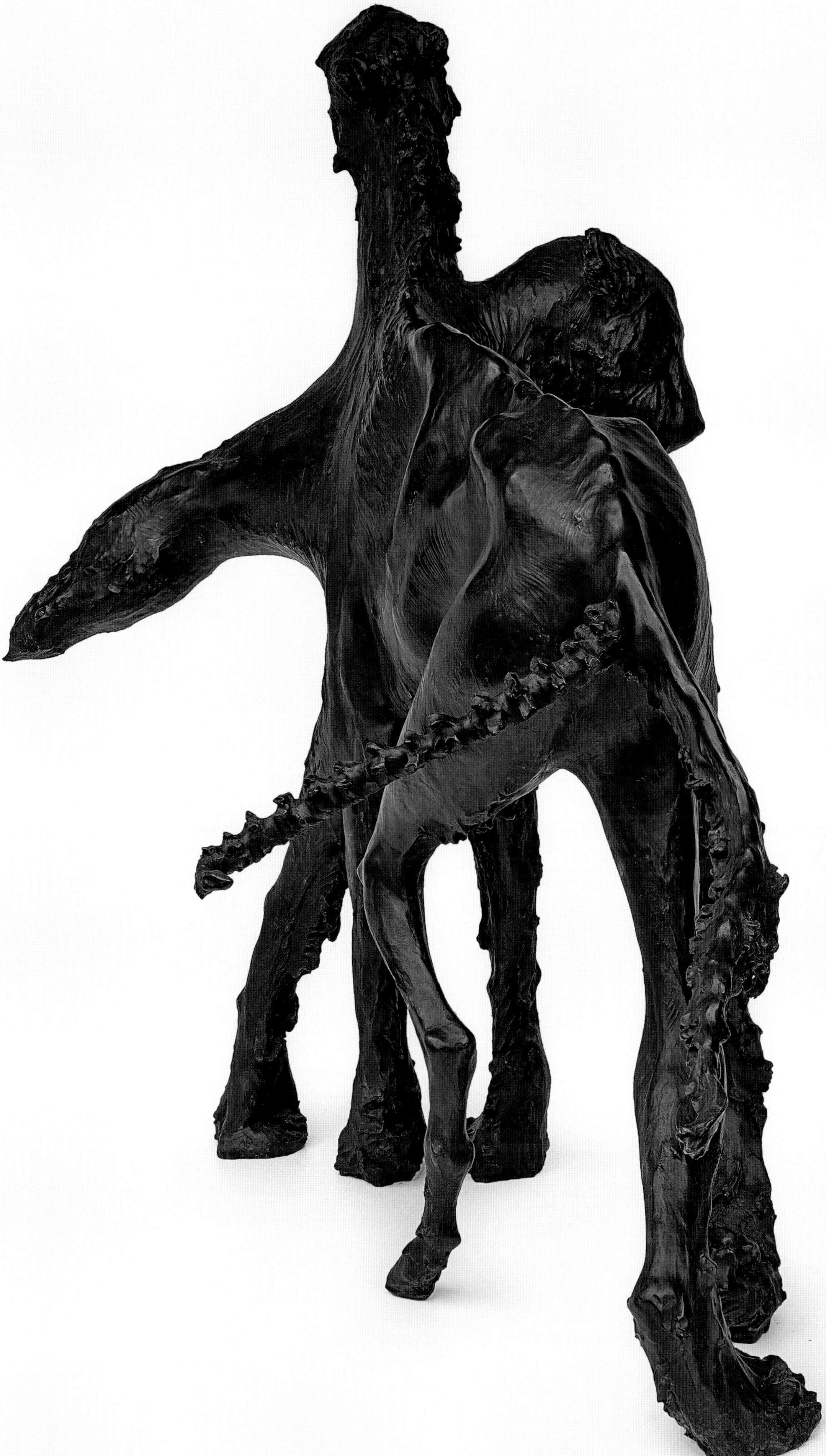

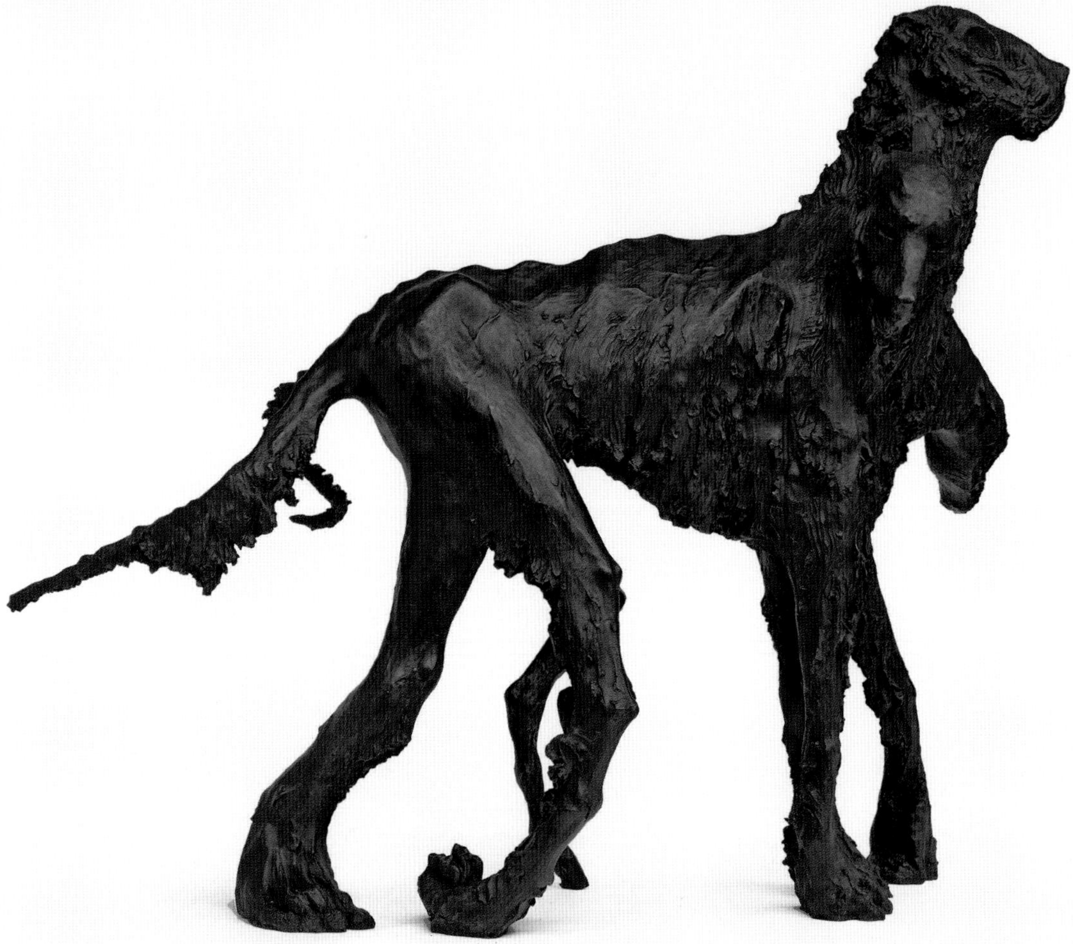

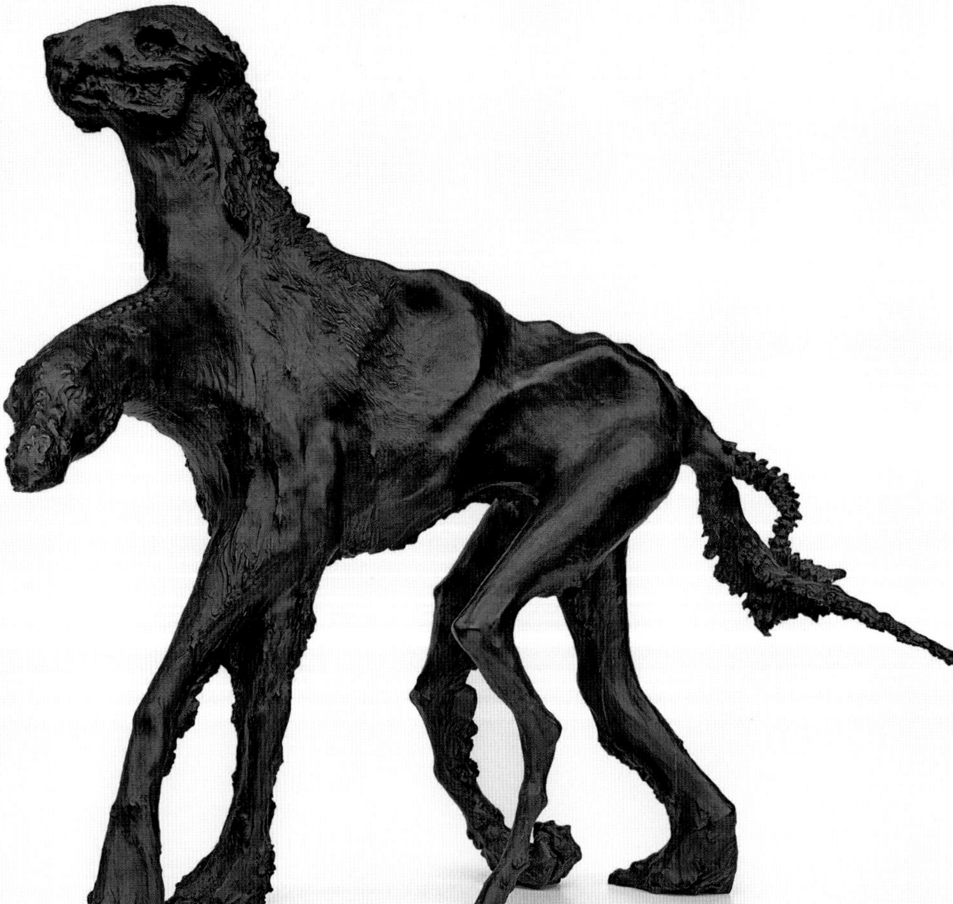

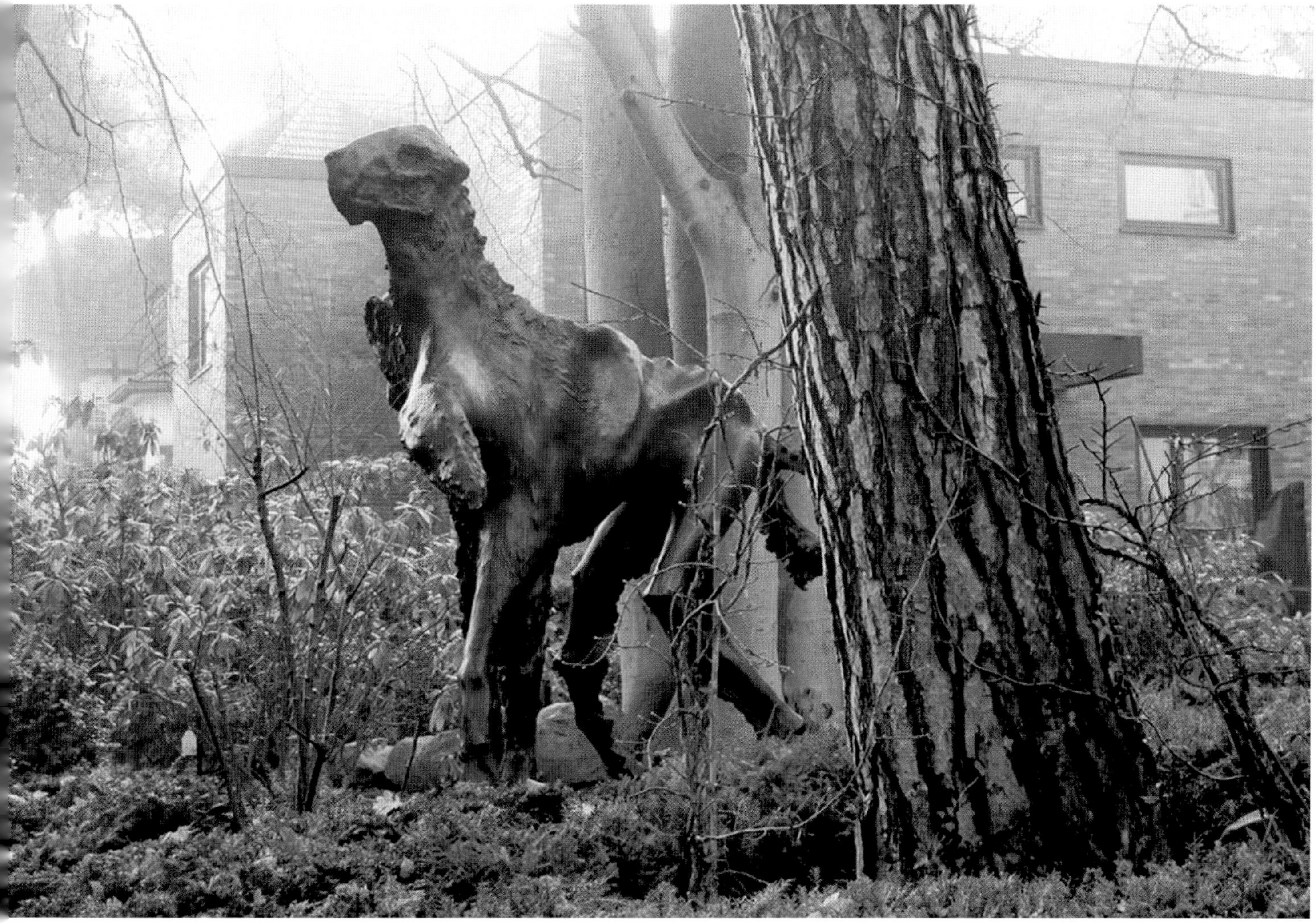

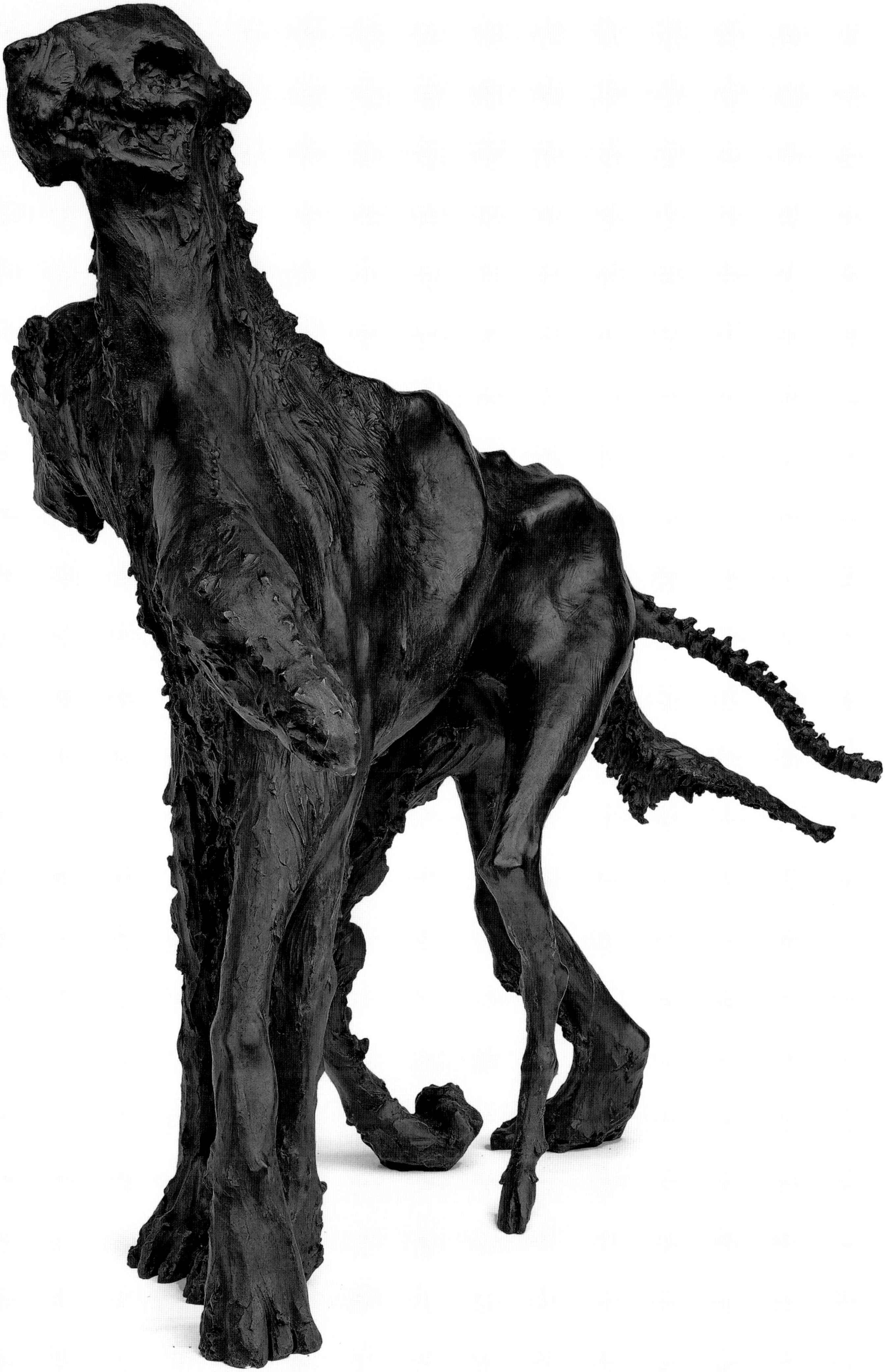

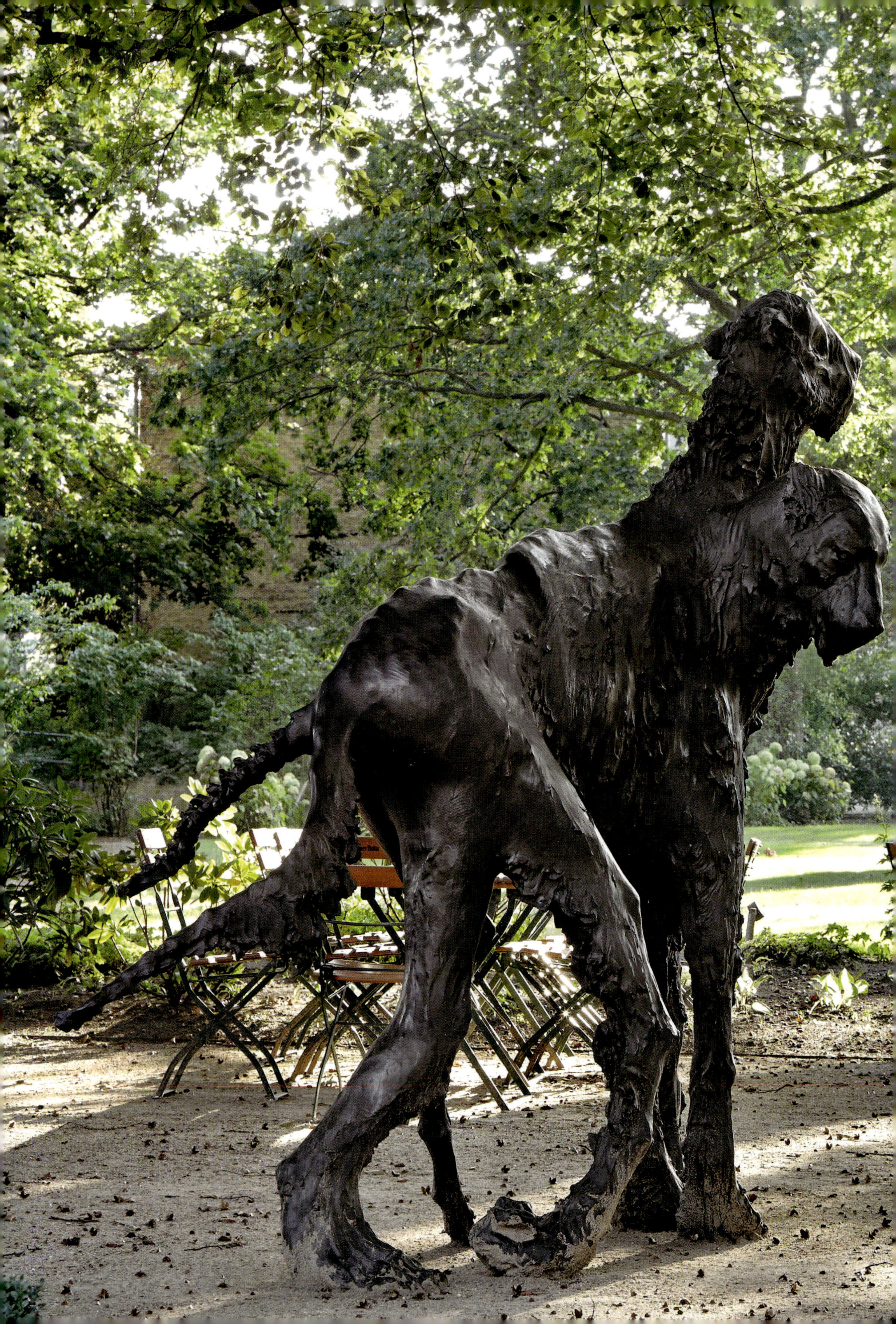

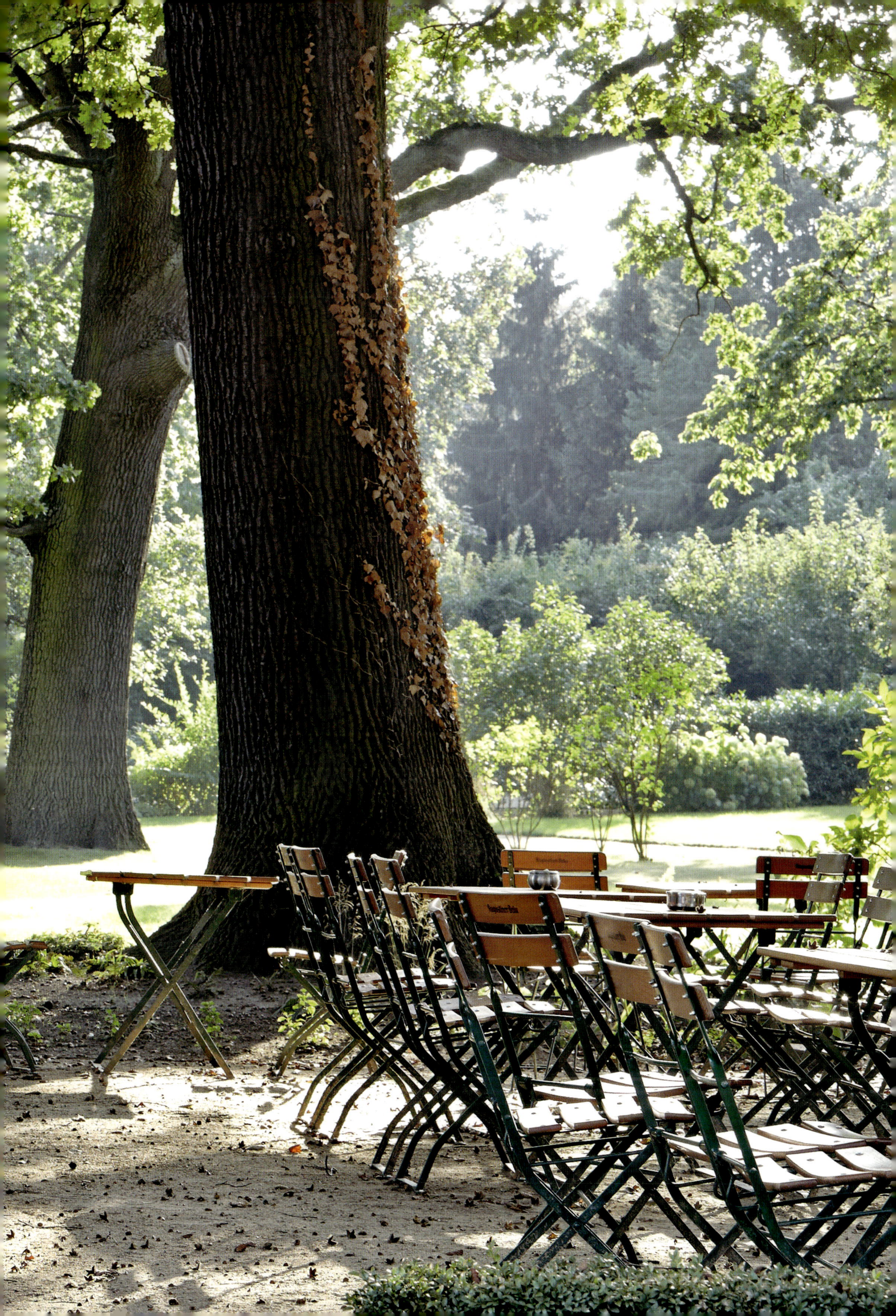

NEUTRON – A NEW DEFINITION OF SCULPTURAL CONCEPTS

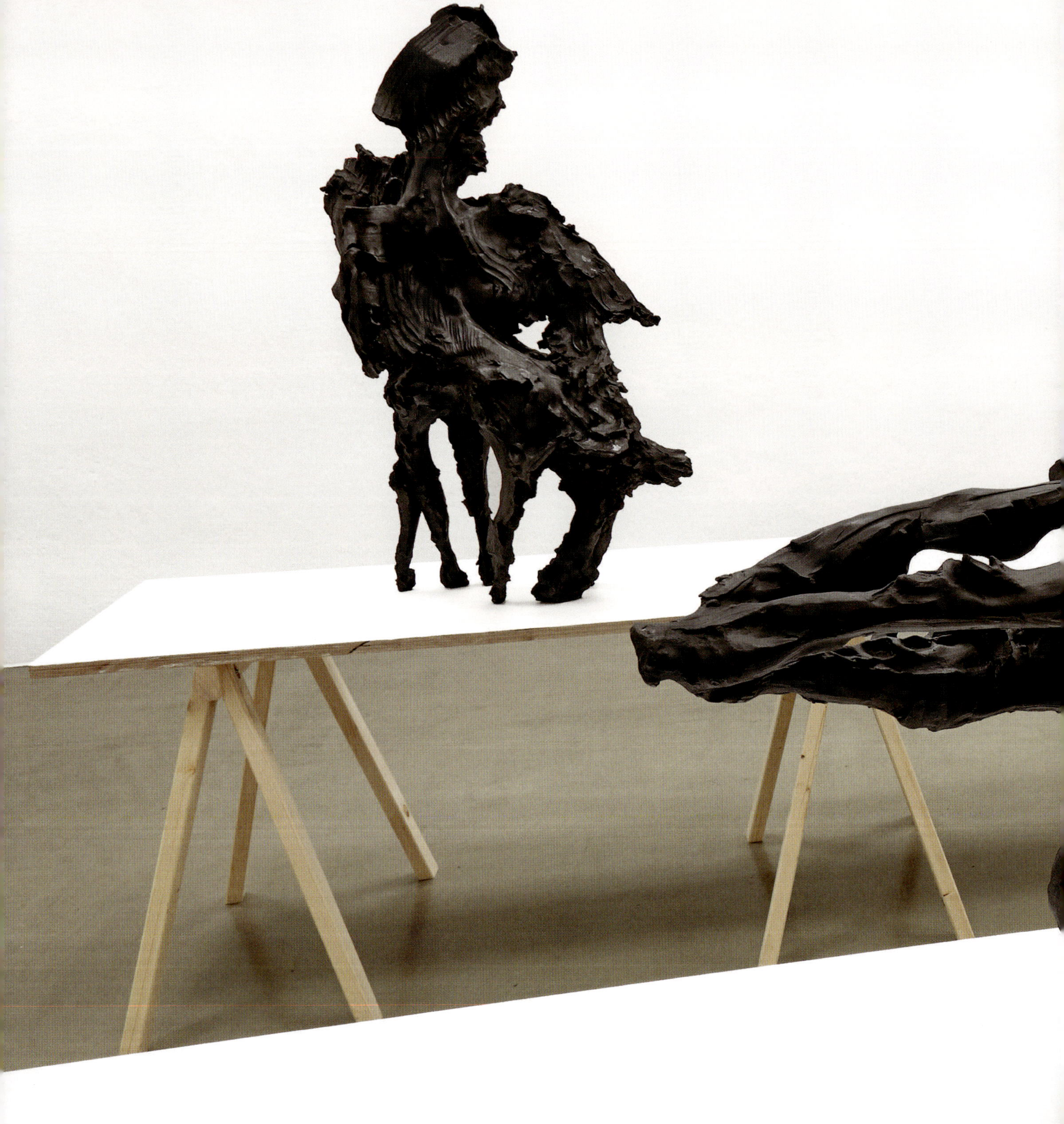

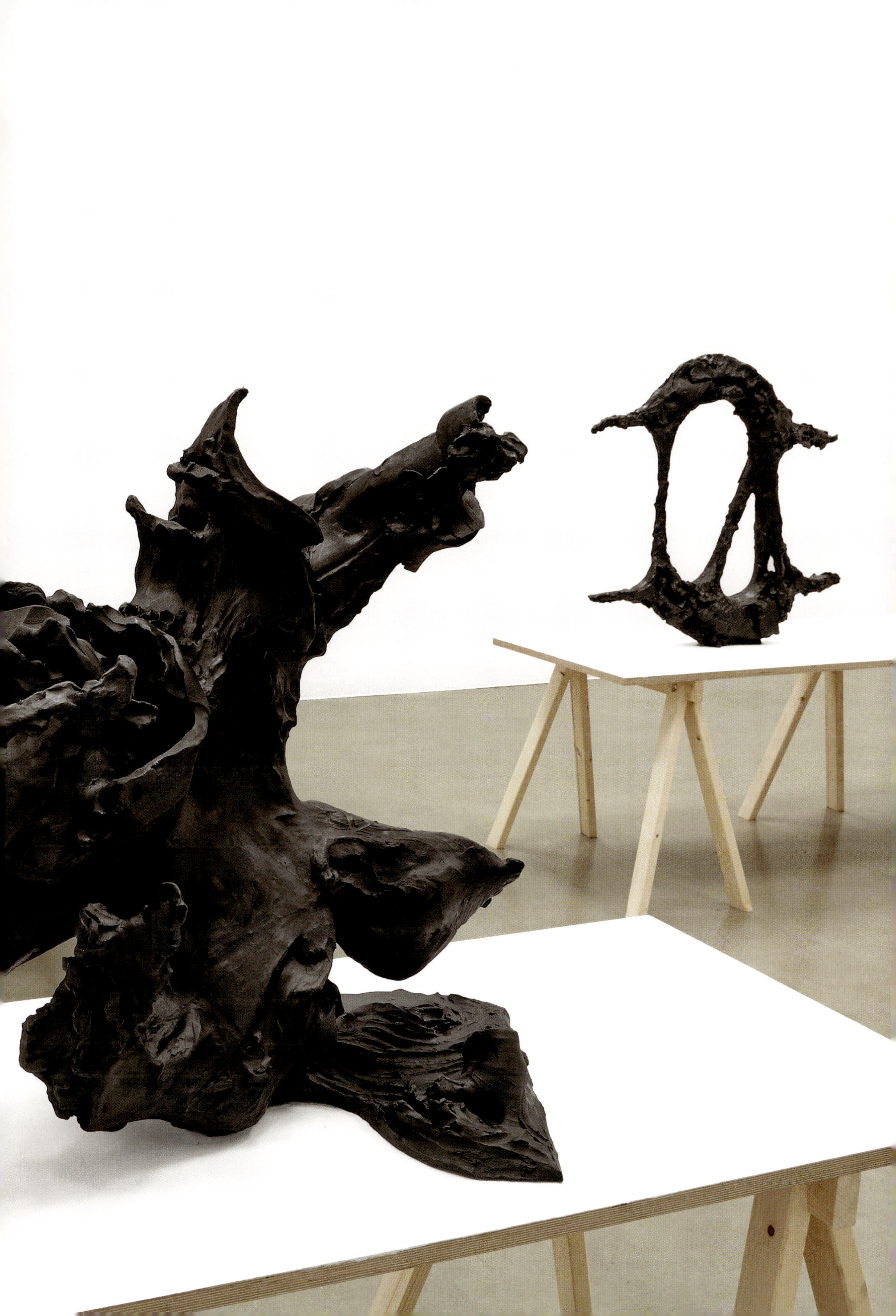

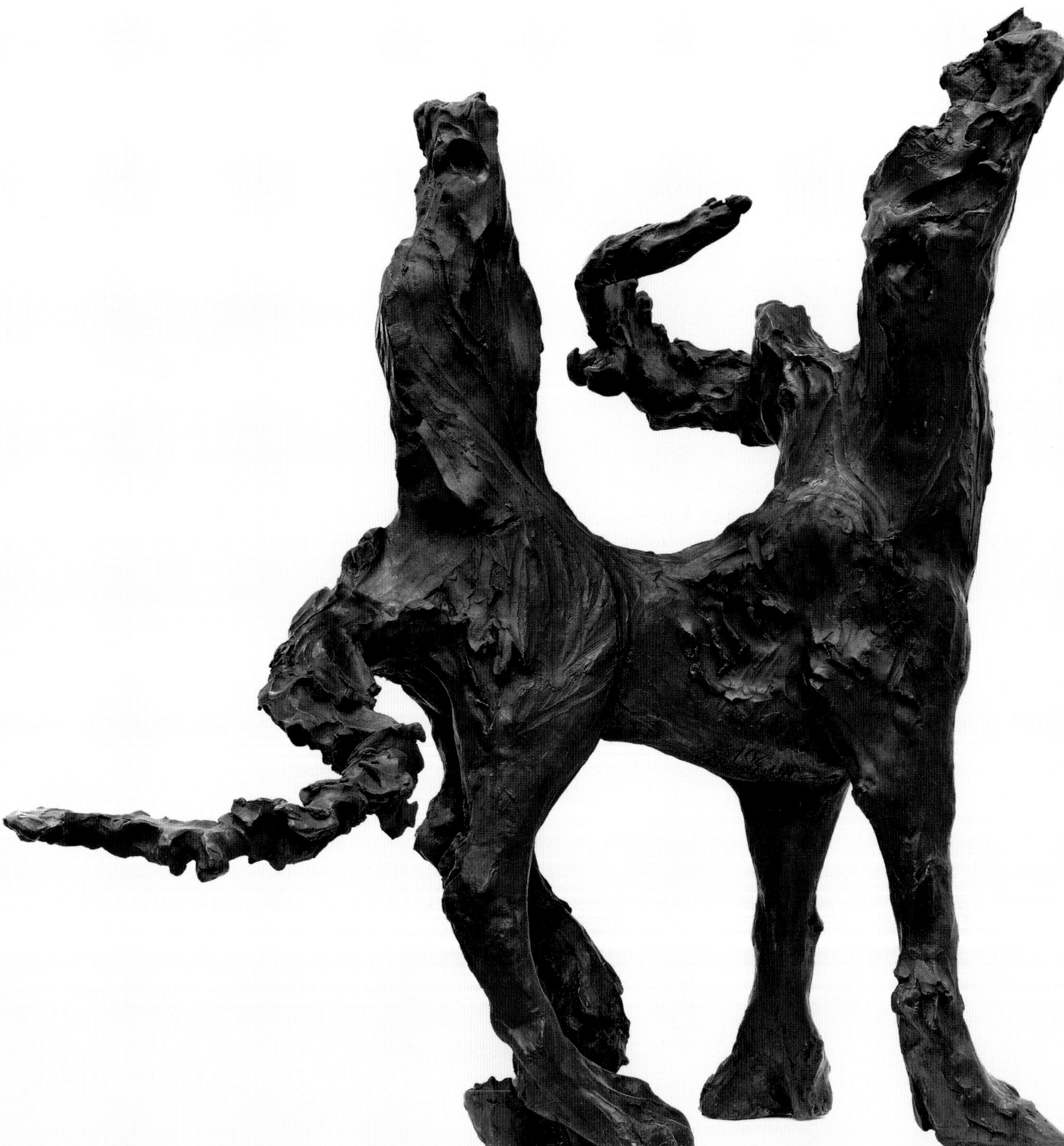

For Hamberg, every sculpture, quite apart from its motif or narrative features, is a "concept," a specific mode of three-dimensional formulation. By now she has developed such a large repertoire of ways to concretise and disintegrate forms that it is not surprising to find a range of possible sculptural concepts exemplified in the relatively large number, compared to her output in the previous years, of new bronze sculptures. Instead of striving for a comprehensive solution in a single figure like *Hund* or a small group of figures like the *Berserkers*, in this larger group of sculptures variations on the basic theme are presented, as in a kaleidoscope, that were ultimately intensified in *Hund*. The uniform black patination of all these works accents their purely sculptural form, as does the detailed modelling and the presence or absence of surface sheen, but not a painterly deployment of patina as in *vom Verrecken und der Unmöglichkeit zu sterben*. In this respect, the new sculptures also represent a turn toward formal reduction and abstraction.

The categorical inclusion of time, either as flowing or frozen, recollected or projected into the future, which was taken to an extreme in *Hund*, is an ever-present feature in the twelve sculptures produced in 2015, as is the resulting necessity of viewing them from different angles. For only when circling them does one understand that there is neither a clearly established starting point nor an end point. Yet the abandonment of a single primary view or sequence of views by no means leaves the viewer in limbo, for the figure cast in bronze remains always the same and clearly defined. Also, there is not the ambiguity of puzzling symbols onto which one can project this or that meaning. Instead, the sculptures suggest a degree of perception for which no fixed point of view suffices any longer. One's mental image is formed only through viewing the work in movement, recognising its varied and at times contradictory features.

Motifs from *Hund* are taken up in *the curve I – twilight mountain sculpture* (2015), for example two dogs' heads visible from a certain perspective, but through abstraction it distances itself so far from the motifs of the dog's body that in the metamorphosis of forms one sees, depending on one's point of view, an animal seated on its hind legs, a winged creature striving upward, and even a transition from zoomorphic shapes to those of a tree. In classic contrapposto, with relaxed and tensed, burdened and unburdened elements, as well as a balance between the axes and equilibrium, it always presents a unified, animated figure with a definite expression of movement or the potential for it. However, in this case we find a figure that, depending on which side one views, reveals different degrees of stability or dynamism, of axial stability or instability, and is characterised by differing rhythms.

In *the curve 2 – Stille* (2015) certain individual forms are also derived from forms that originated in *Hund*, for example its disappearing back view, though it makes little sense to name the motifs. From one side the sculpture is built up above a rectangular base slab, only to then contract from other perspectives, extend far out into space in one direction or another, or even to perform a capriole, like a bit of choreography in a modern dance performance. Contraction and expansion of form are likewise themes in *the curve 3 – echoes in my head* (2015), a sculpture that evolves primarily from bottom to top like a three-rooted tree and culminates in a spirited spiral tip. To judge from other Hamberg sculptures, in which large, fateful questions of human existence are addressed, one could imagine being allowed to witness here sheer joy in the dance of sculptural forms. As long as Hamberg's sculptures include references to natural forms or take them as a starting point, the pendulum swinging between these and pure sculptural form can either emphasize the motif, as in *Frau*, or free form, as in *the curve 2 – Stille*. *das ist das* (2015), a ferocious open shark's maw with pointed teeth, is surely among the works with a more defined motif and those that also let the artist's roguish humour and sense of the grotesque shine through, like *Dämon I* and *Dämon II*, *out of season*, and *reset* from her earlier work. *das ist das* does not have the sculptural or contextual weight of such works as *Berserkers* or *Hund*, but immediately presents itself as an artistic artefact. In the Potsdam exhibition (2016), the shark's maw, through which one can look, stood atop an iron base with a surface plate that seems to float. The overall image had not only the suggestion of a Jack-in-the-box, it also described the fascination for the monstrous as a high-wire act between pathos and the grotesque – a tension that Hamberg takes up again and again with different emphases. This also explains the self-irony in *me* (2015), a crude depiction of a kiwi that always looks lost or displaced, no matter in what context it is positioned, or in *out of season*, where the grotesqueness of human effort is part of the pictorial poetry. In this context, one might also mention *großer Schatten* (Large Shadow; 2015), a Janus-like sculpture of a theatrical mask with a tall forehead and hollow eyes, like a dream vision by Max Klinger, and a dog's head.

Also *my dear fellow* (2015), one of the sculptures in this series with a more clearly identifiable motif, is not entirely free of grotesque features, but in small format also represents an inscrutable interpretation of an age-old sculptural subject, the equestrian monument. From antiquity to the Renaissance and Baroque, and on up to its formulaic torpor in the 19th century, this genre was used above all for the depiction of rulers. Given Stella Hamberg's proven skill in depicting extremely powerful and dynamic animal figures, as in *prayer* and even in *Hund*, this horse, with its fragile body characterised by cracks in the drying clay, stands out mainly for its unstable stance on thin, stilt-like legs. When the figure's right flank is viewed, the horse's head and that of the rider, who, without legs, is conjoined with its back and who recalls the thin-as-a-rail Don Quixote, turn into death's heads.

The dynamic alternative to this sculpture is *fortune* (2015). This sculpture is also clearly a free variation of *Hund*, whose six-legged figure is here transformed into a kind of Pegasus, a ghostly winged horse, either rising up or shying, depending on the side from which it is viewed.

The motif of the wings of a large bird is taken up once again in grandiose, animated forms in *Nacht* (Night; 2015). In profile an altogether static, fixed figure, seen from the front the bird recalls the motif of the pelican in Christian art, which tears open its breast in order to feed its chicks. But from behind one sees a powerful bird of prey spreading its wings and rising upward in flight.

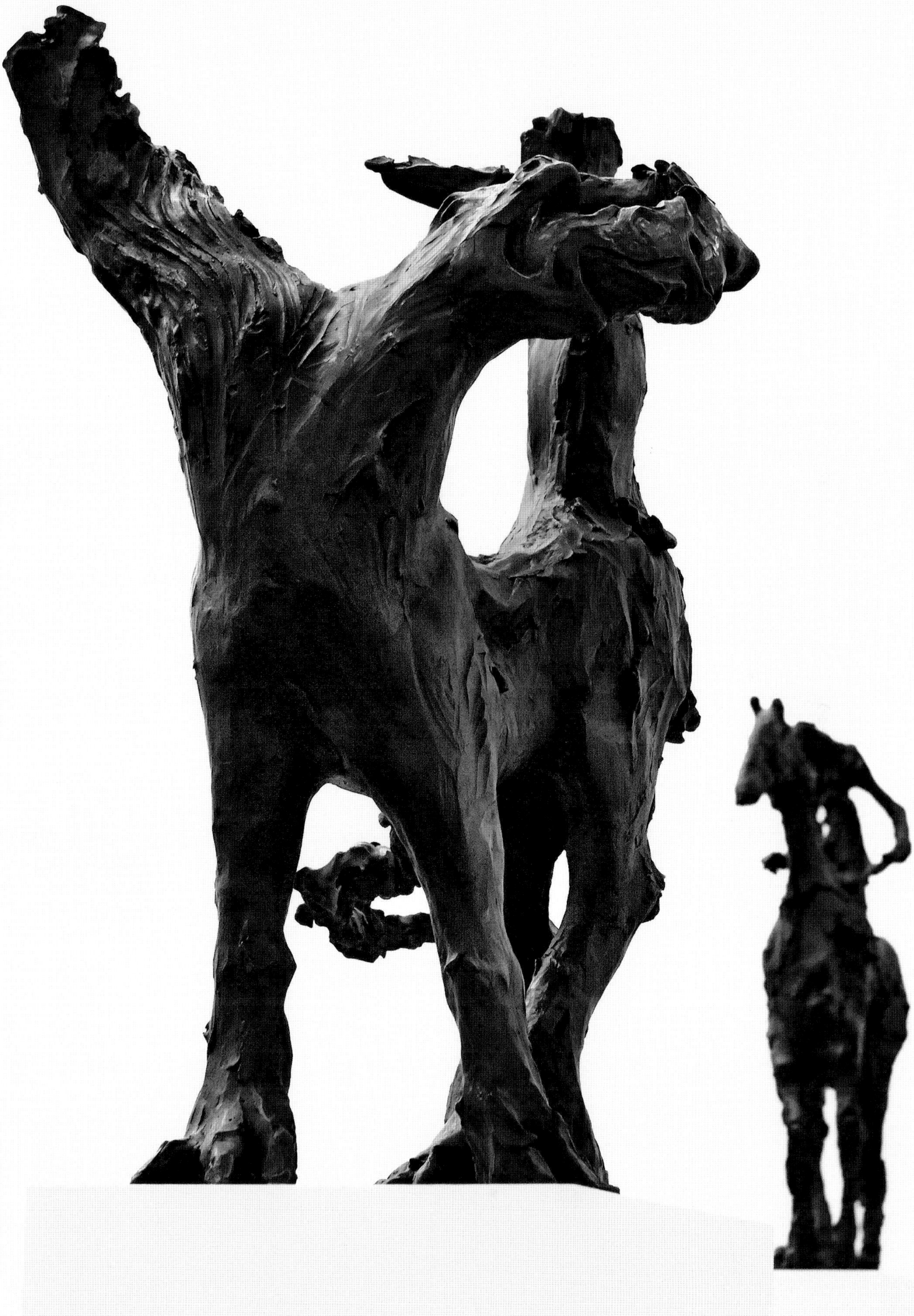

knotty network (don't think twice) 2015

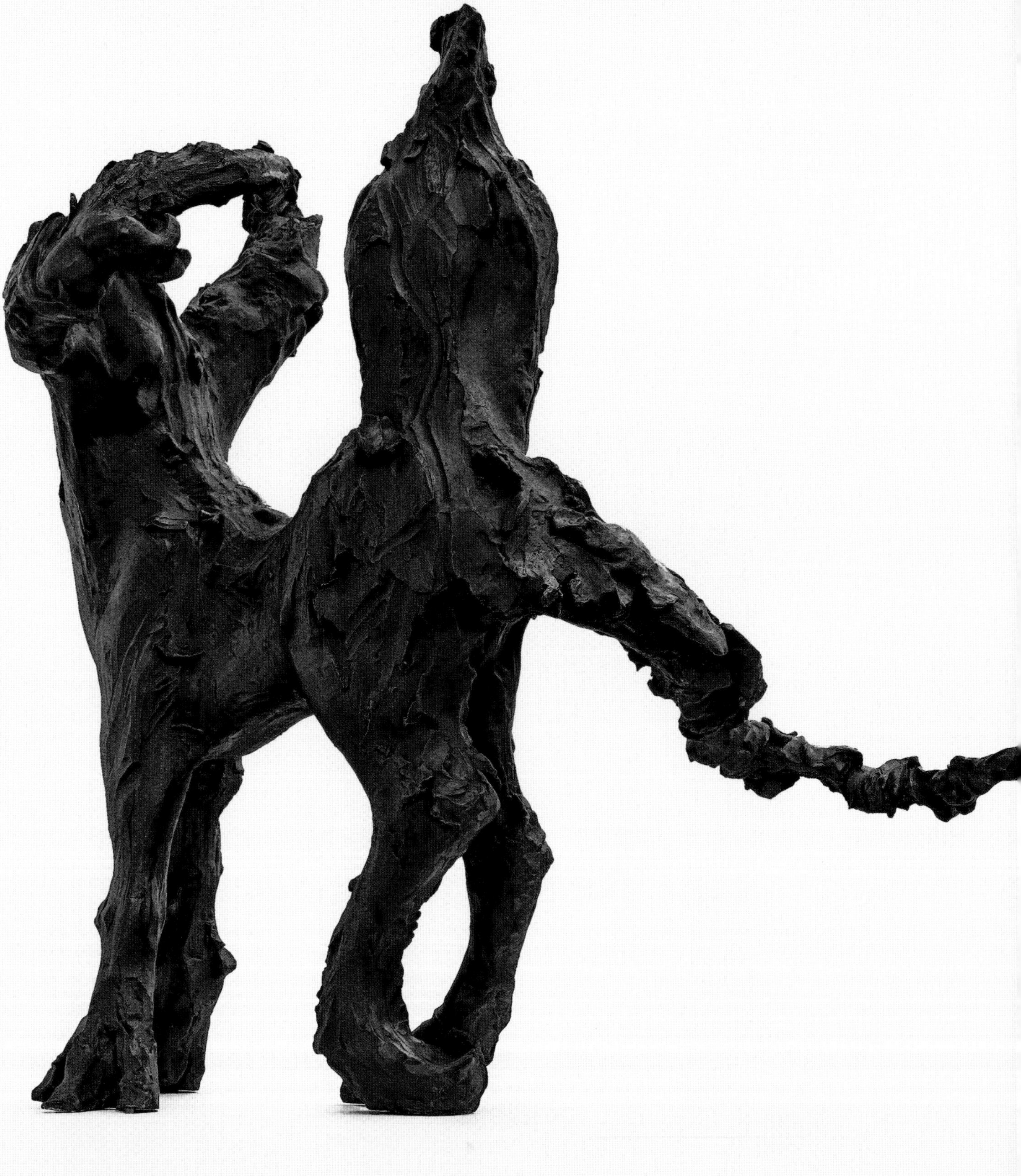

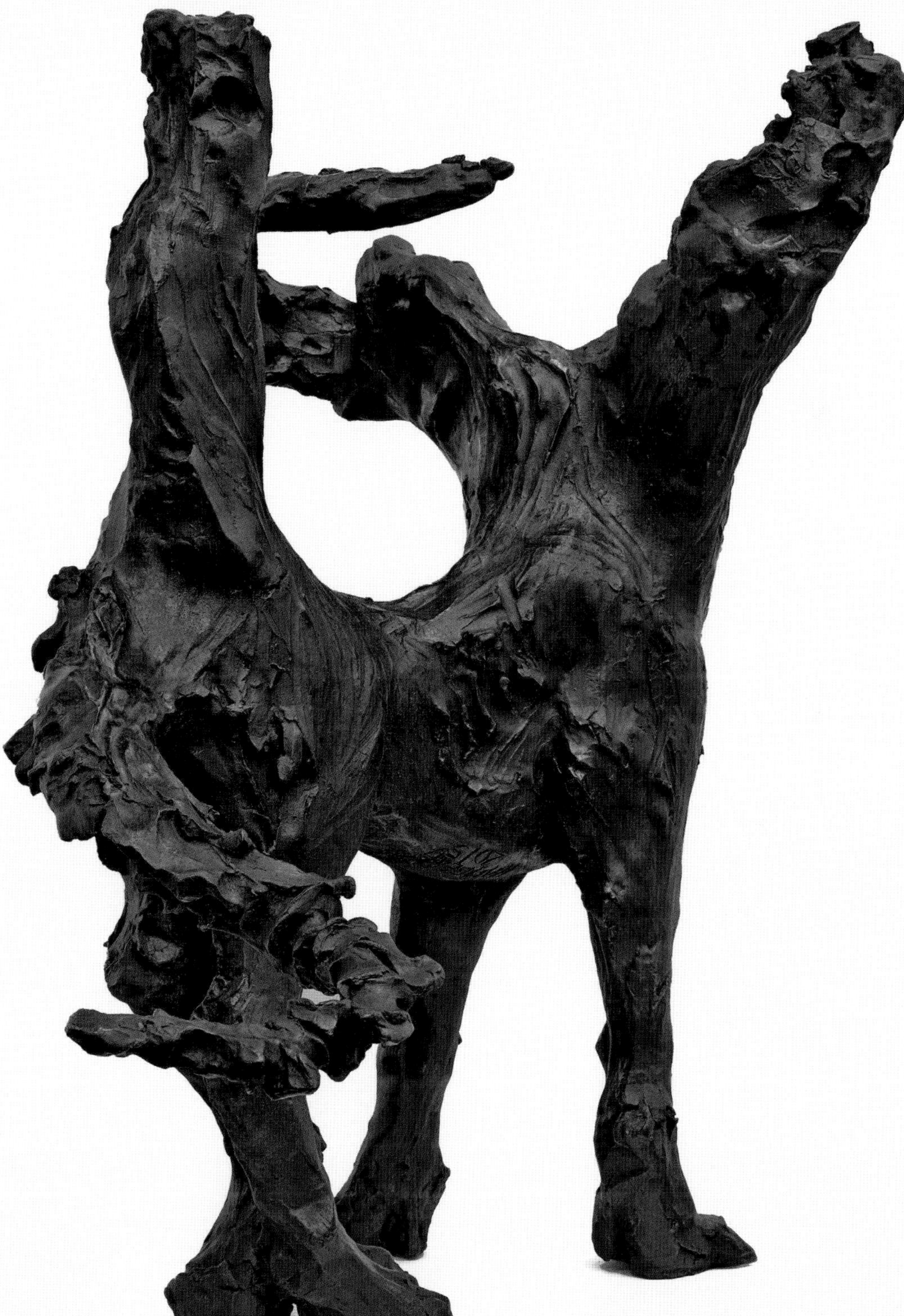

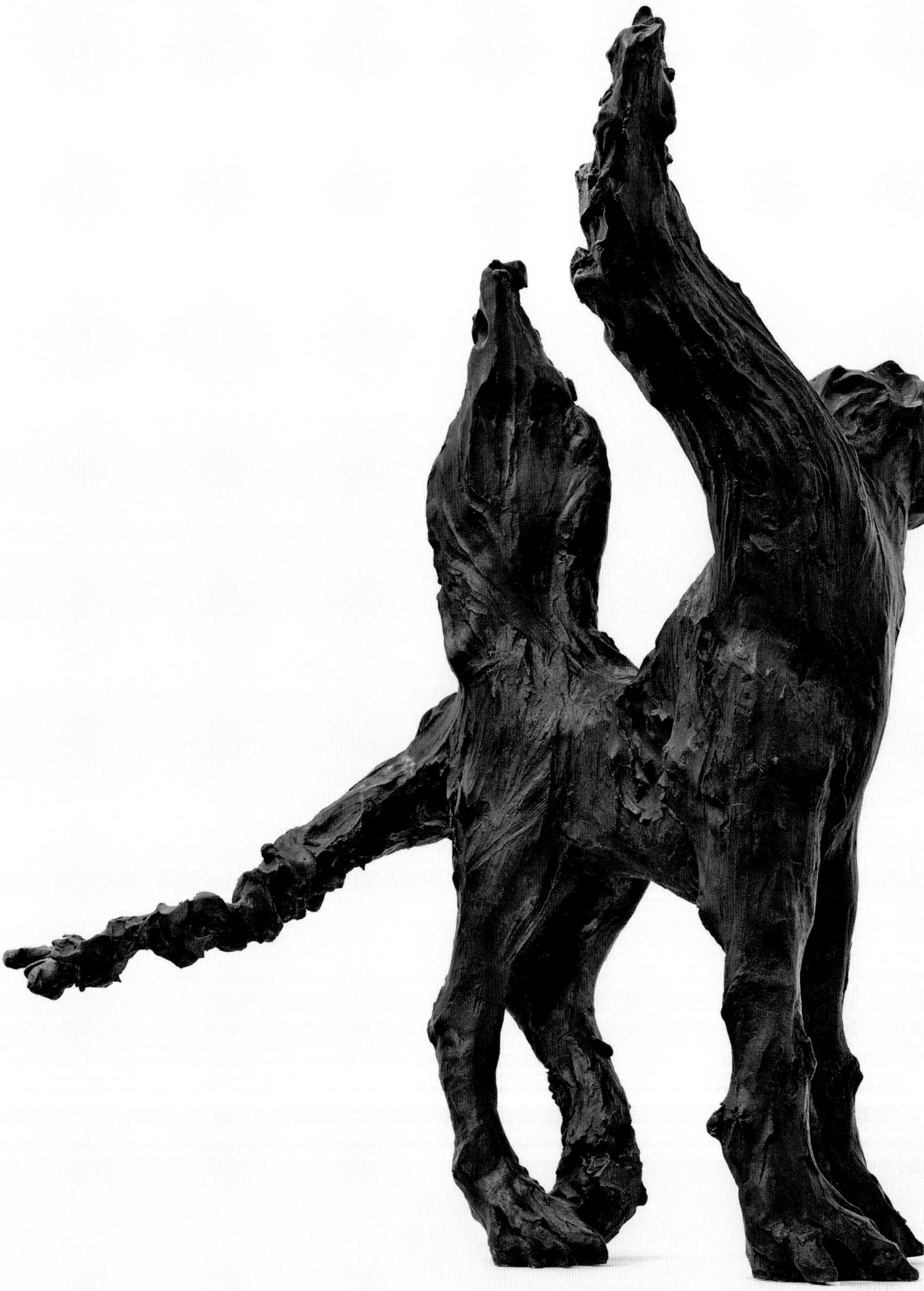

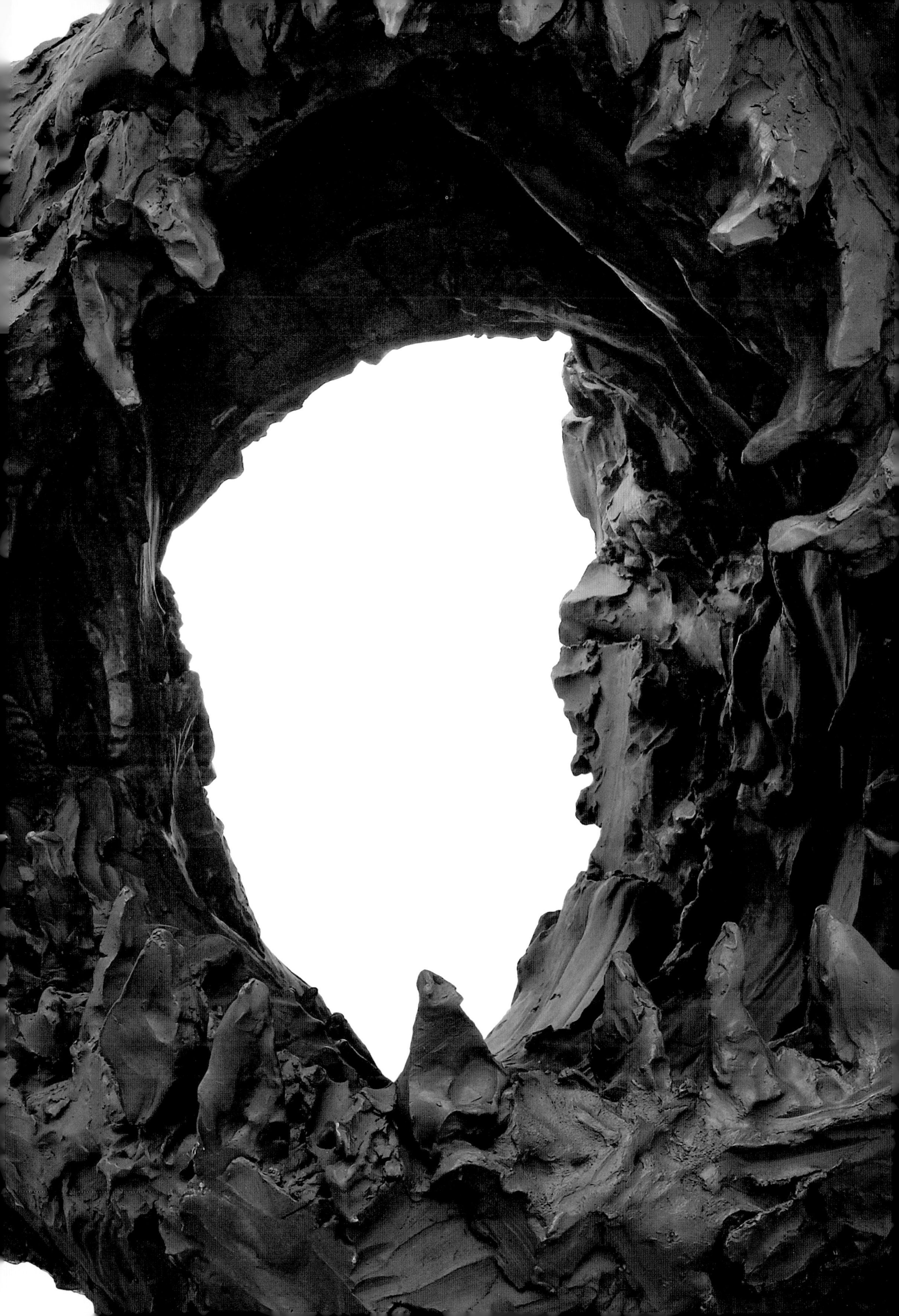

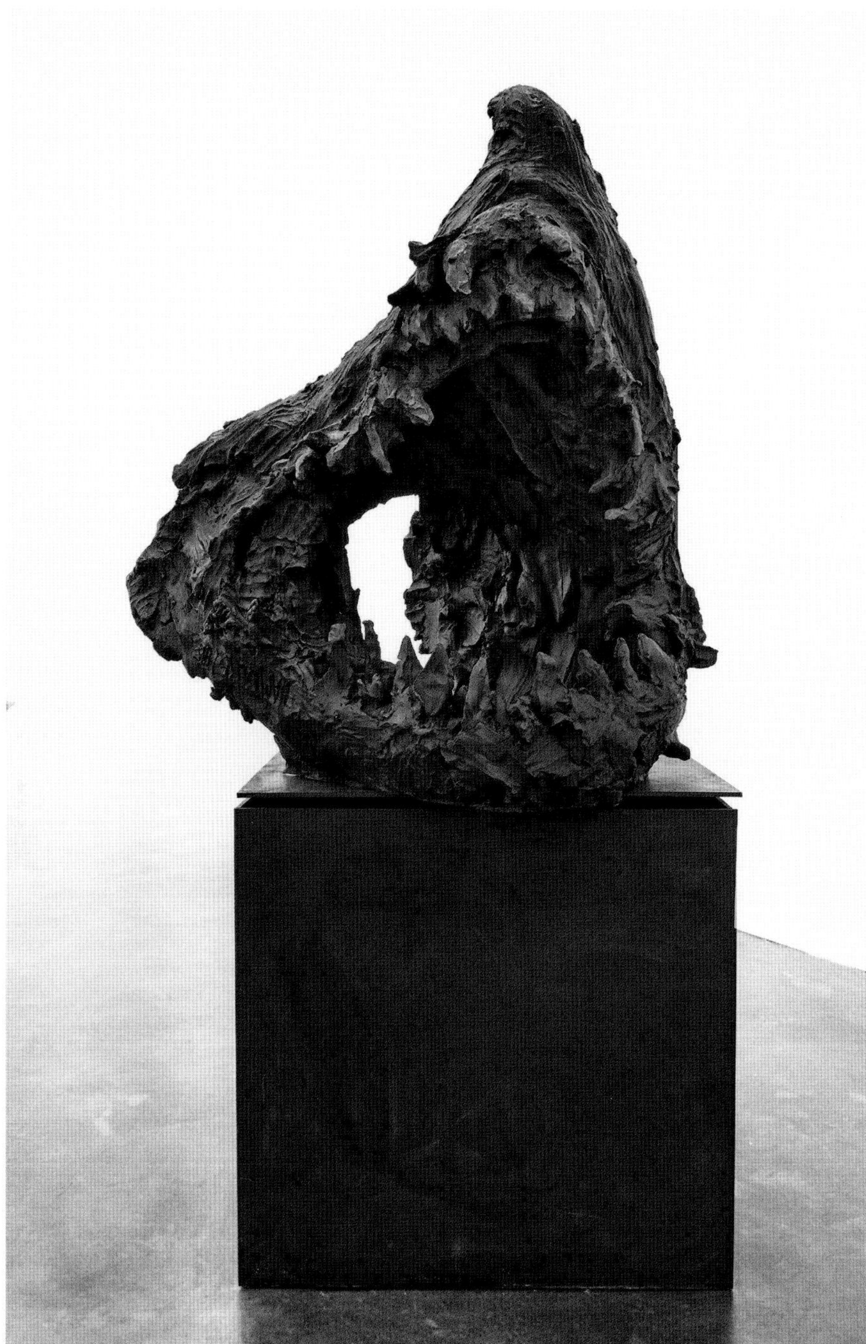

my dear fellow 2015

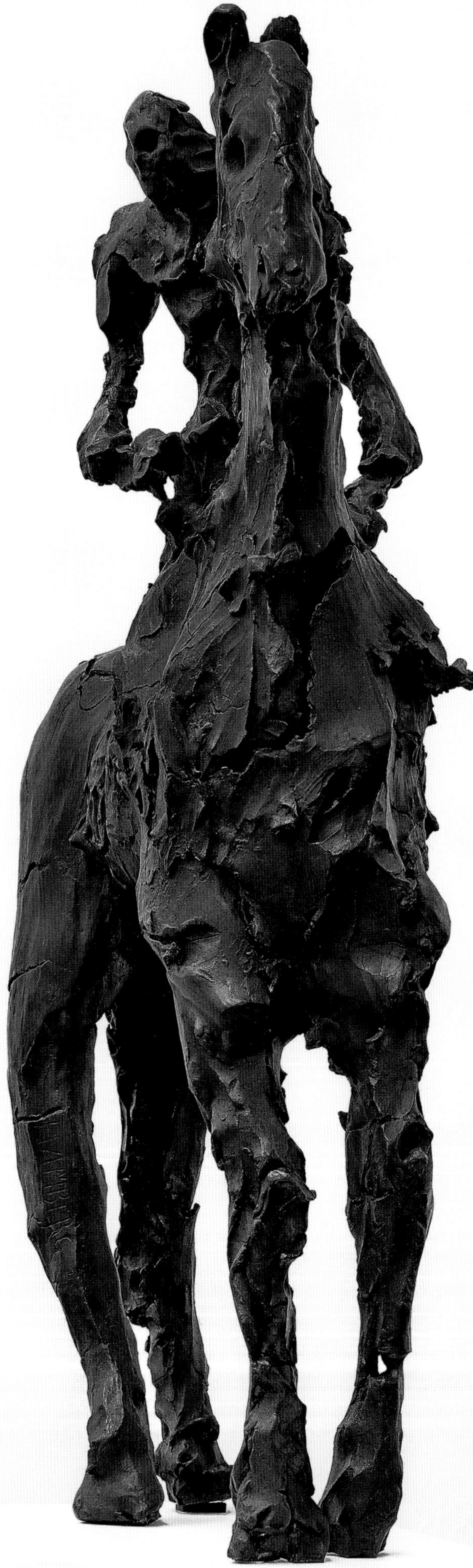

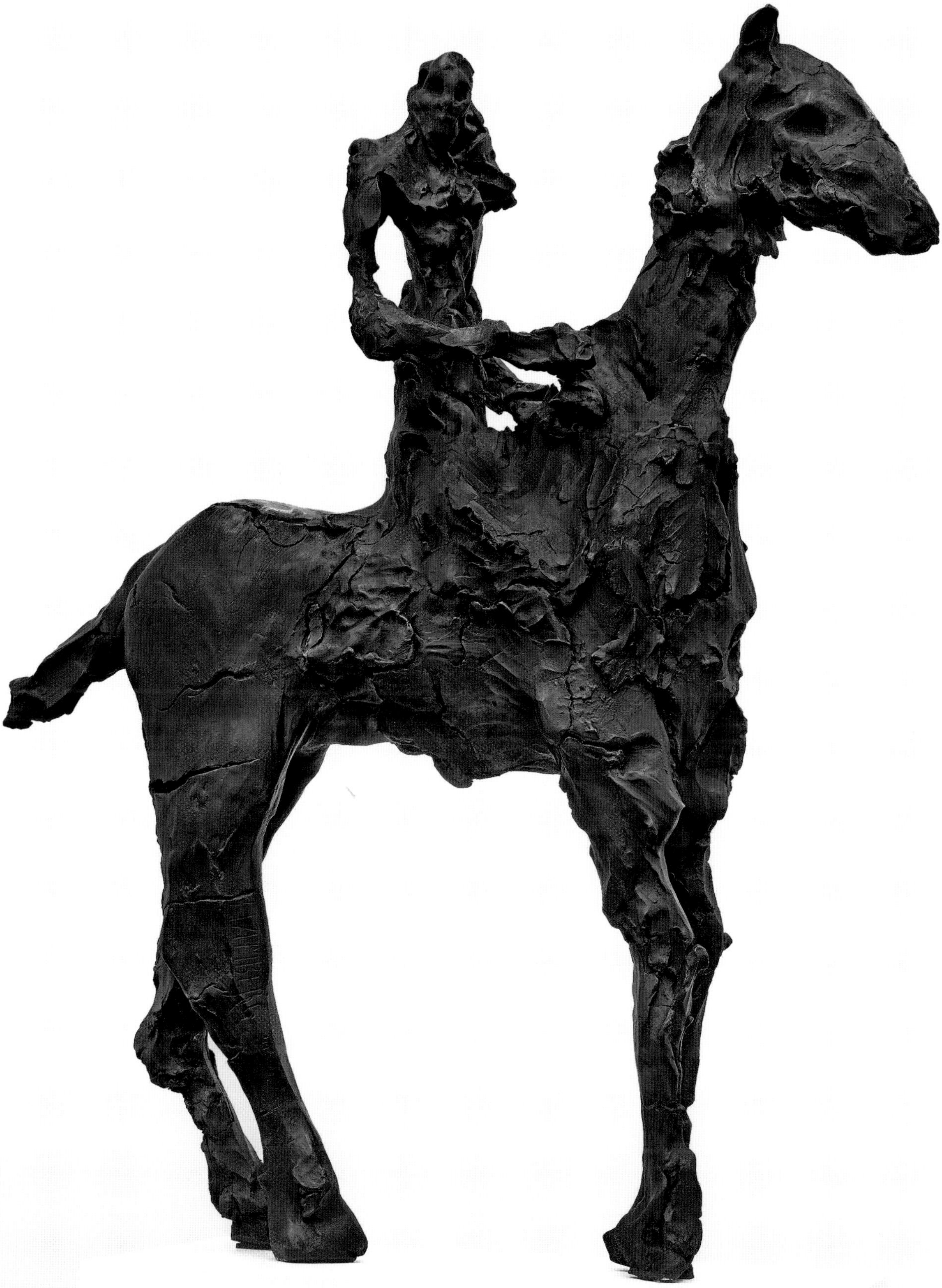

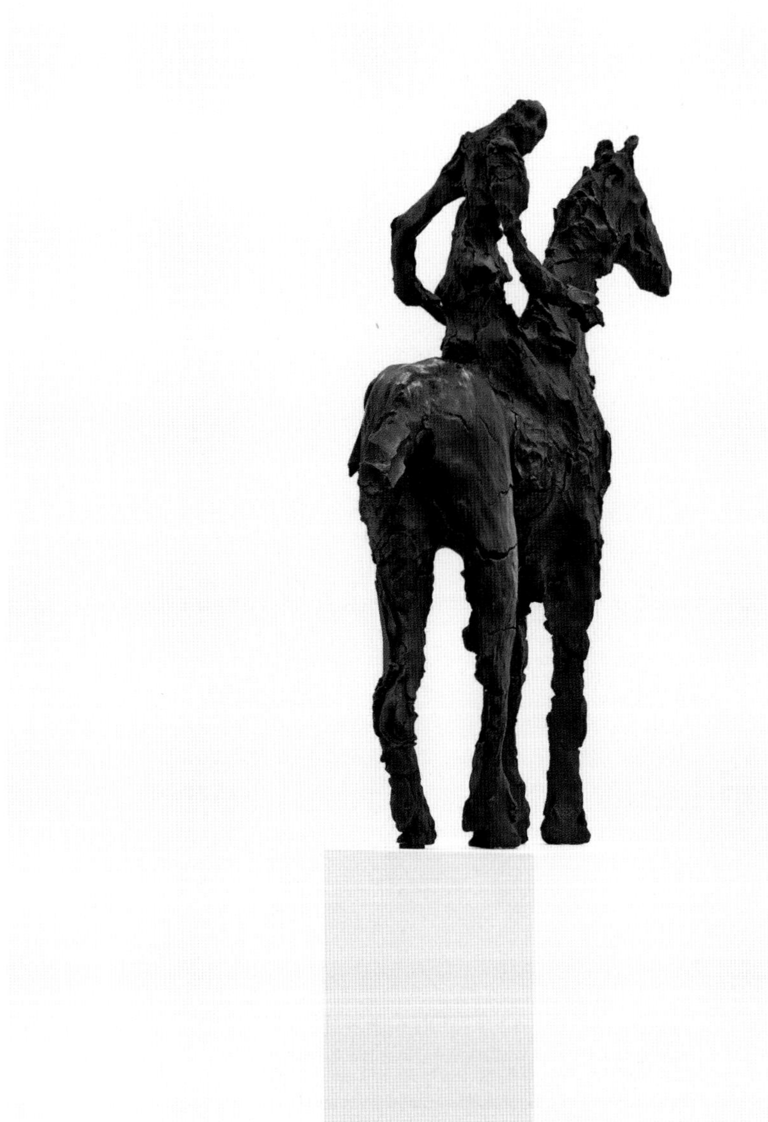

the curve 3 – echoes in my head 2015

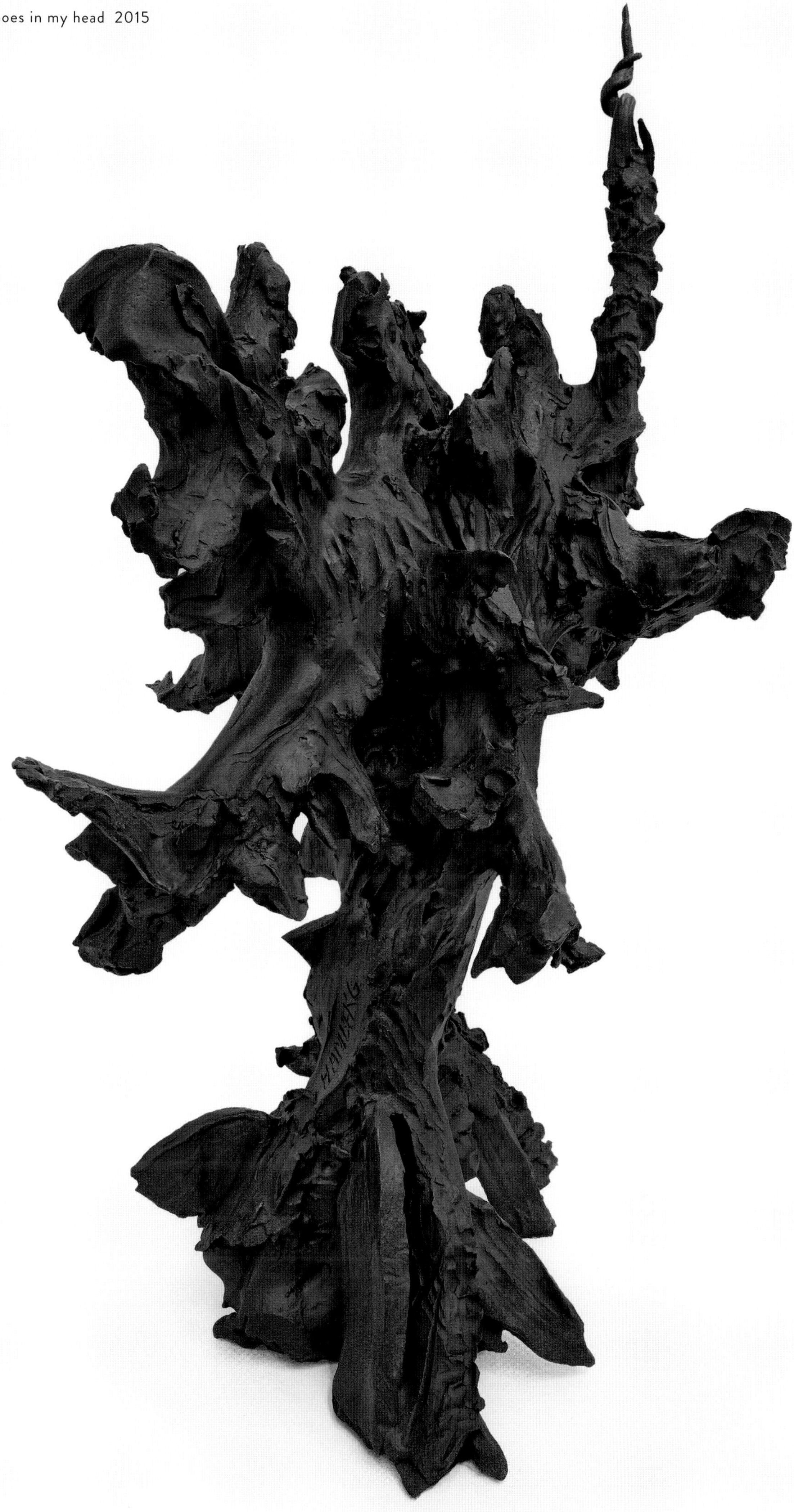

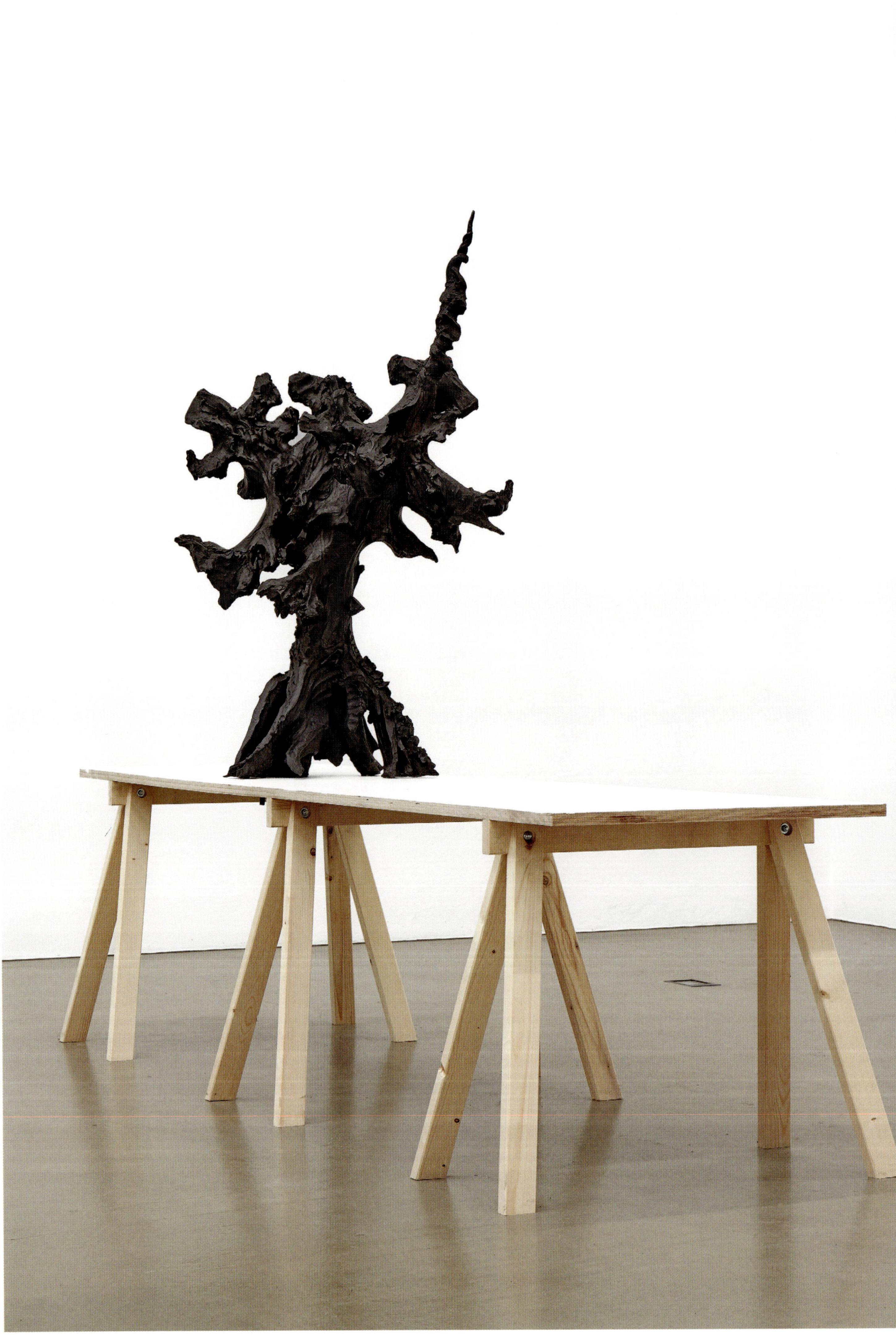

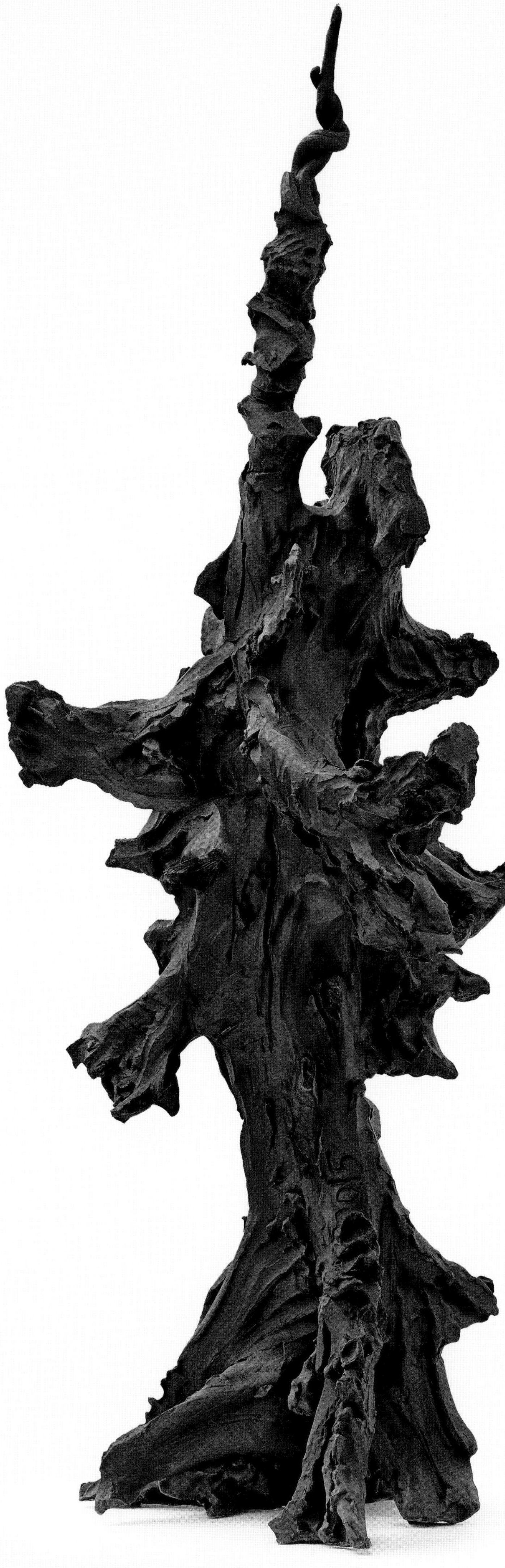

the curve 1 – twilight mountain sculpture 2015

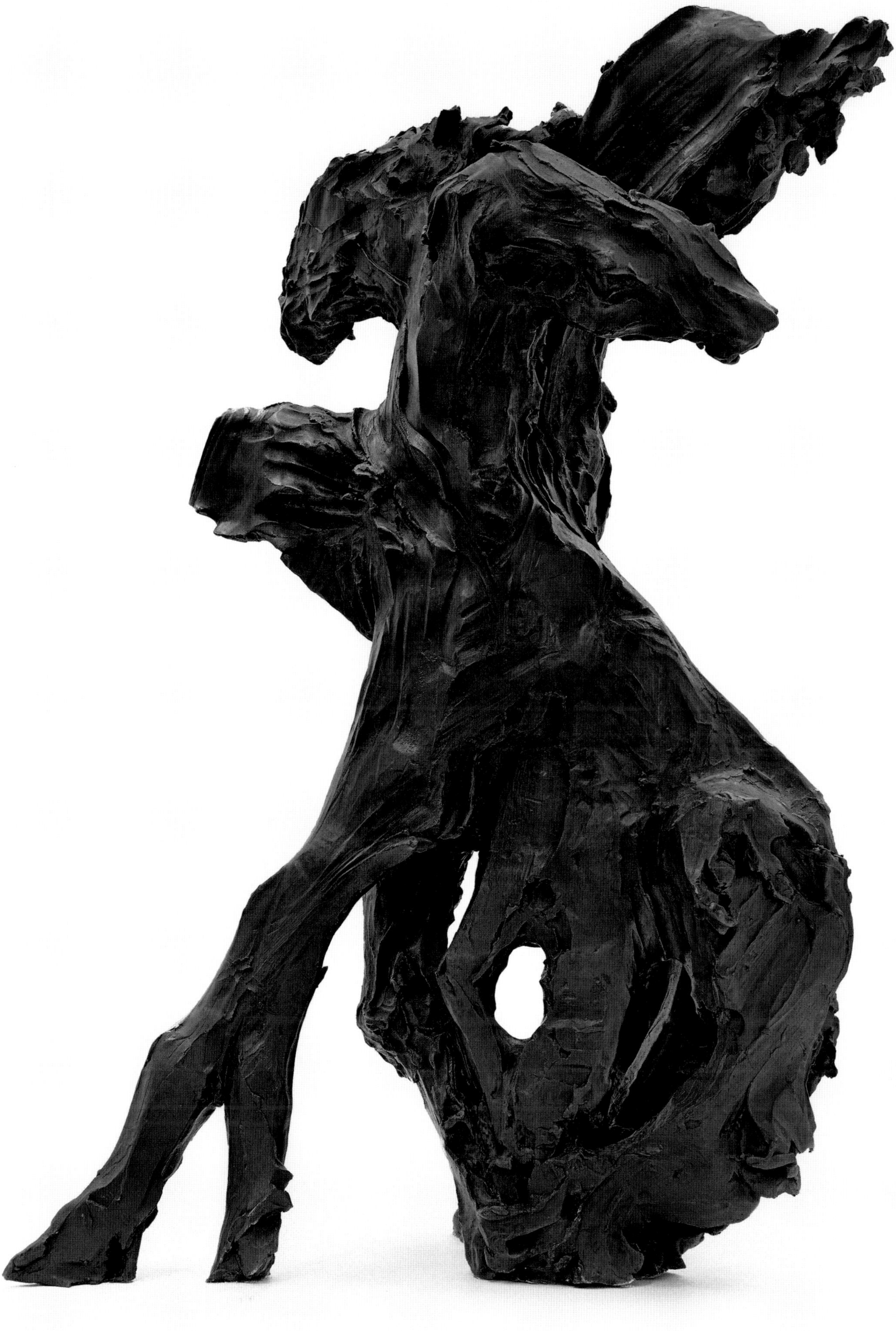

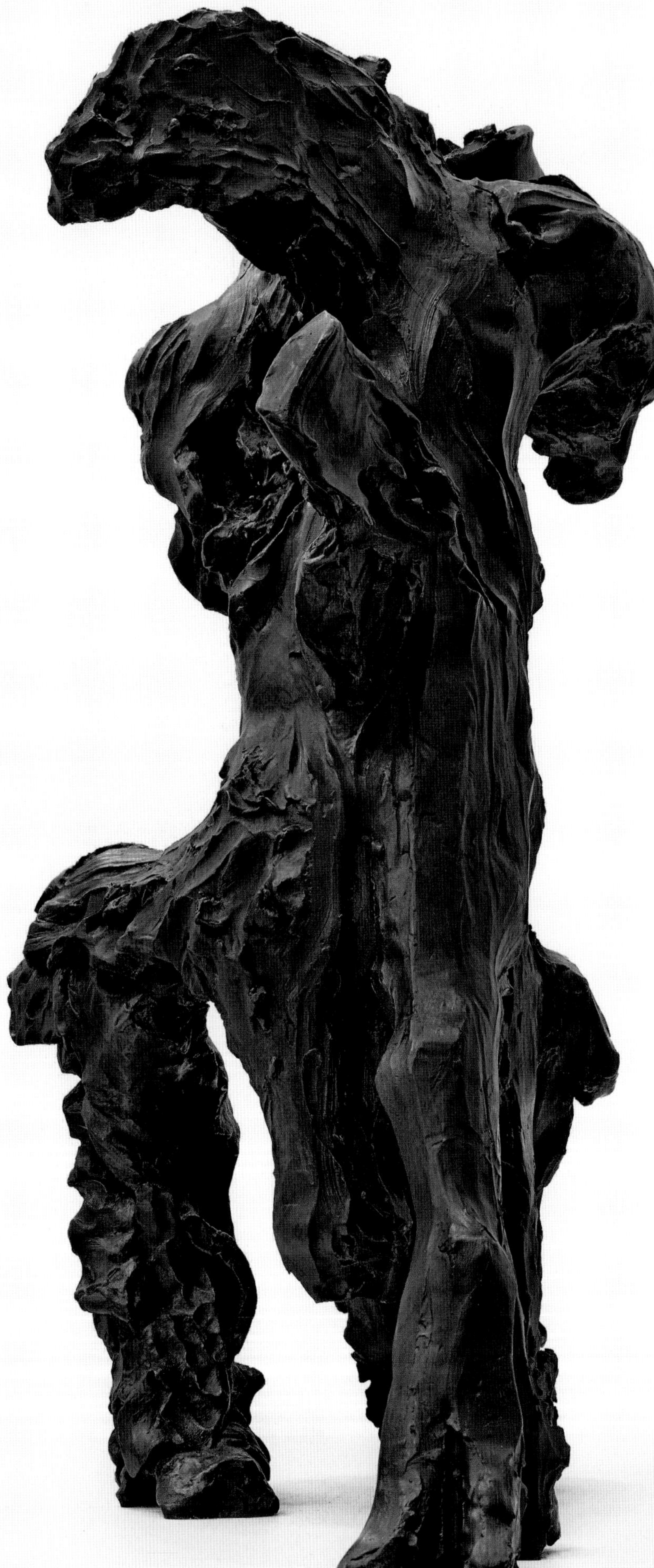

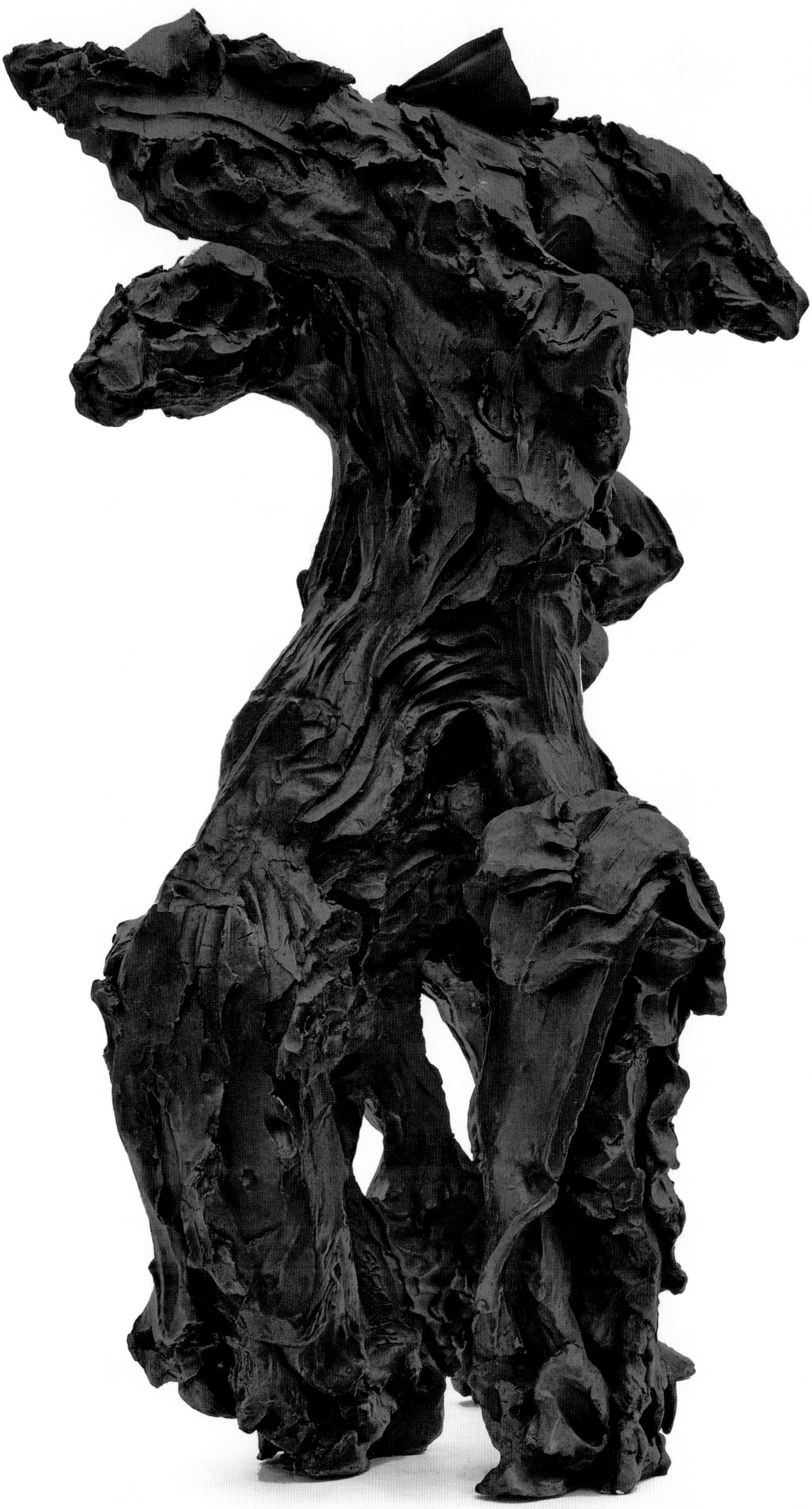

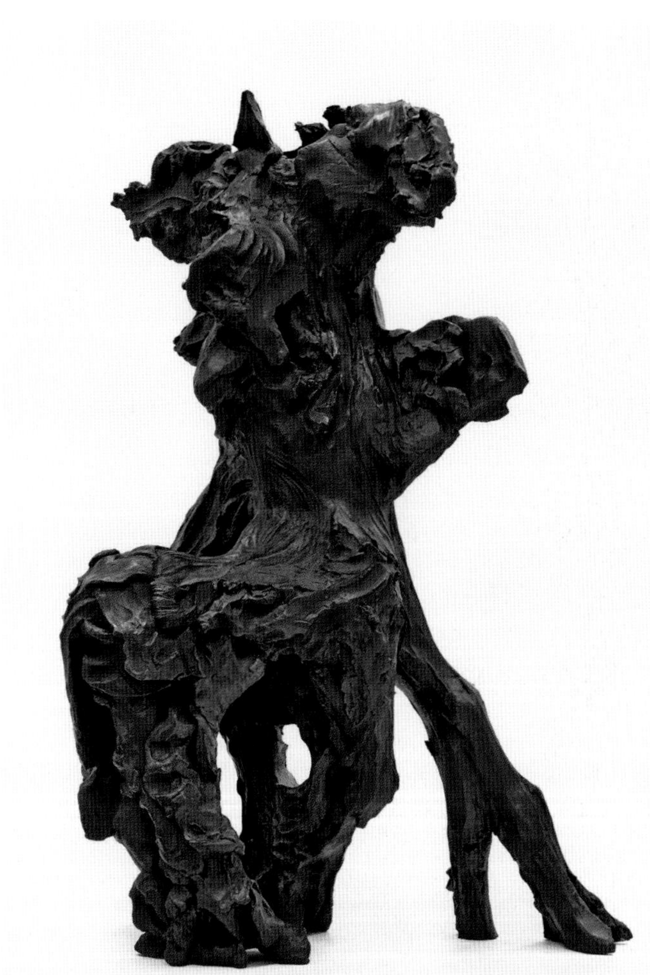

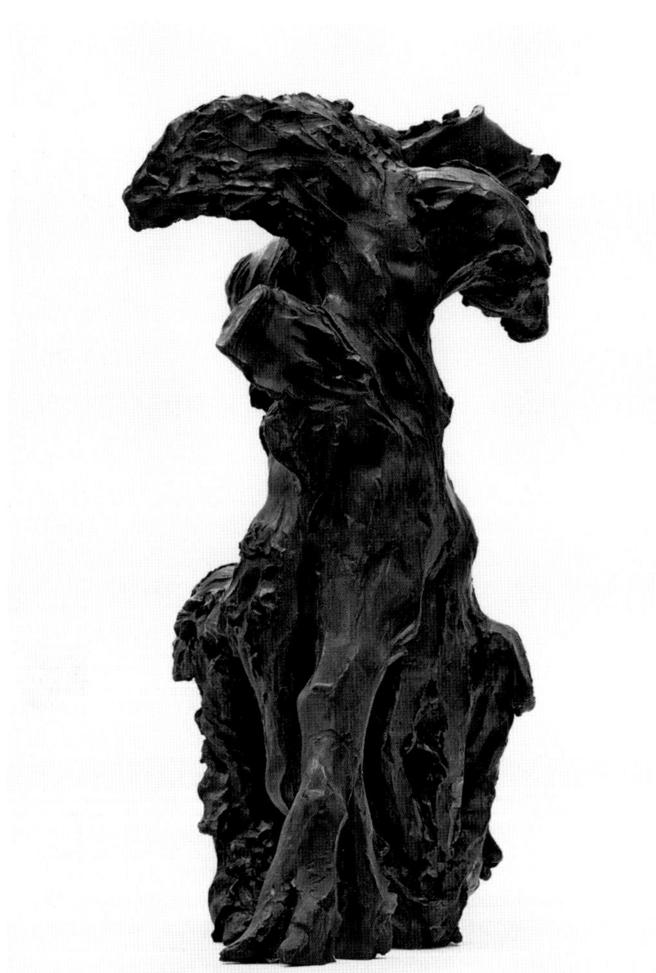

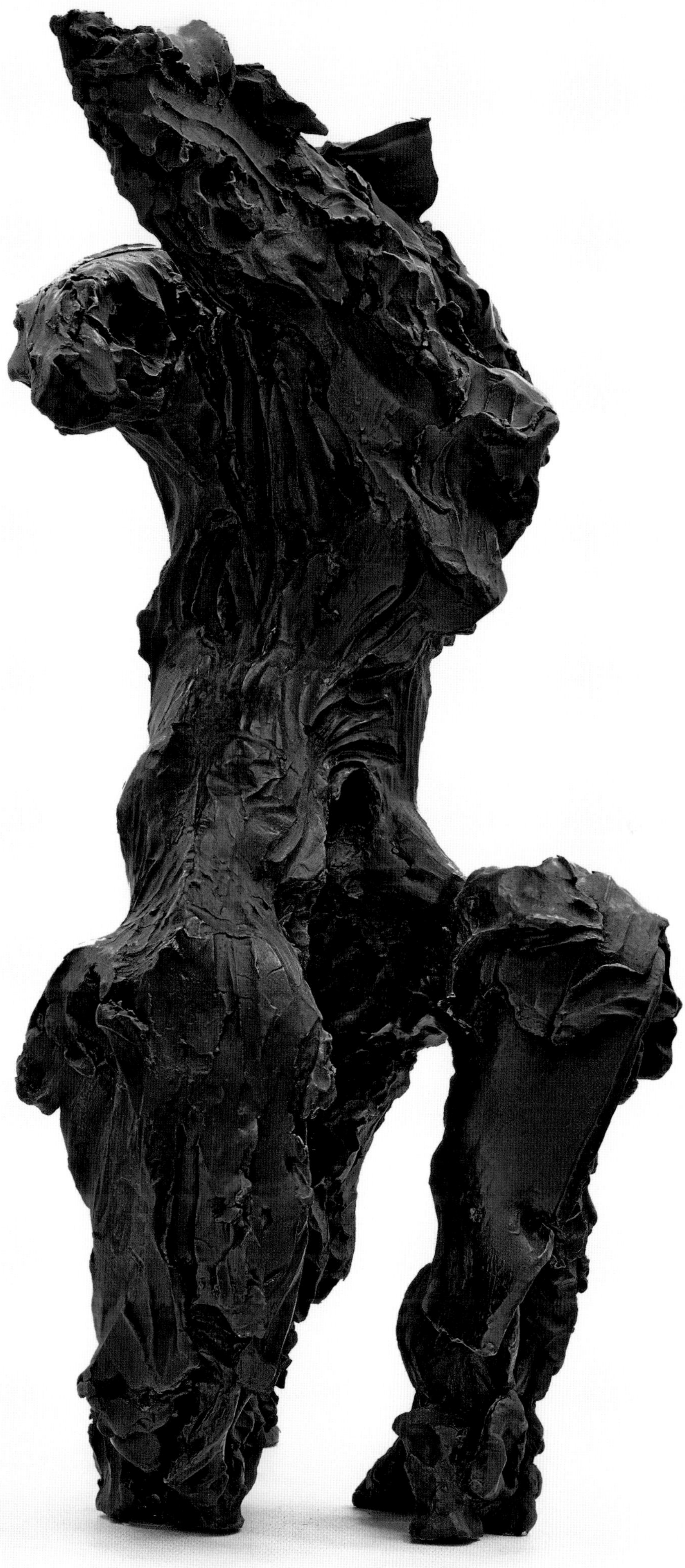

großer Schatten 2015

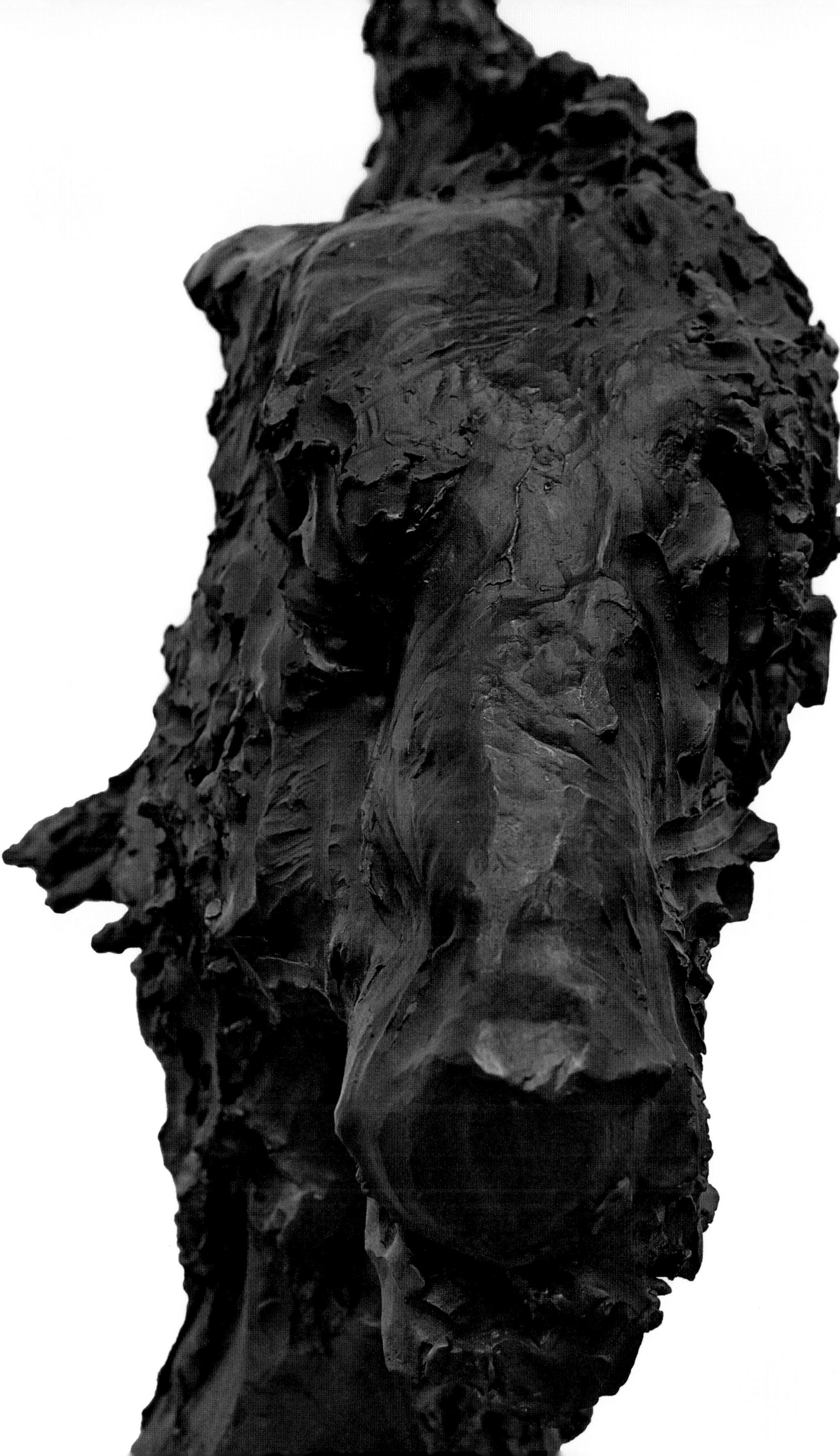

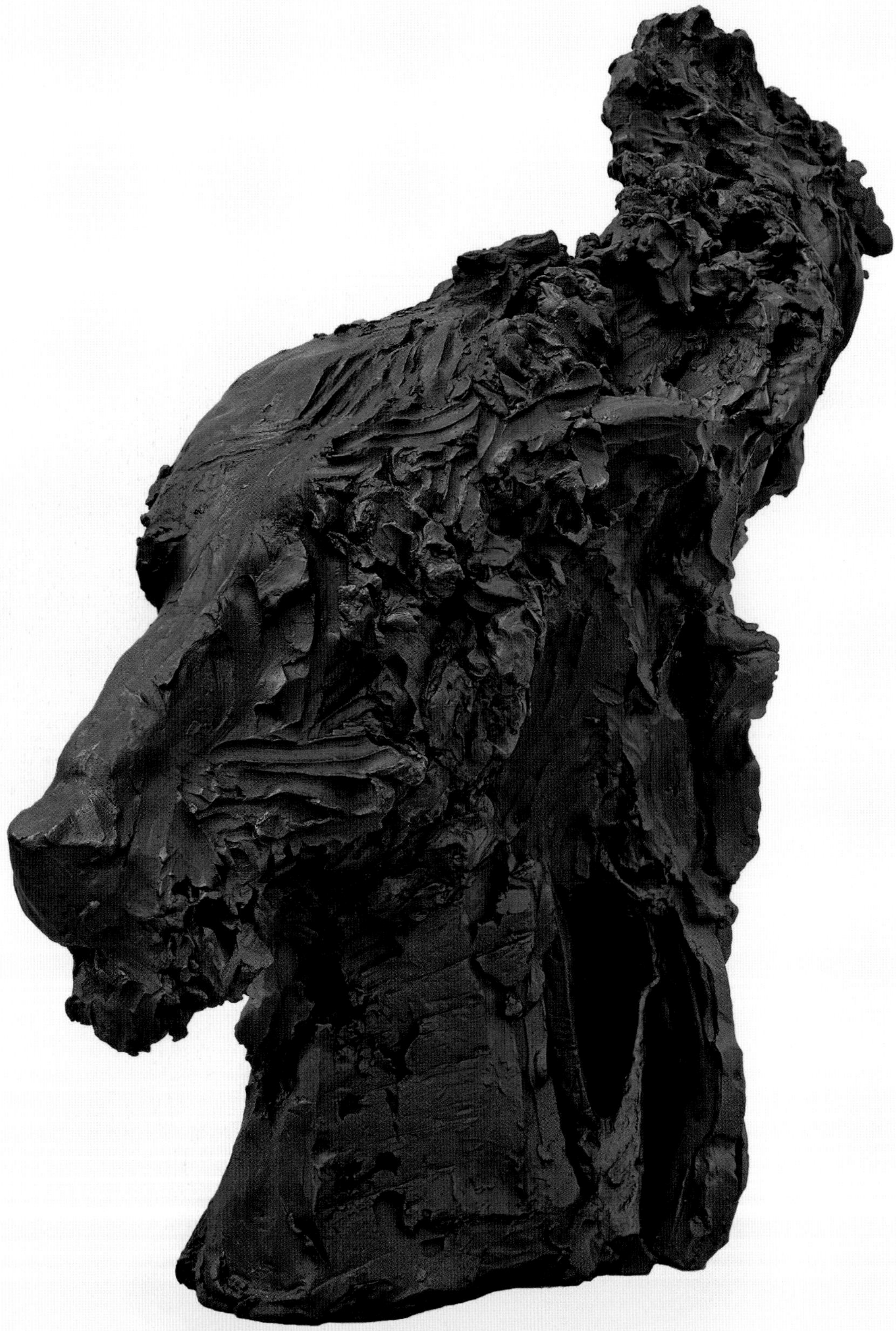

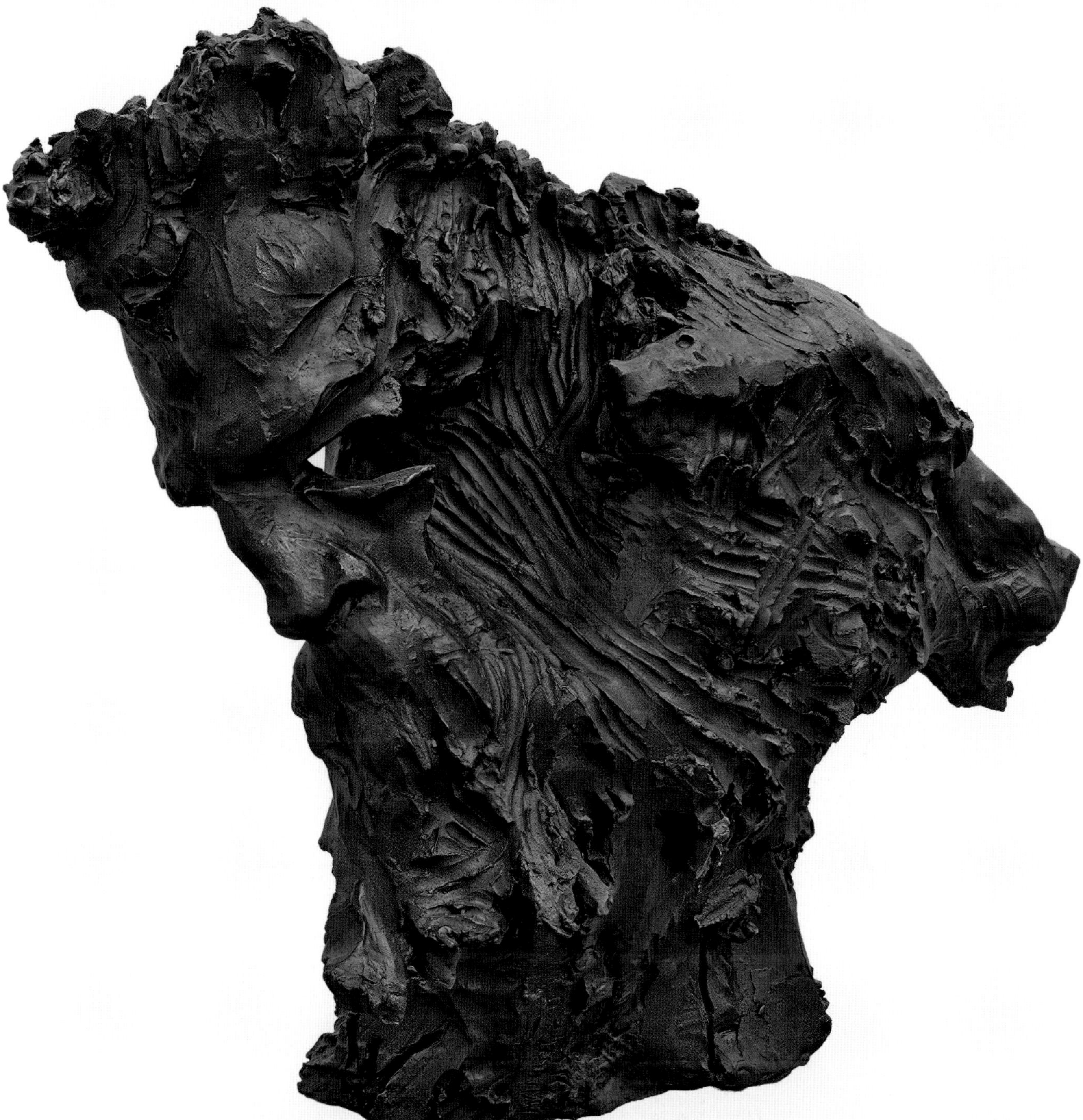

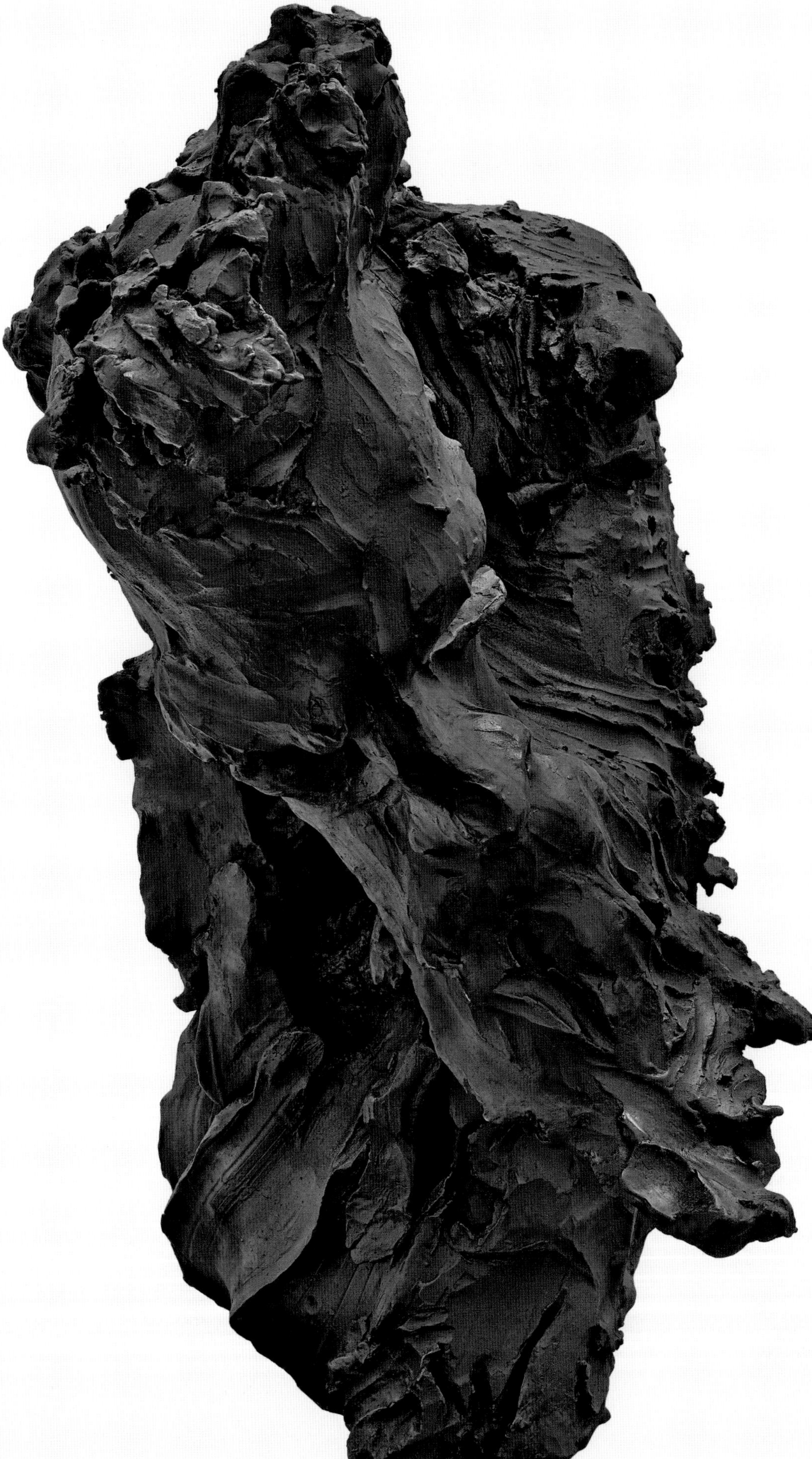

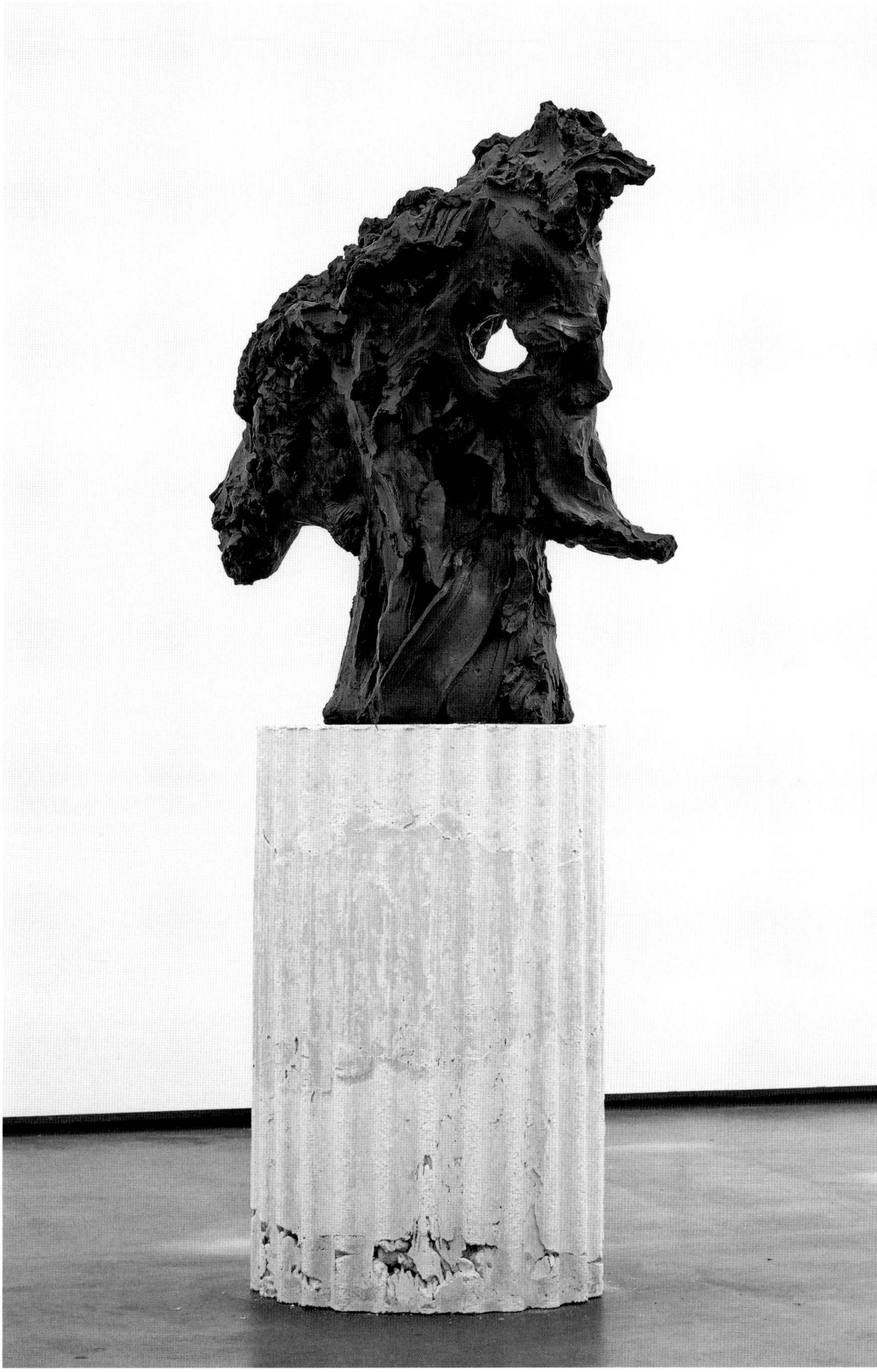

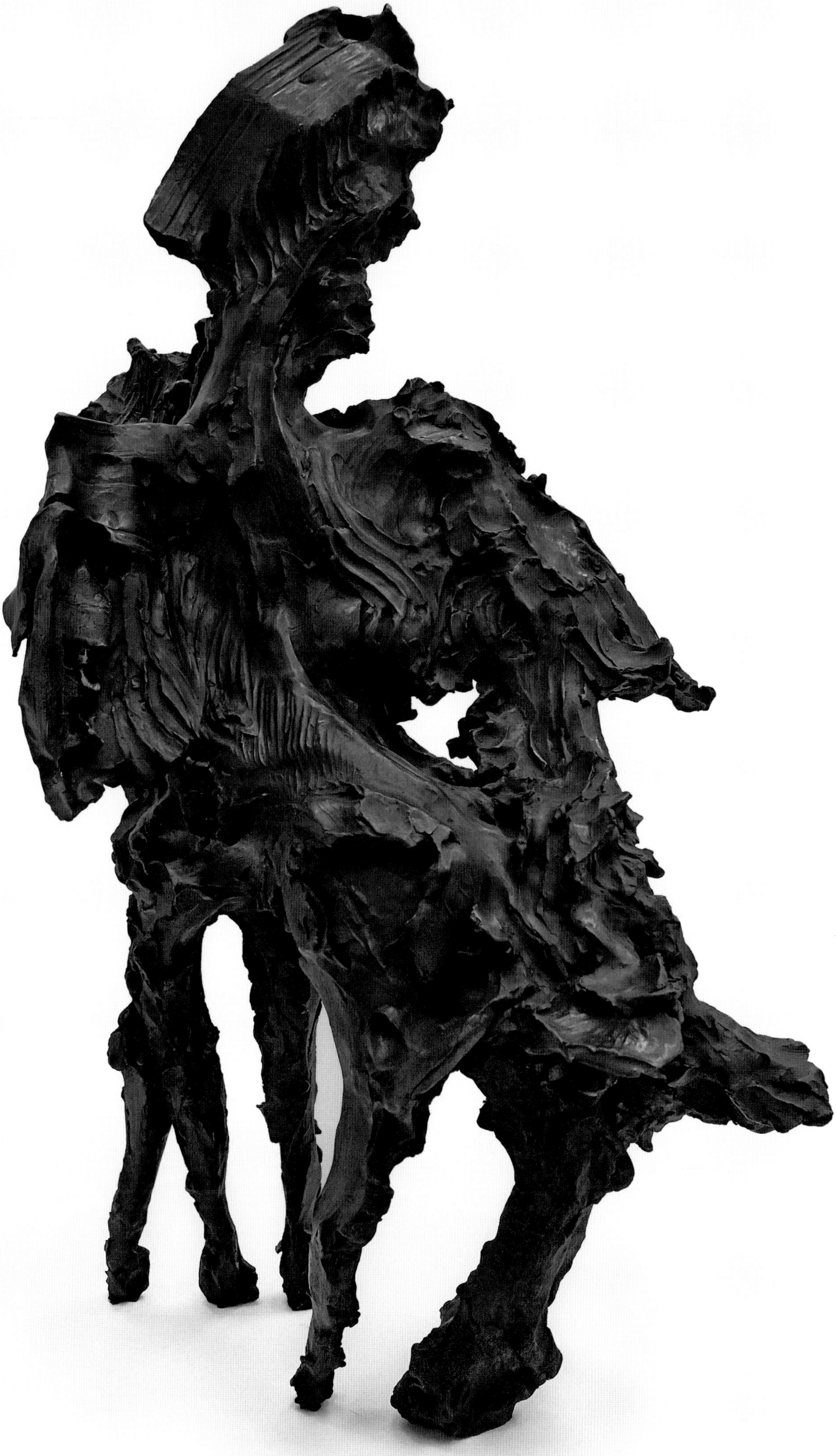

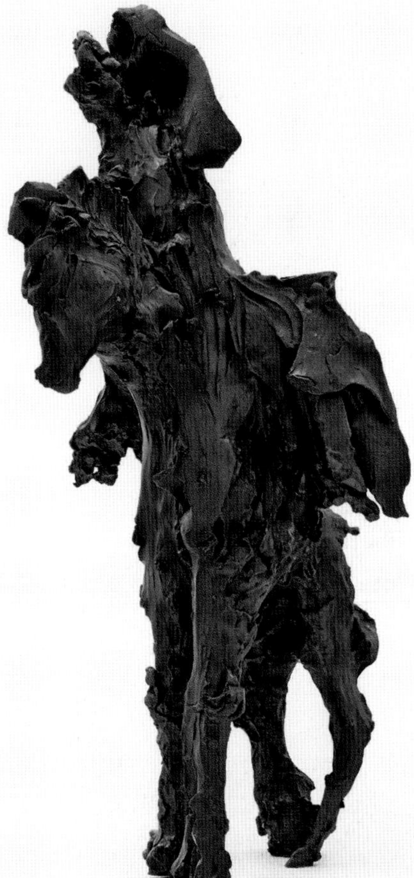

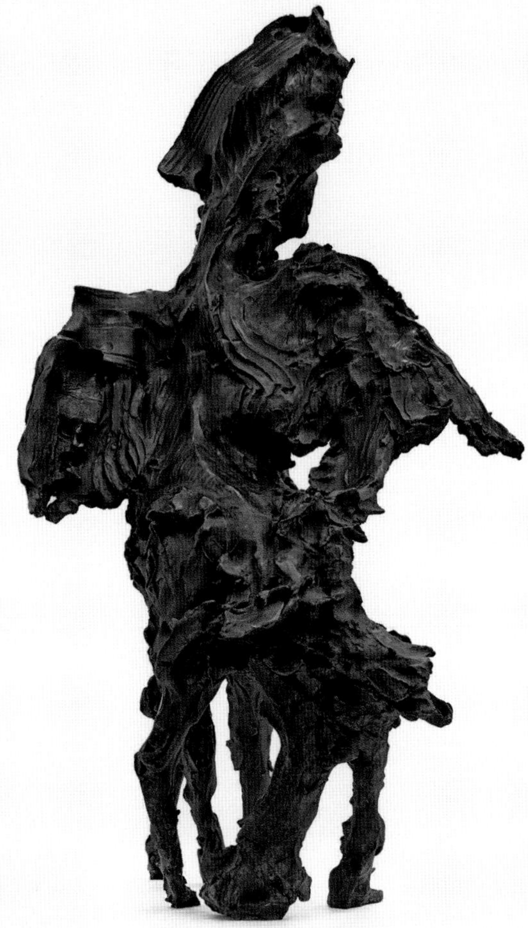

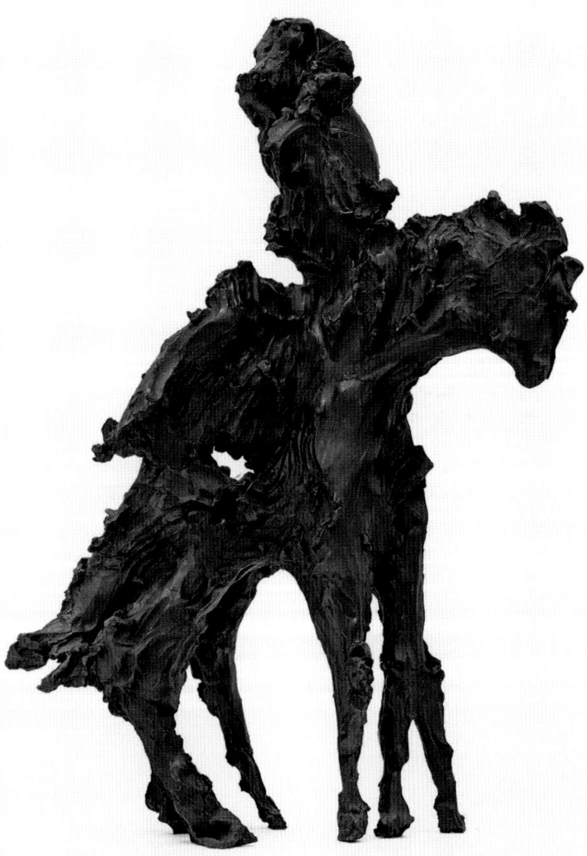

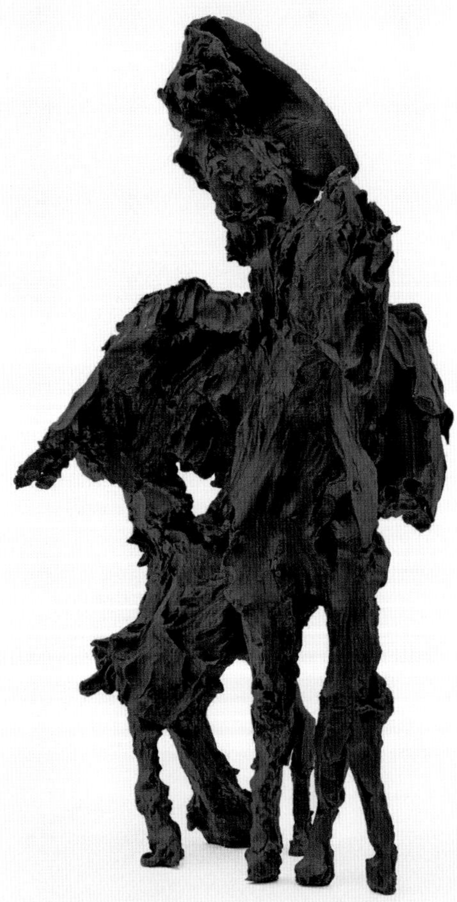

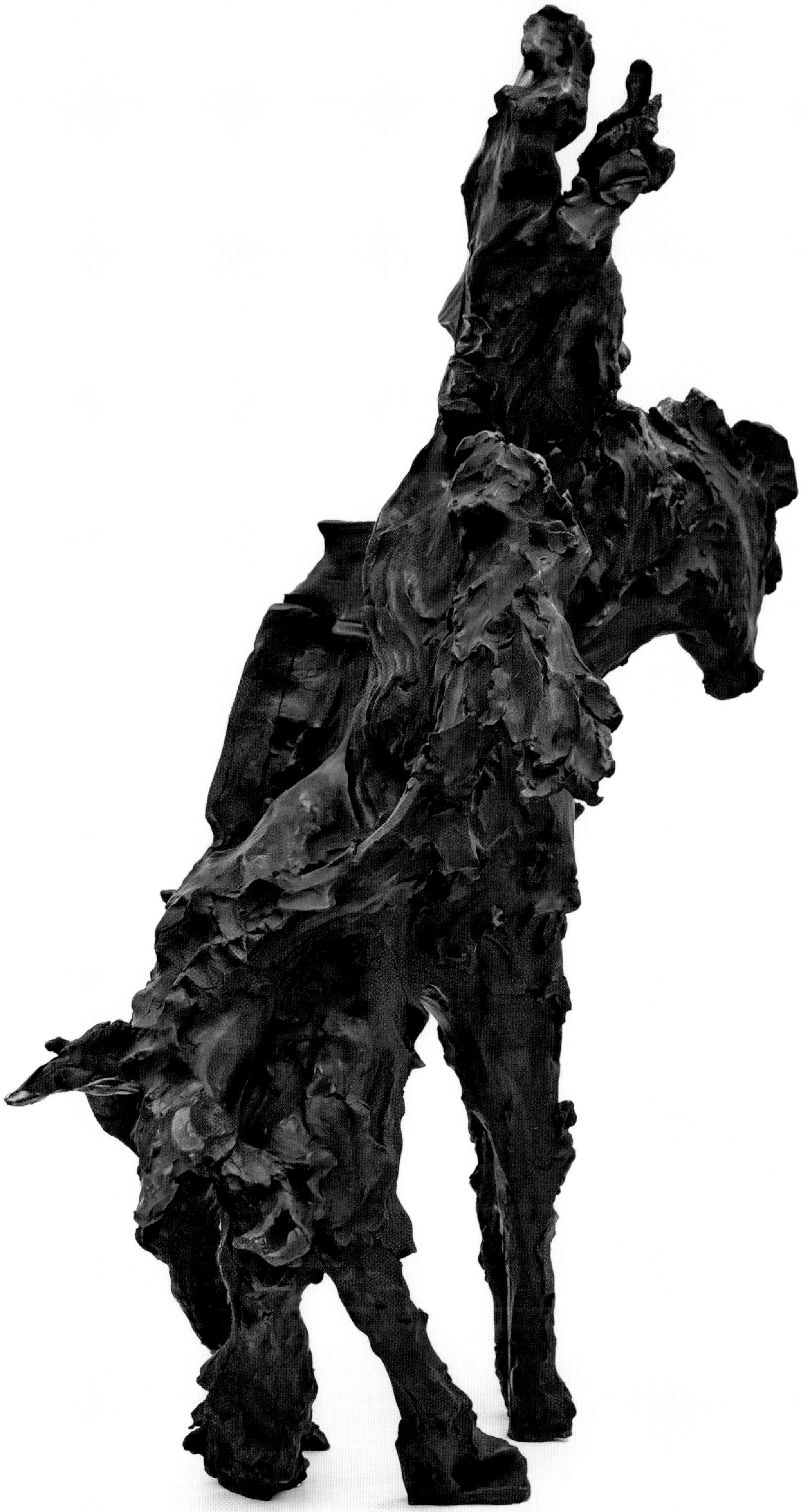

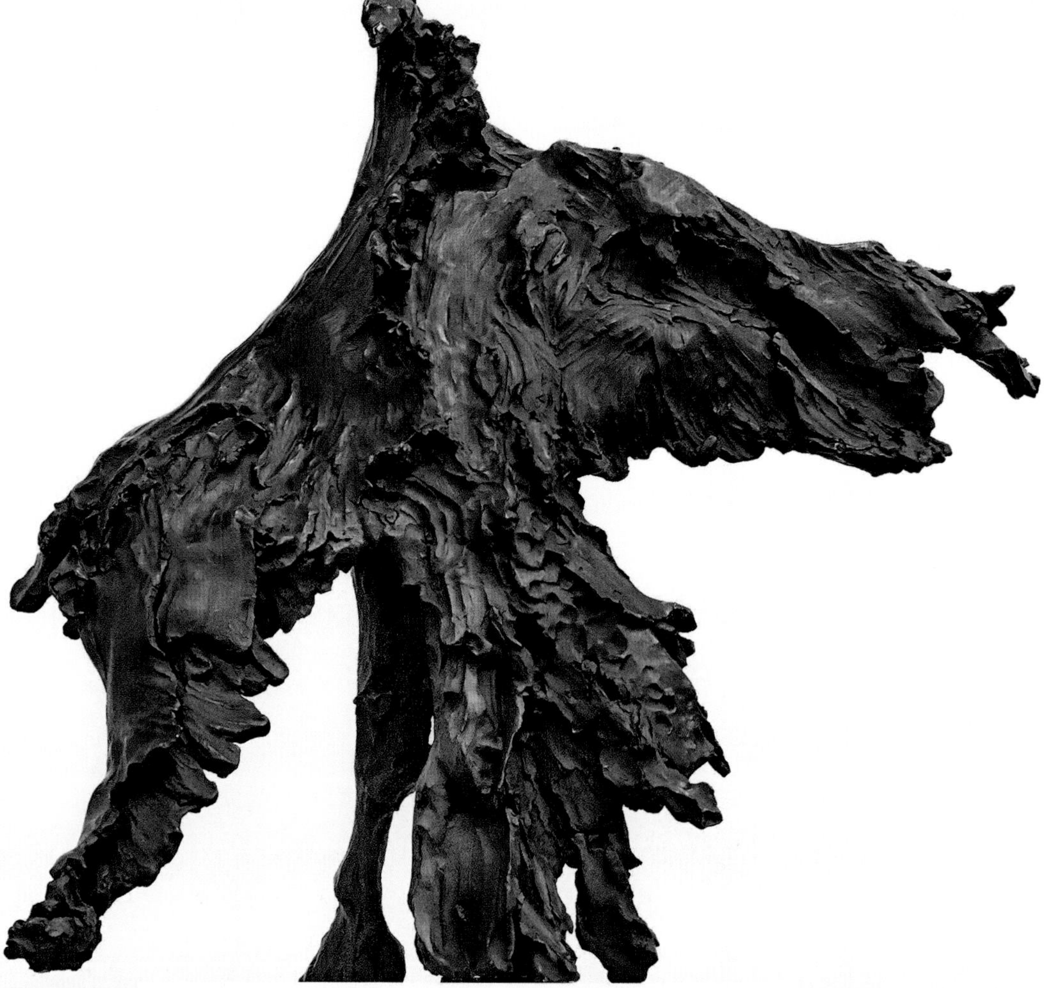

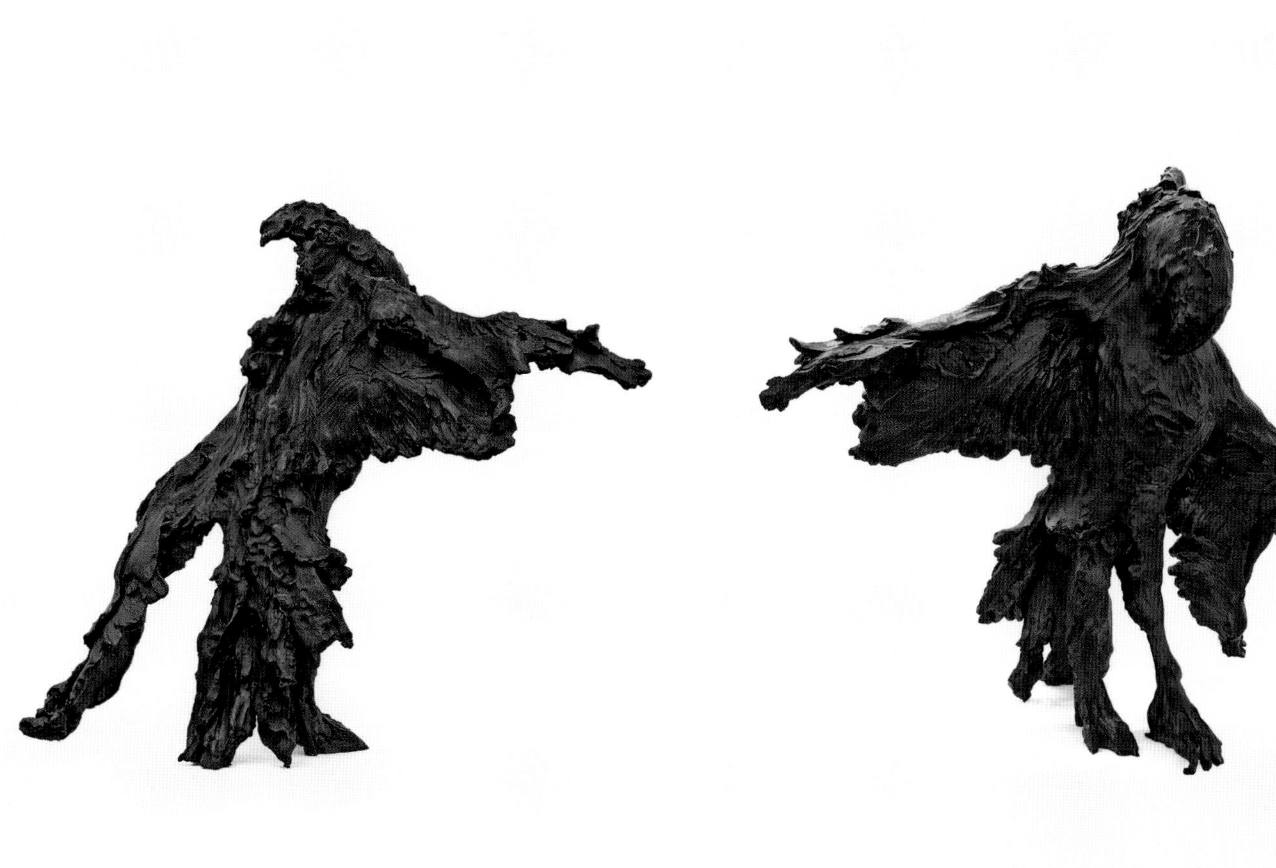

kein Titel (großer Dank) 2015

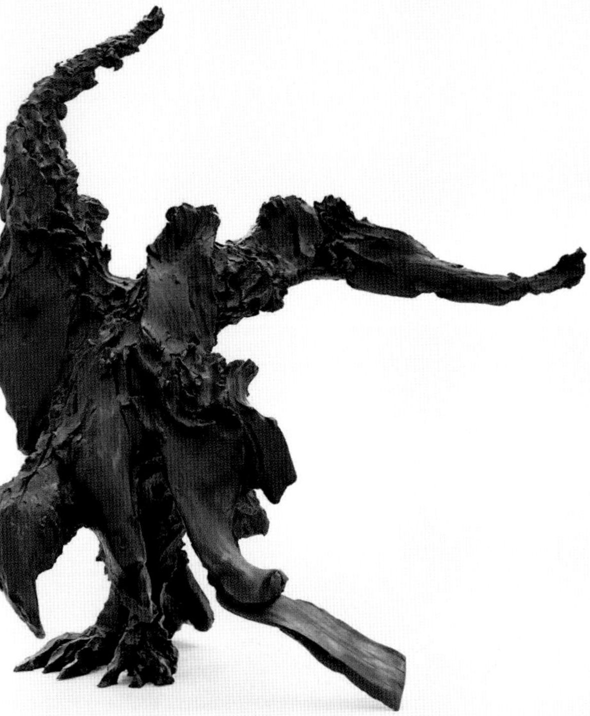

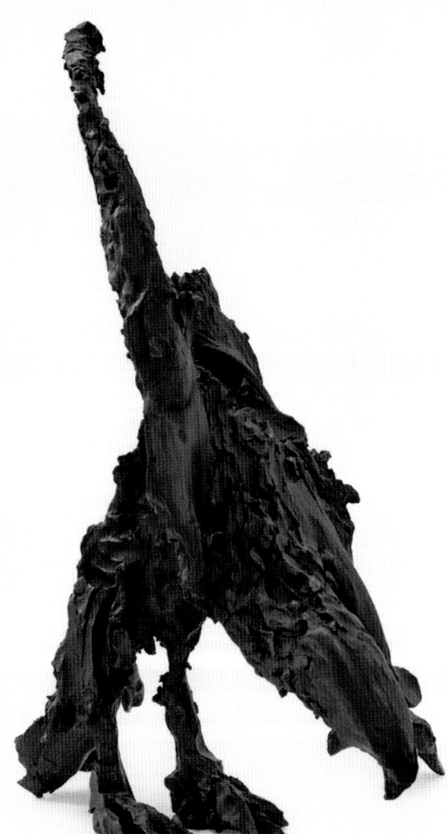

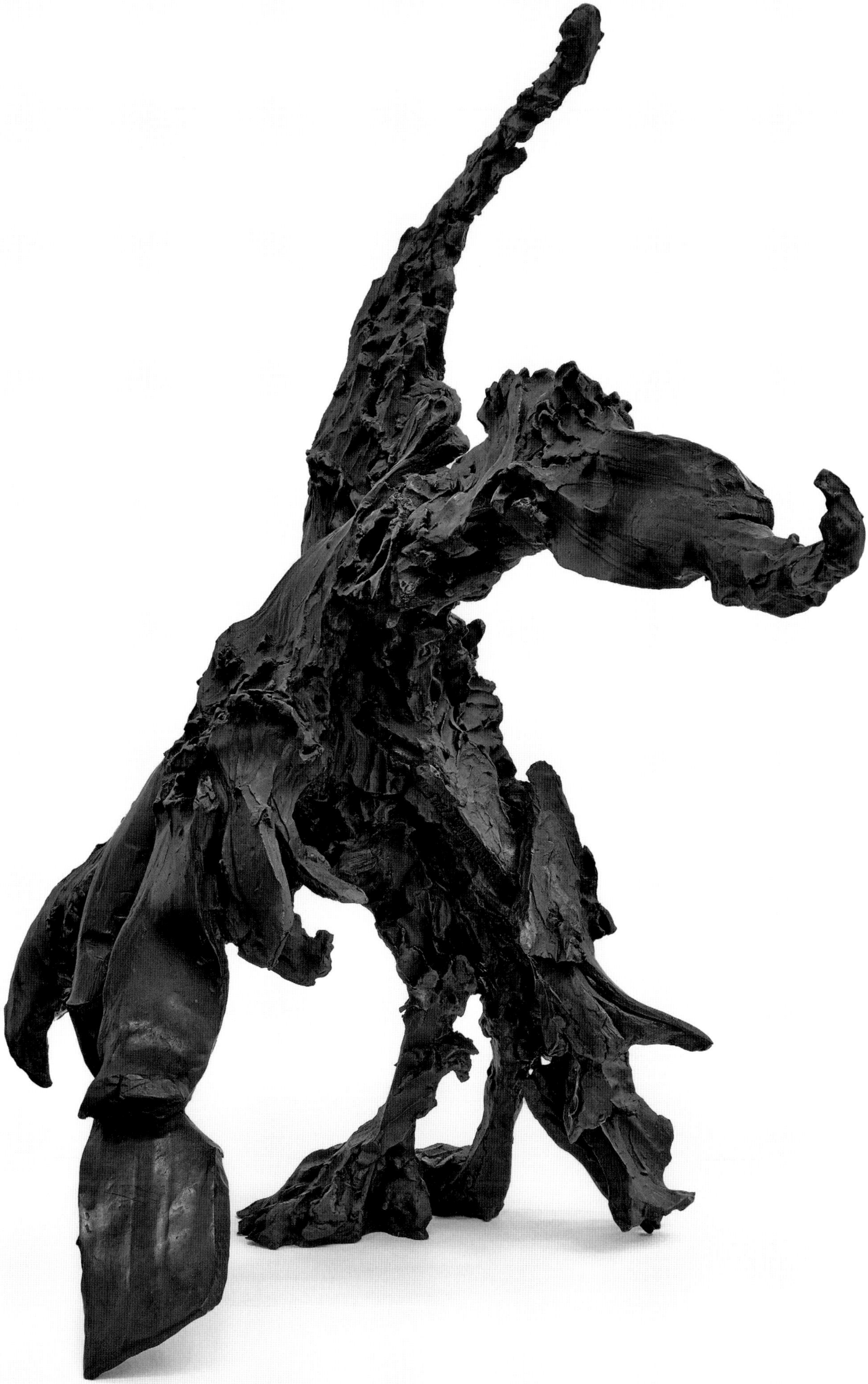

the curve 2 – Stille 2015

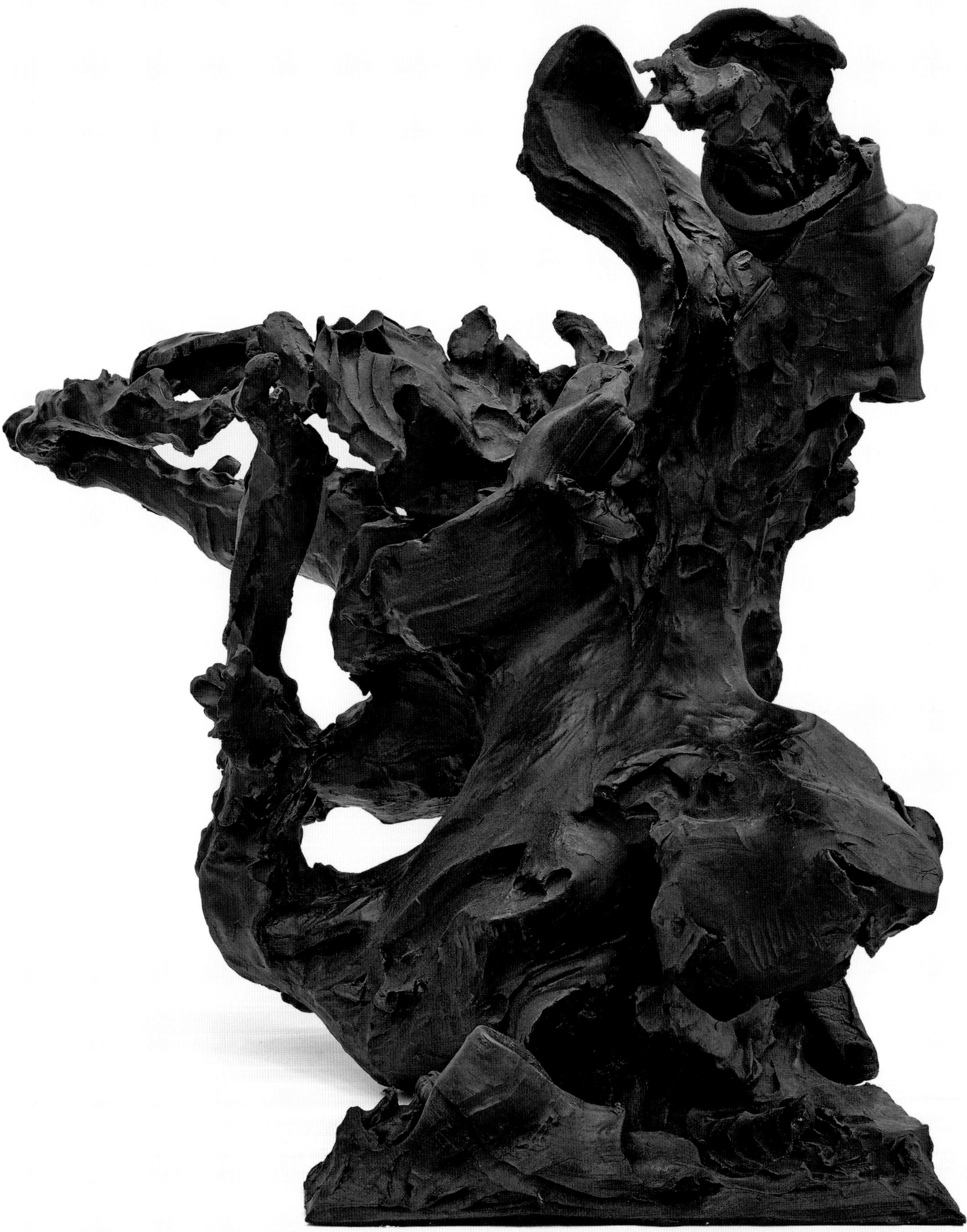

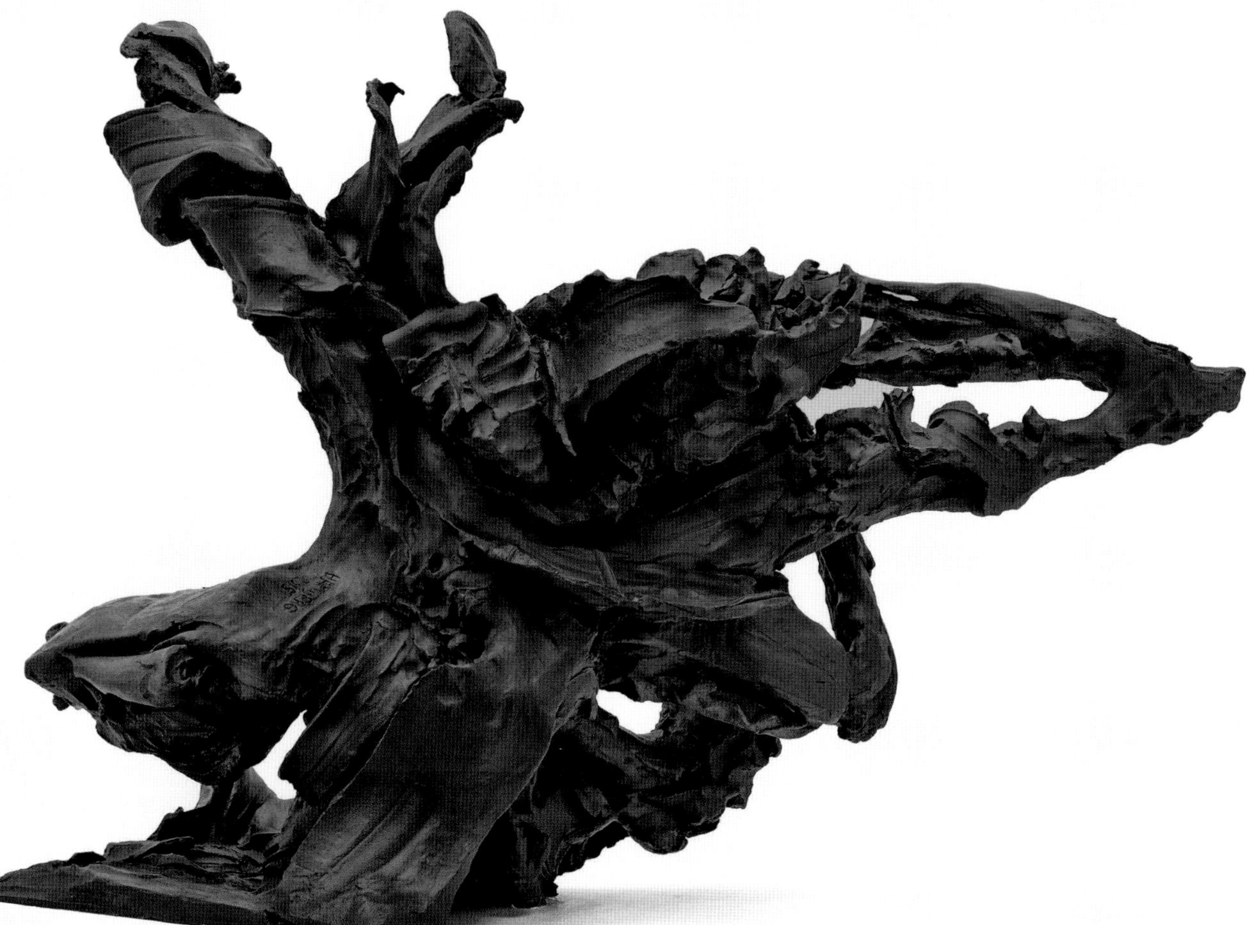

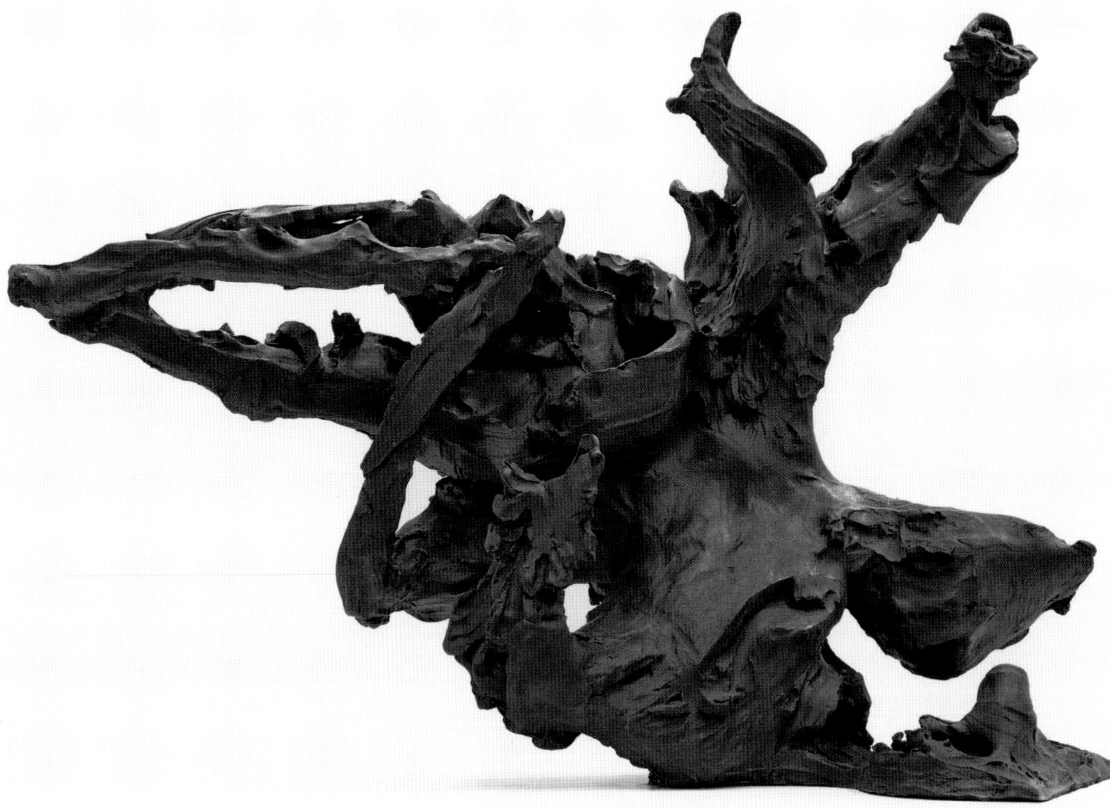

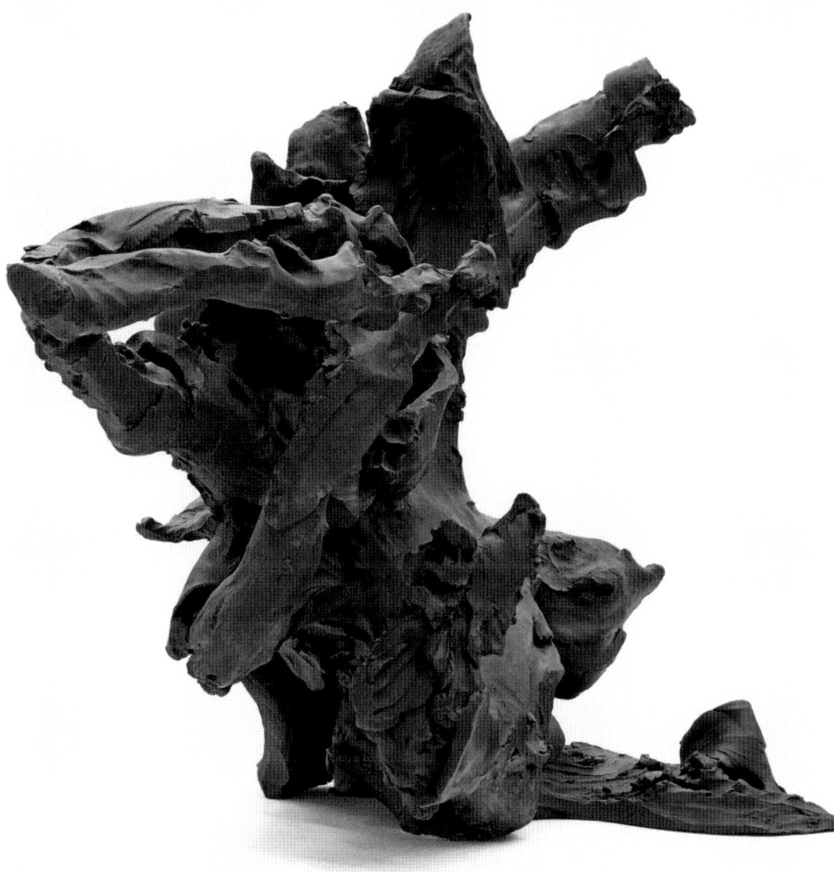

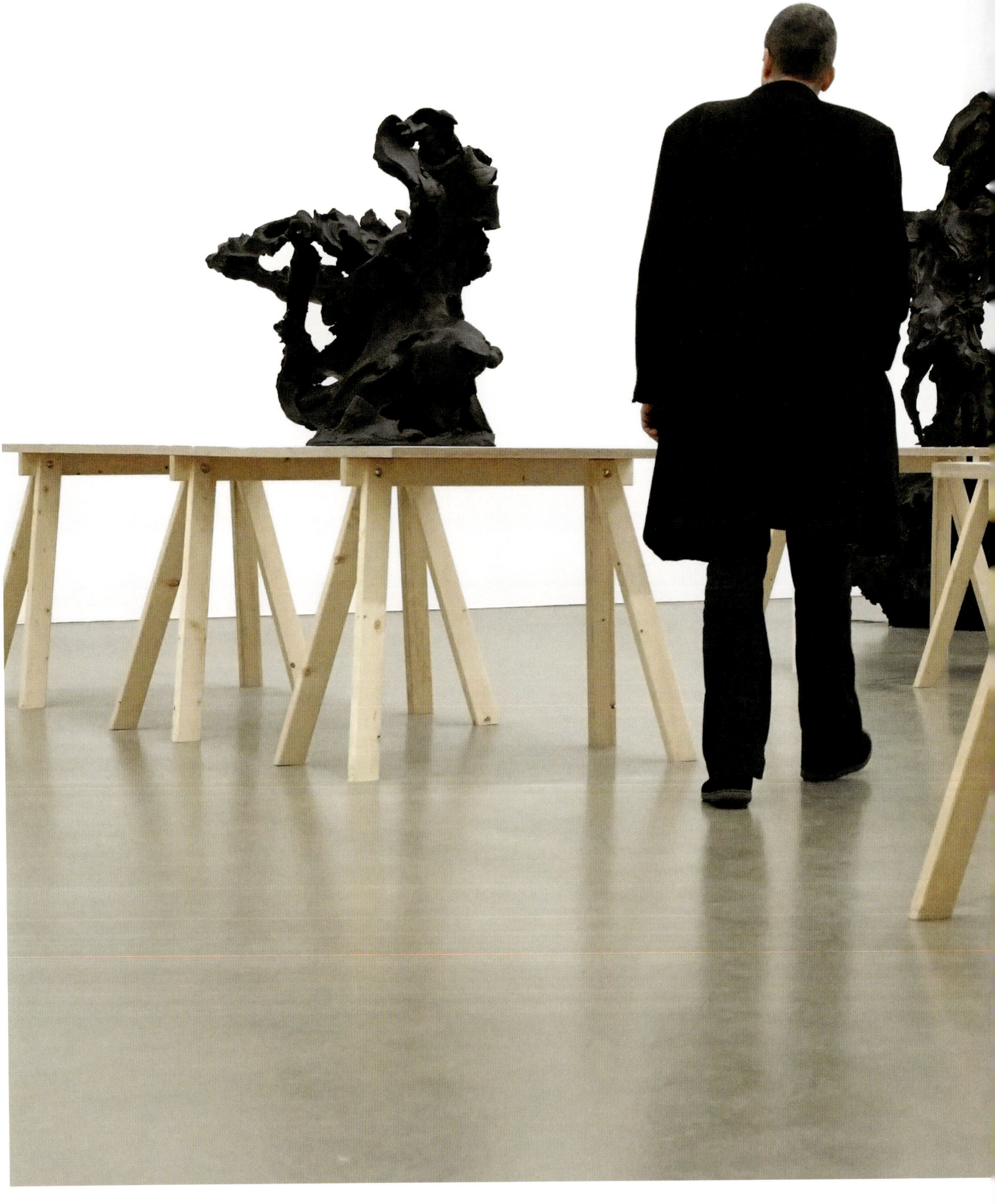

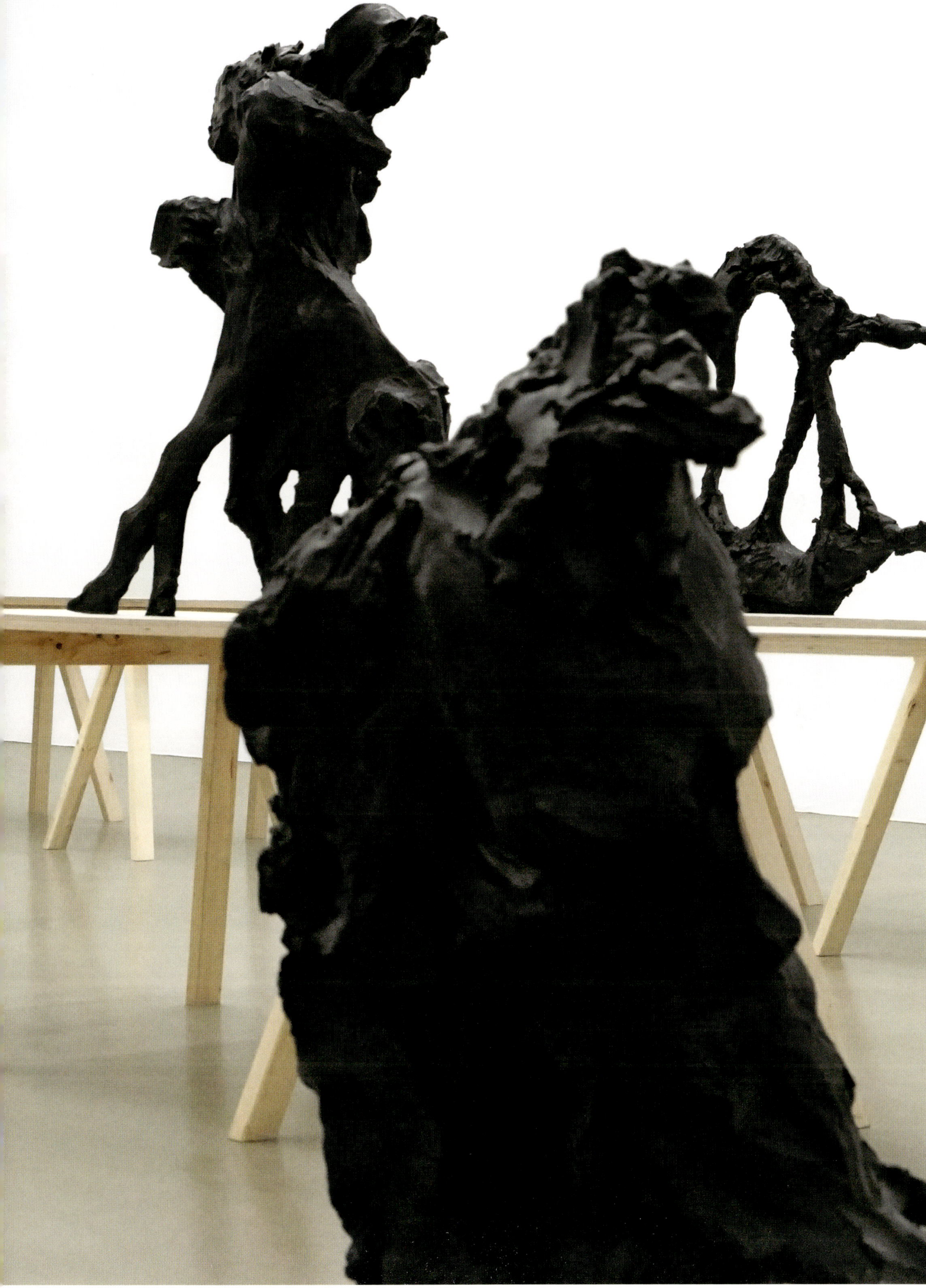

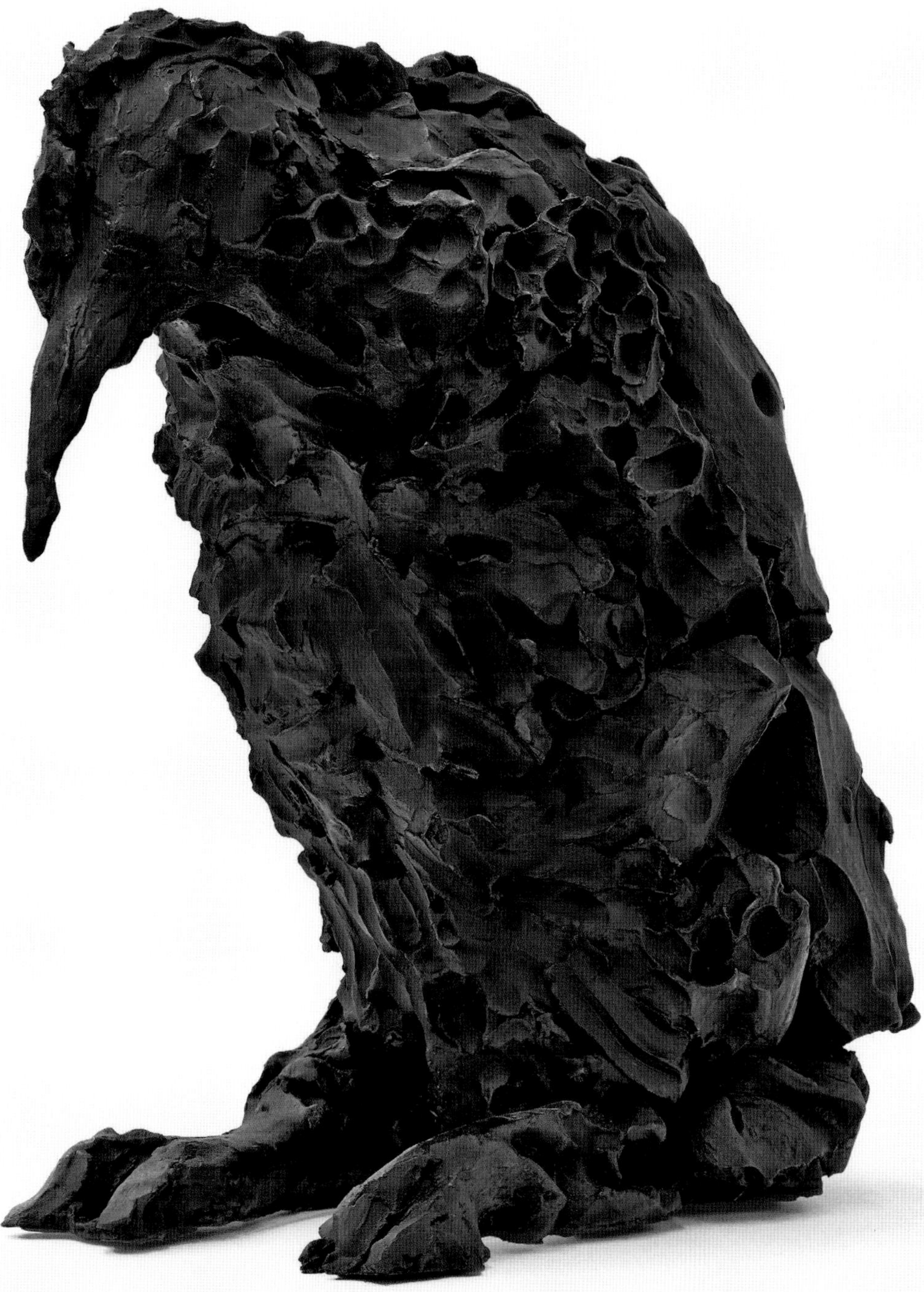

A NEW CHAPTER – PHOTOGRAPHY AND ABSTRACTION OF SHAPE

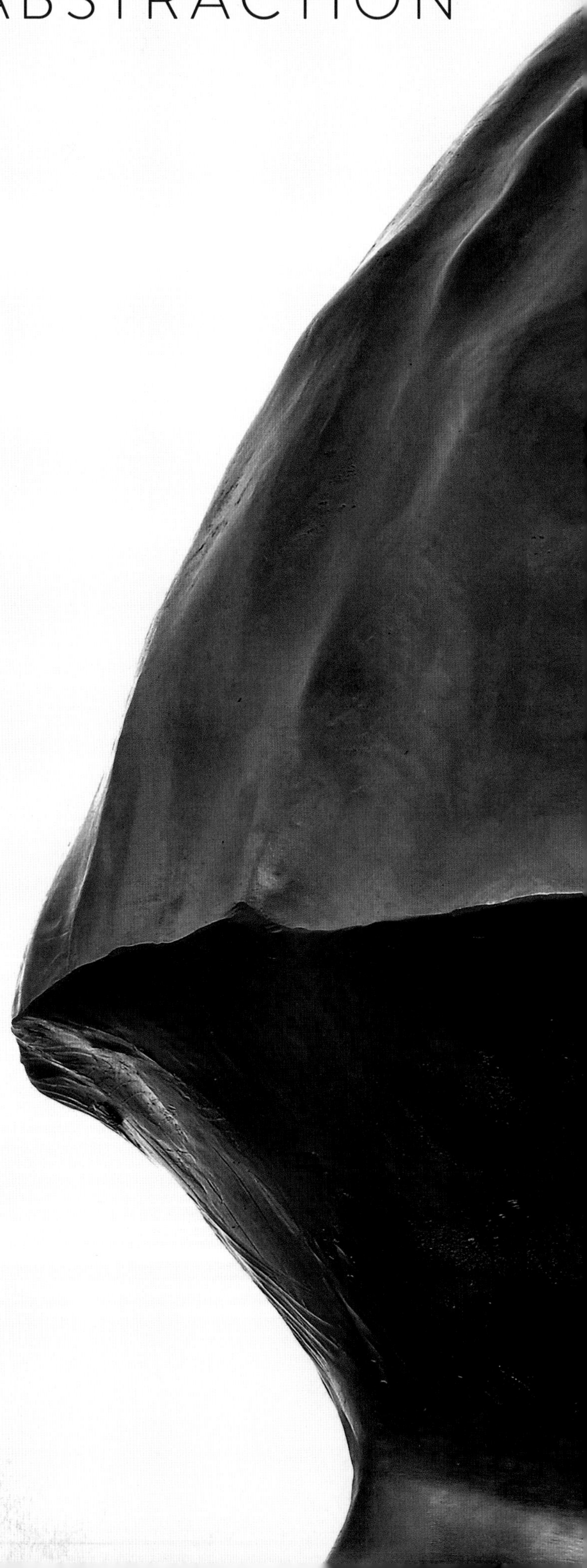

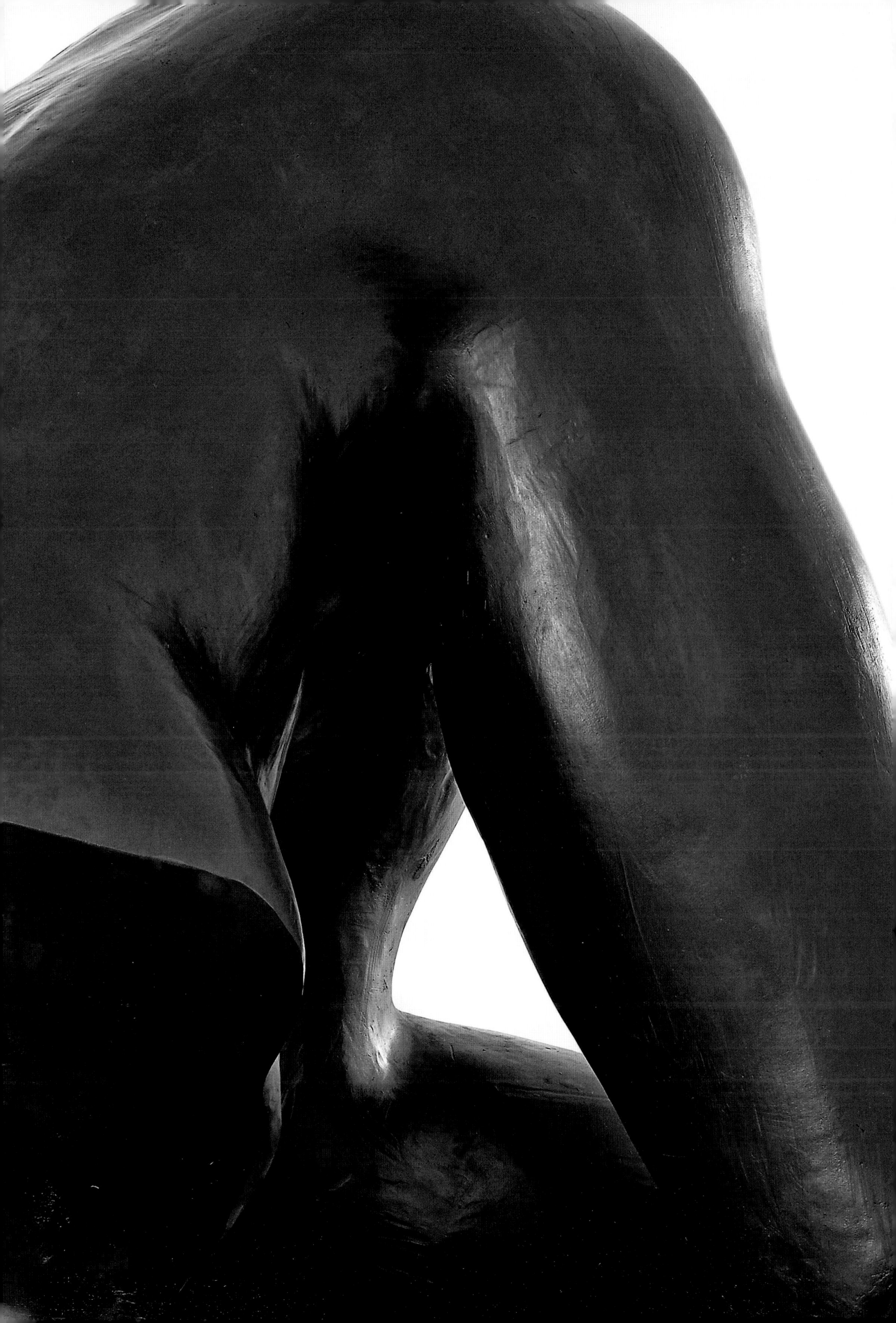

Reflection on the relationship between sculpture and viewer has accompanied Hamberg's work from the beginning. The roughly life-size figures with names like "Alexander," "Abel," "Tatú," "Maria," or "Martha" are artworks, but at the same time they encounter the viewer on another level, like people to whom he/she is forced to relate either consciously or unconsciously. Their communicative gazes and their curious clothing and attributes facilitate this direct contact, while their unrealistic elements – for example their combinations of materials, proportional discrepancies, or mix of costumes from obviously different historical periods – elicit confusion.

Such relationships with the viewer, to some extent physical, are created by the bronzes as well. At least a slight shudder, the feeling of not being able to take possession of the artwork with one's gaze but potentially being dominated by it, arises with the larger-than-life figures the *Berserkers*, *Hund*, or *Frau*. But playful communication is also possible, comparing oneself with the figures, observing them openly or almost furtively. The various pictures of sculptures together with people scattered throughout this book suggest as much.

In all her works, Hamberg, in contrast to hyper-realistic artists from Duane Hanson to Ron Mueck, always makes it clear that, despite their sensual presence, they are created works of art. She is not attempting to overwhelm the viewer. Her striving for a maximum intensity is always thwarted by a deliberate creation of distance. In reflection on the desired and possible relations between the artwork and viewer, this alternation between involvement and shielding comes close to the theme of the gaze discussed above: direct eye contact lasts perhaps only a fraction of a second.

In the exhibition in Potsdam in 2016, the sculptures were accompanied by photographs by Mick Vincenz that pictured the bronzes against a white background. These pictures relate to the sculptures in much the same way as a film still to a movie. They concentrate in a single image the flow of the event into a few important moments. Supplementing the physical presence of the sculptures in space, in this way two of their additional qualities are especially emphasised: their outline and their independence from the contingencies of the exhibition space. An entirely separate narrative is created when the sculptures and photos of them are displayed together. The art historian may be reminded of the inclusion of photographs by Eugène Druet in August Rodin's exhibitions. The visitor is encouraged to make a simple comparison between the sculpture and its photograph, which in itself can be instructive on a simple level, since one becomes aware of how often the perception of three-dimensional sculptures is influenced by photographs. In many cases these are today more or less careful and conscientious visual notes made with a smartphone, which not infrequently replace the original visual experience and postpone it to a later time. In addition to their documentary qualities, the extremely virtuosic photographs by Vincenz, which manage to capture the painterly black-on-black of their surfaces together with their physical form and outline, represent very personal interpretations of the sculptures. They appear, almost without casting shadows, in surroundings of pure white, detached from any setting, like works of pure poetry. Accordingly, the artist's book *Stella Hamberg – Neutron. Skizzen und Plastiken* (2016) that appeared at the time of the exhibition consists of a suggestive alternation of Hamberg's sketches and Vincenz's photographs. After the promising group of composite early works, beginning with *Alexander* (2004), came fundamental major works like the *Berserkers* (2007), *sieben100millionen* (2008), and *vom Verrecken und der absoluten Unmöglichkeit zu sterben* (2008), and then, as a first summing up and synthesis, *Hund* (2013) as a four-dimensional sculpture – an experiment that underwent multiple variations in the sculptures from 2015/16.

The inclusion of photography, and the concomitant reduction of perception and partial dematerialisation of the sculptures opened a new chapter in Hamberg's career. An analytical eye for details and excerpts that can themselves become the main sculptural motif had appeared in her work already in *sieben100millionen* or *Das Tabu*. An especially pointed three-dimensional formulation is the torso *Trance* (2016). As a motif, it may recall torsos from classical Modernism or a figure like Wilhelm Lehmbruck's *Der Gestürzte* (The Fallen One; 1915), yet in that era a hundred years ago one would never find a form bent at such an unnaturally sharp angle. Flexion that is perfectly possible in heavily modelled sculptures with a reduced reference to motif cannot be accomplished in such a classically modelled human body without violence. Put another way: despite its seemingly strong figural presence, *Trance* employs a high degree of formal abstraction. Because of the artist's decision to present this sculptural study with a rectangular base plate on a triangular steel pedestal set at an angle with the plate further emphasises the sharpness of the sections and the geometrically plotted changes in the direction in the figure's axes. This work once again shows that Hamberg does not attempt to establish a recognisable "trademark style," but rather continuously explores, proceeding from a stage once achieved, the possibilities for articulating ideas by way of sculptural concepts.

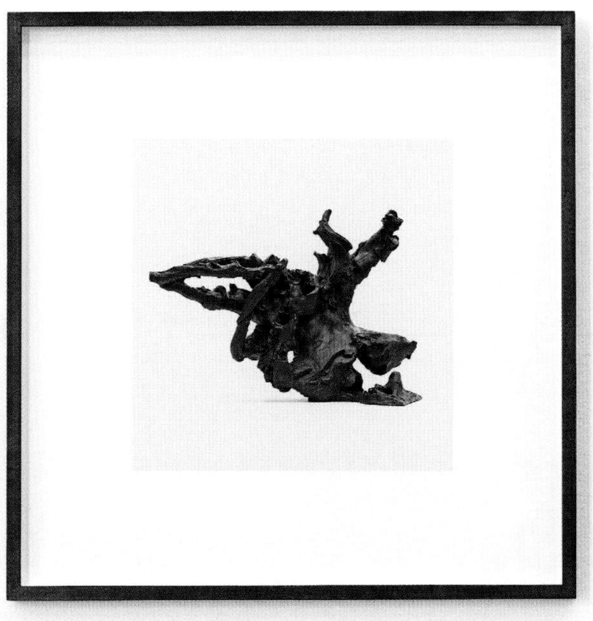
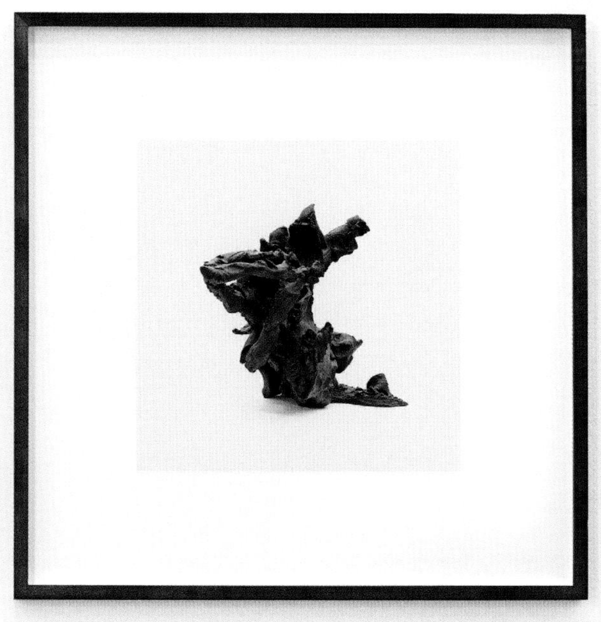

szenischer Ausschnitt (Blitzlicht) 1 2015

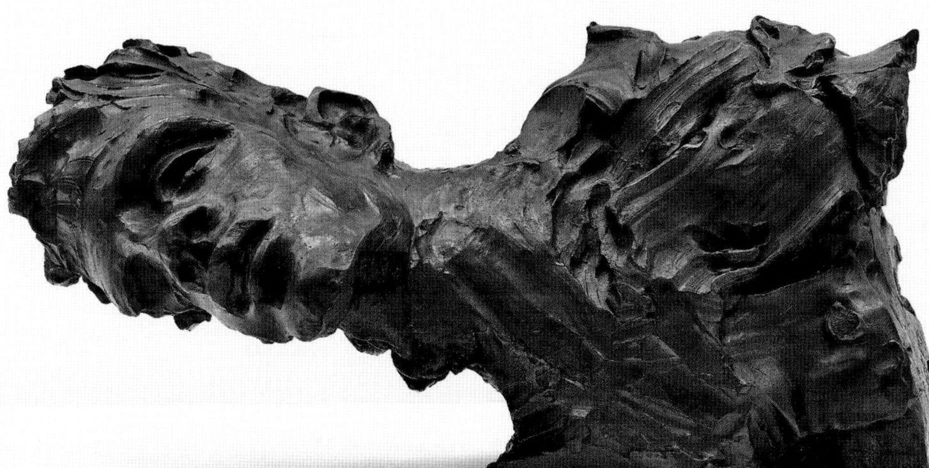

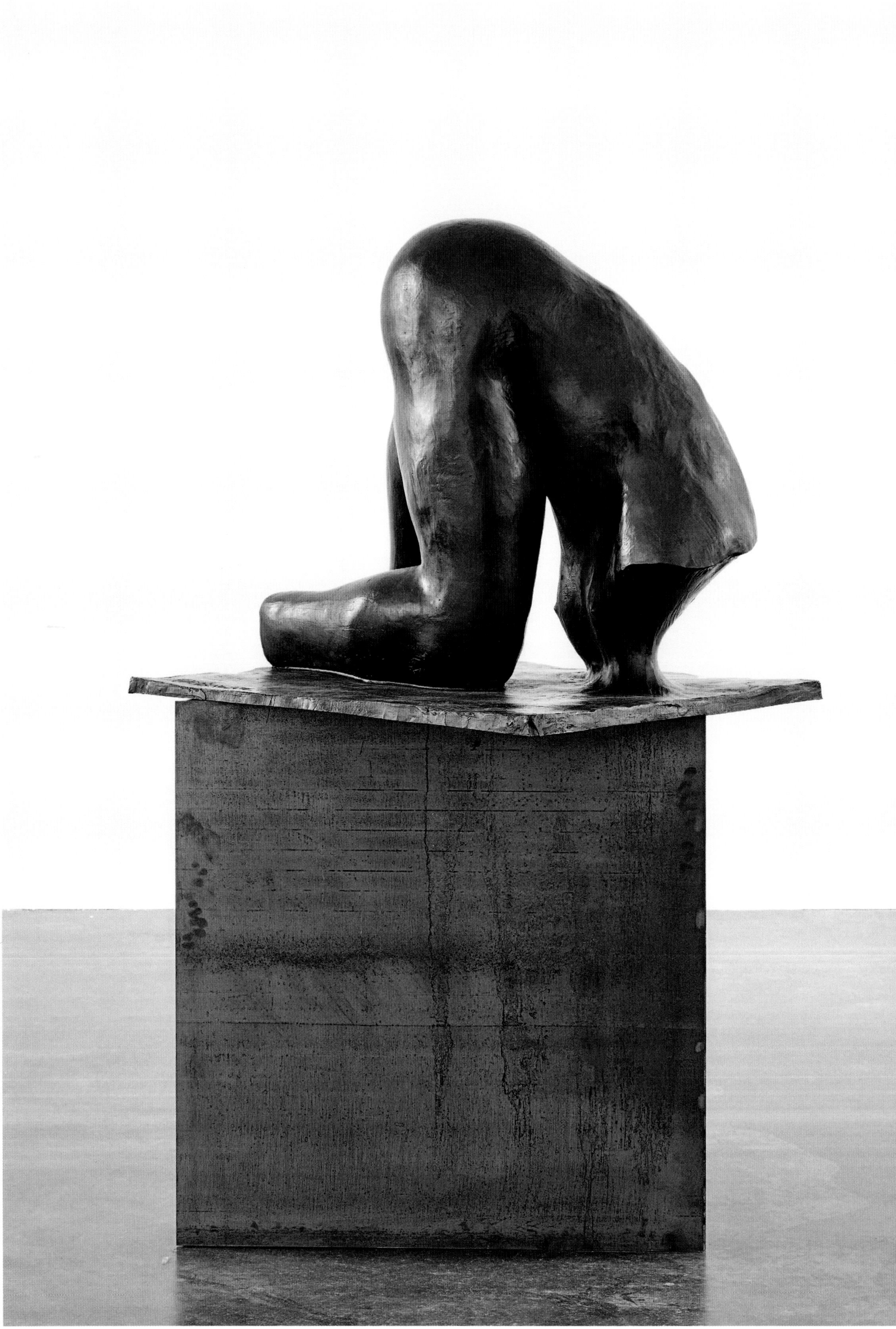

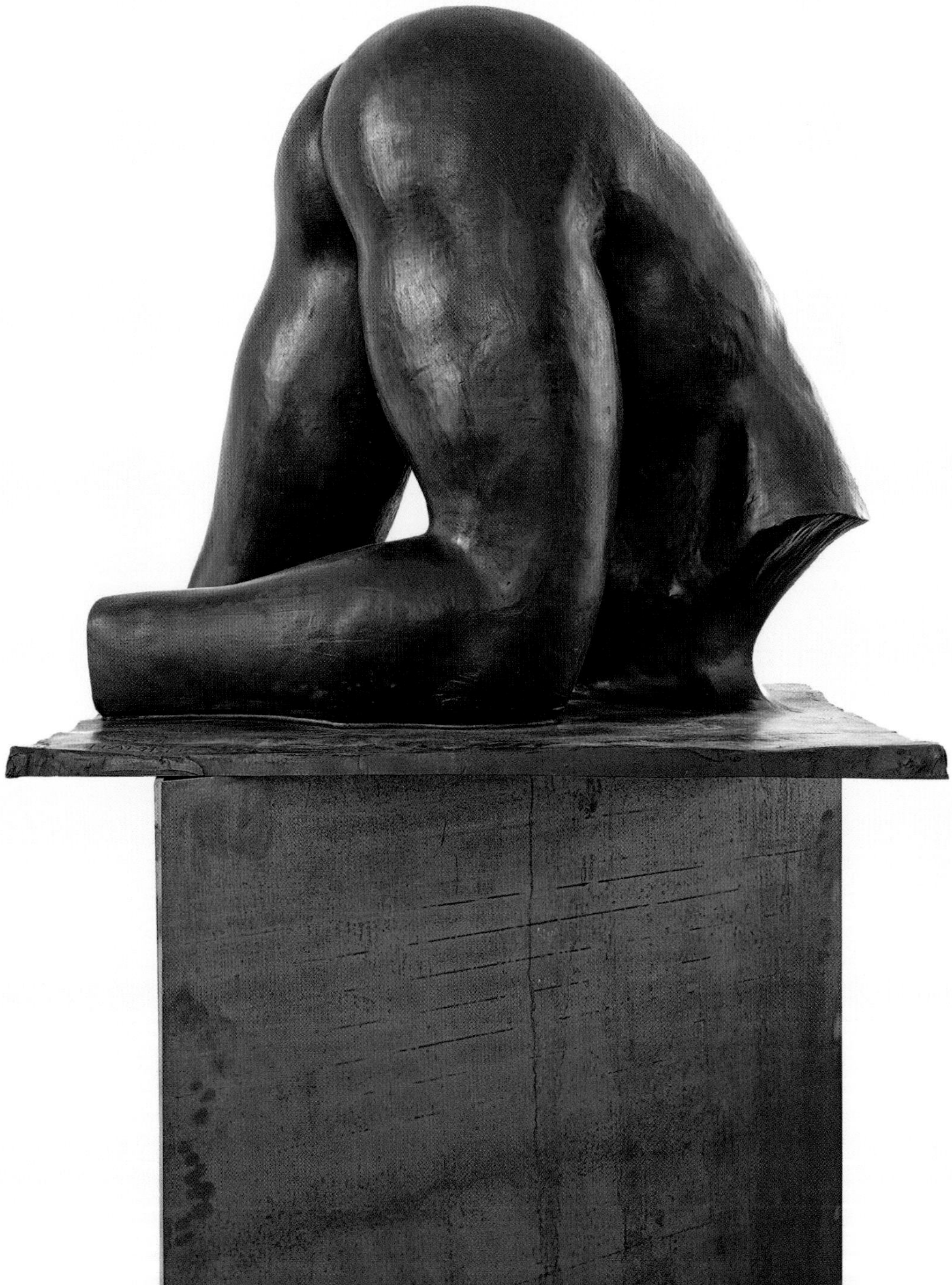

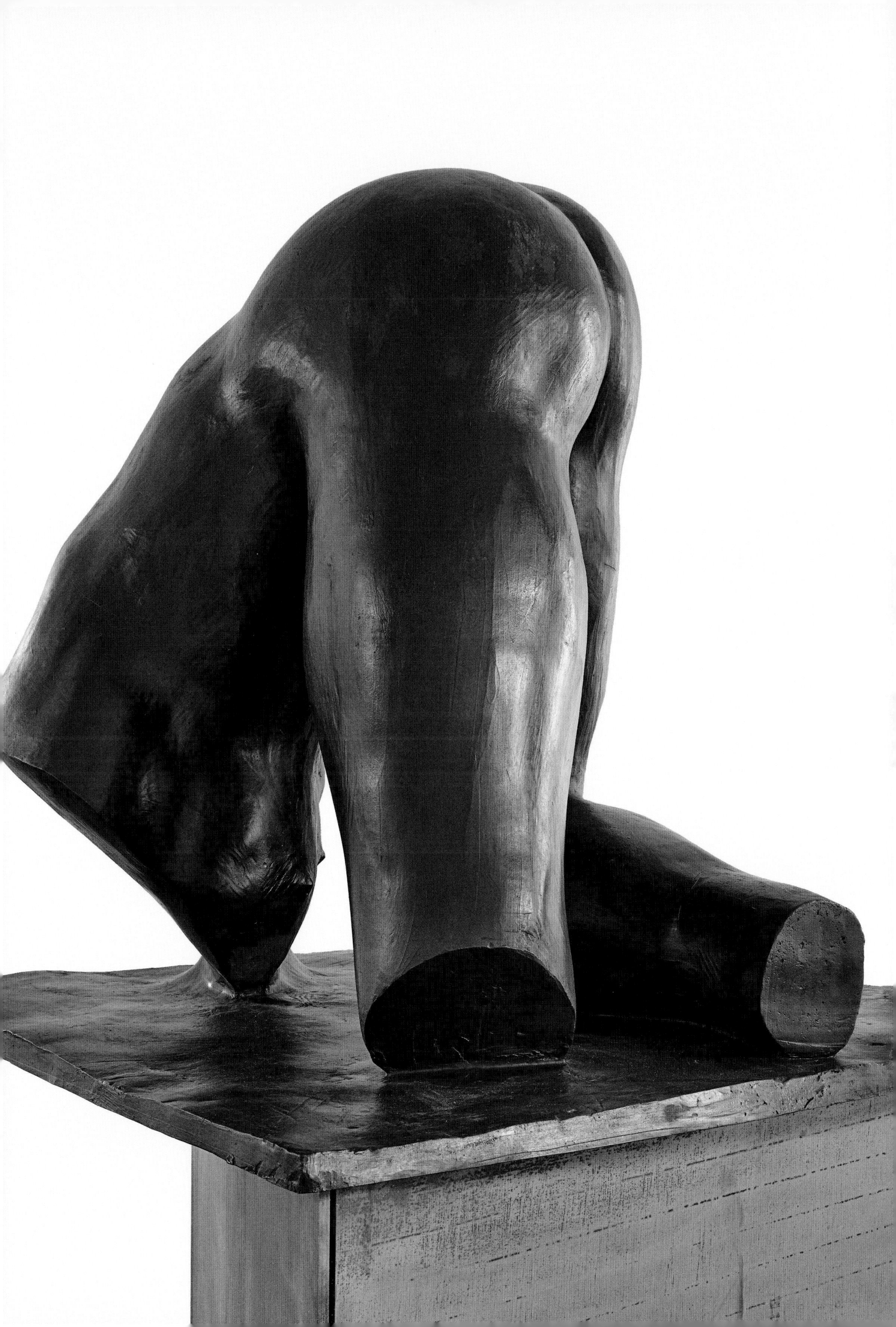

À TRAVERS LA TÊTE

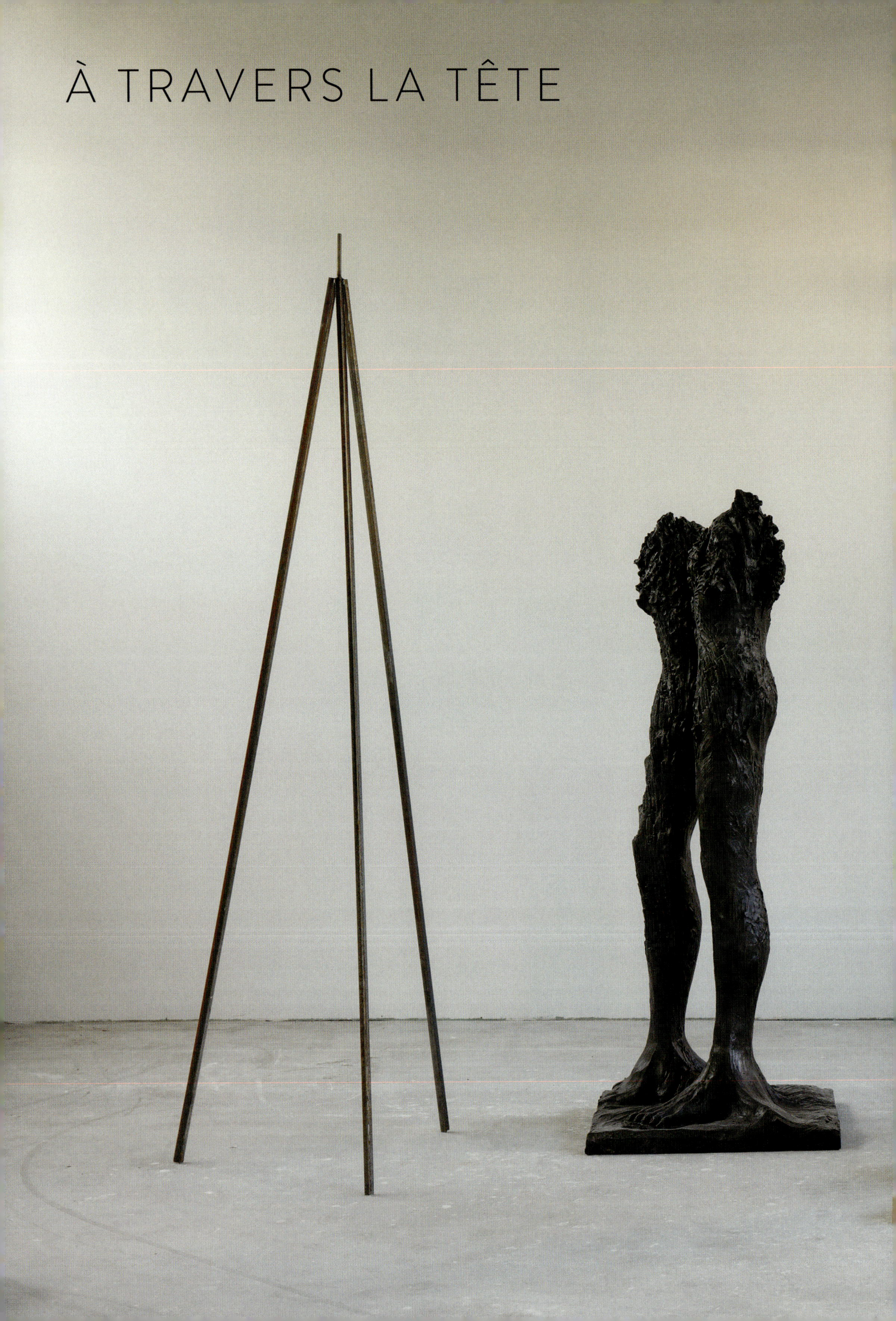

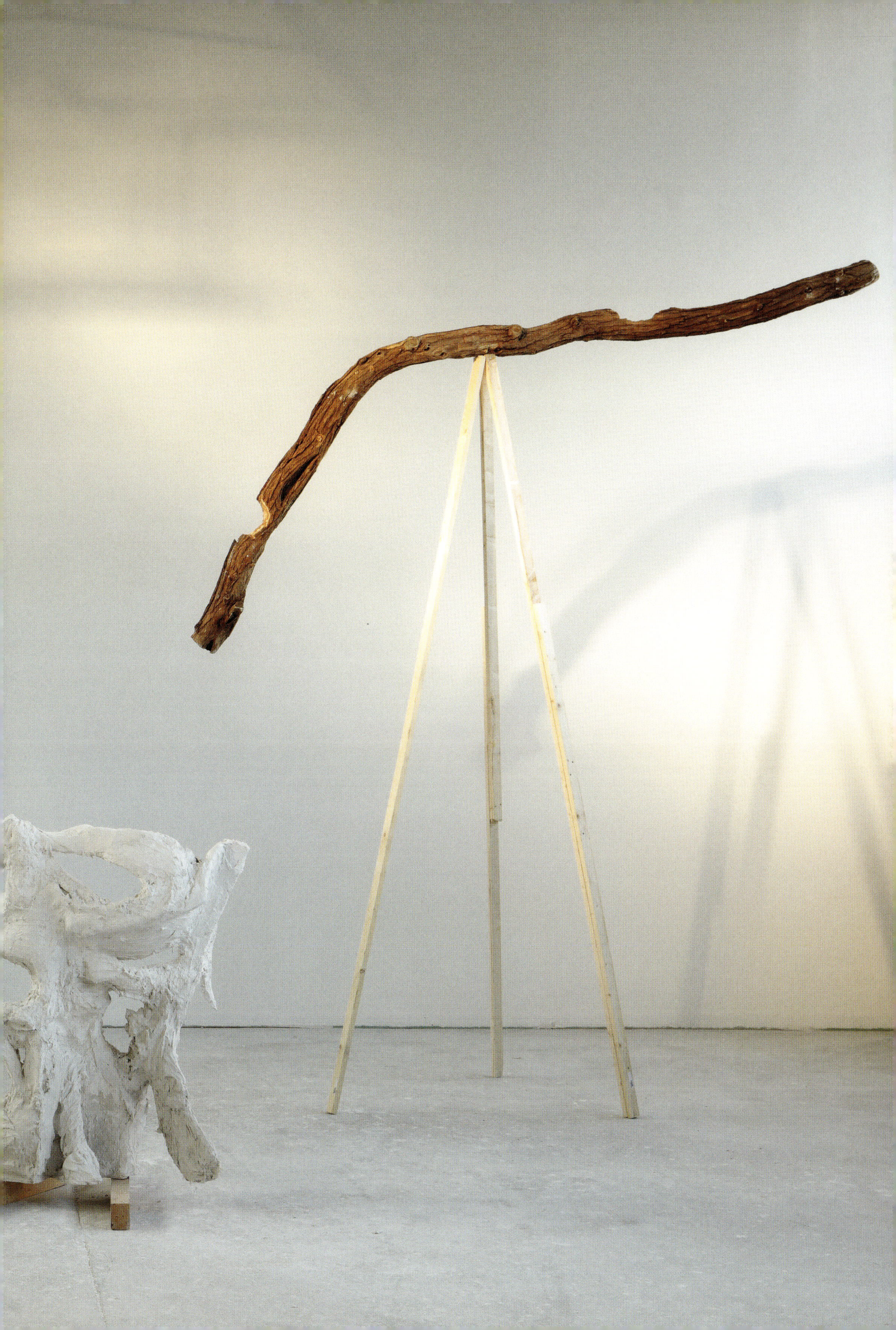

2017 in Stella Hamberg's studio, a hall next to the Skulpturengiesserei in Berlin. Two unconnected bronze legs loom up some 2.3 meters into space out of a base plate. Rough surfaces alternate with distinctly structured ones. The statement is loud, almost blatant. The two steles end at waist level, widening toward the top. The gap between the columns, a narrow line of light, draws one's attention to both the figure's surrounding and internal spaces. It stands securely on suggested feet pointed in different directions, yet appears to resolve itself into pure contrast with the surrounding space. Above it, a tree trunk is balanced at a height of 3 meters, supported by a fragile tripod. Hamberg comments that it is black locust wood, long used to fence in fields and pastures owing to its imperviousness to weather.

On the floor are seemingly amorphous sculptures in plaster. Some are suggestive of heads, others maintain a puzzling balance between negative and positive forms. In these new works the sculptural vocabulary has been simplified, reduced to essences. Detailed execution has disappeared in favor of structure as such, and with the decision to employ plaster and wood instead of clay and iron in the sculptures' composition the methods have fundamentally changed.

Plaster, which offers little time for alteration, and which Hamberg otherwise employs only in the construction of negative forms, is now used for the actual image. At the same time, however, it is also part of a meditation on negative and positive spaces that continues beyond the individual sculptures into the surrounding space, creating ensembles of different objects. For the first time since *Alexander* (2004) there are again scenarios, stage sets, pictures in space composed in constant engagement with the object.

Once again it becomes clear that formal changes in direction necessitate new methods of presentation suited to the given object, the creative process itself attuned to the specific concept. It is not merely a matter of different motifs or subjects; a particular approach appropriate to each new line of thinking assures a bond between method and content, the poles of art.

The juxtaposition of ephemeral and long-lasting materials – bronze, glass, wood, plaster, iron, cardboard, artificial and natural stone, along with objects of everyday use, both industrially produced and handcrafted – in itself touches on core artistic issues. But here it is never exclusively a conceptual combination based on a sensitivity to materials and formal concerns. Hamberg's works remain close to the figure, to narrative, the object, and in her highly effective treatment of the various forms and of synthetic and natural materials, both intensively worked and raw, create an altogether idiosyncratic, inscrutable poetry.

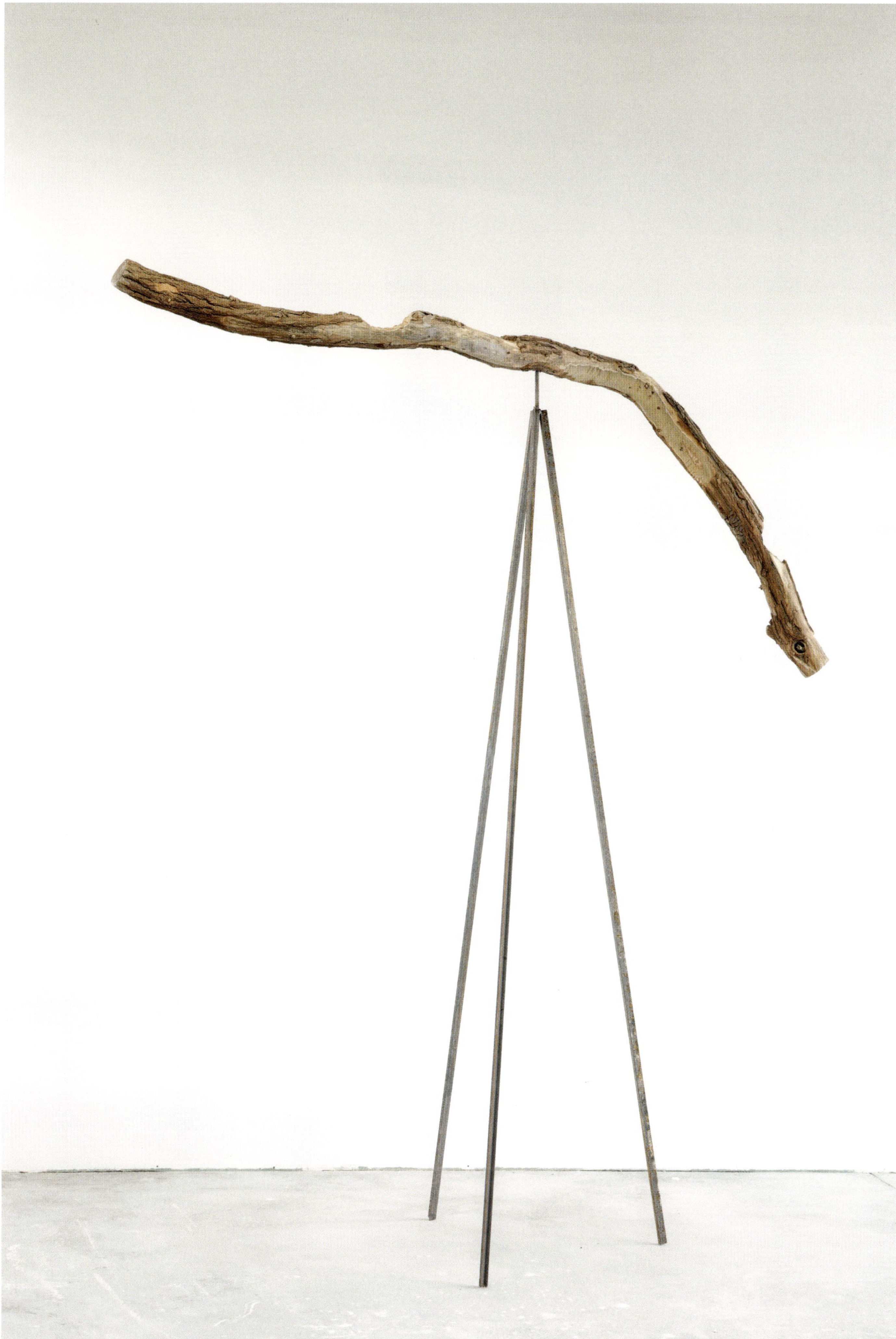

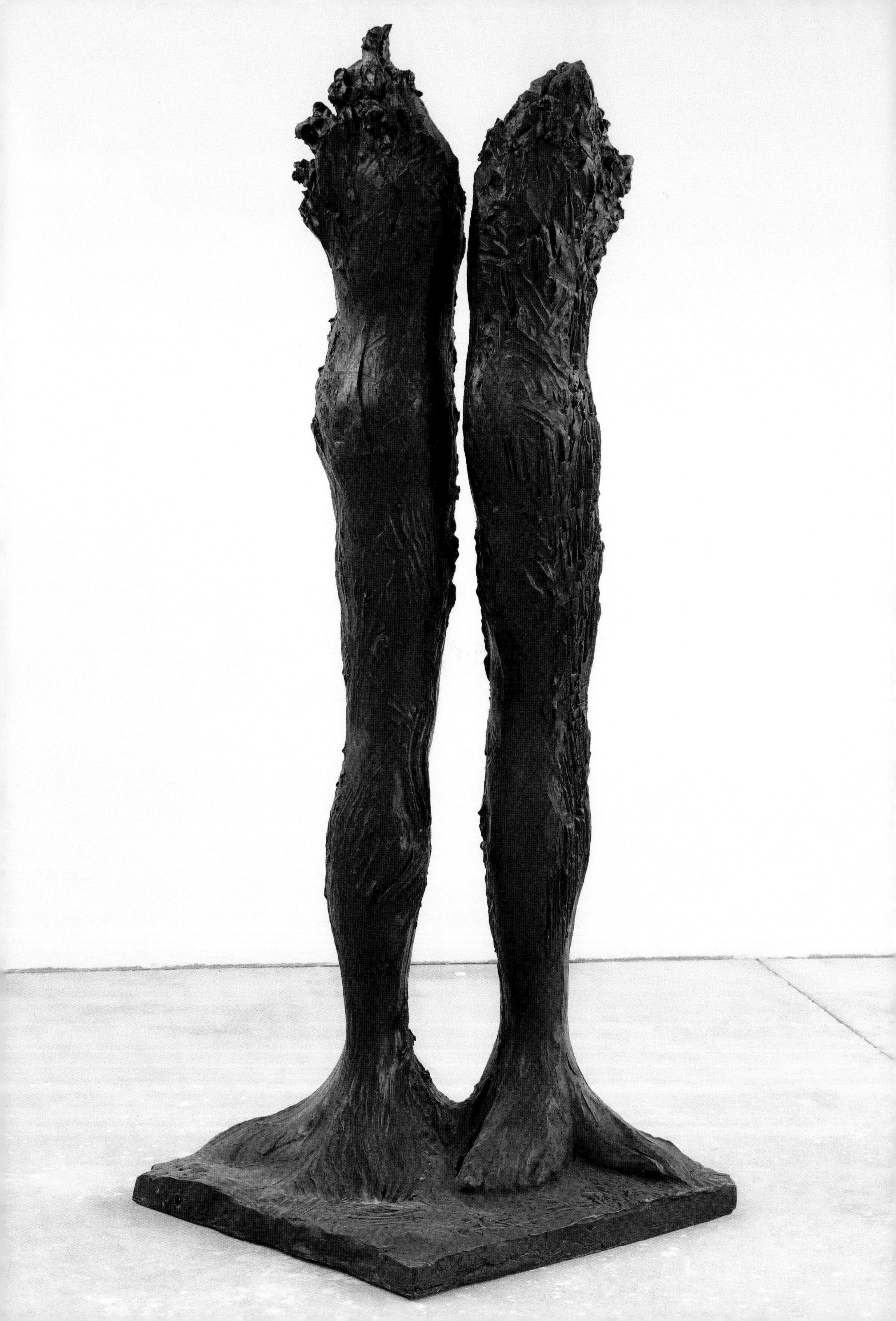

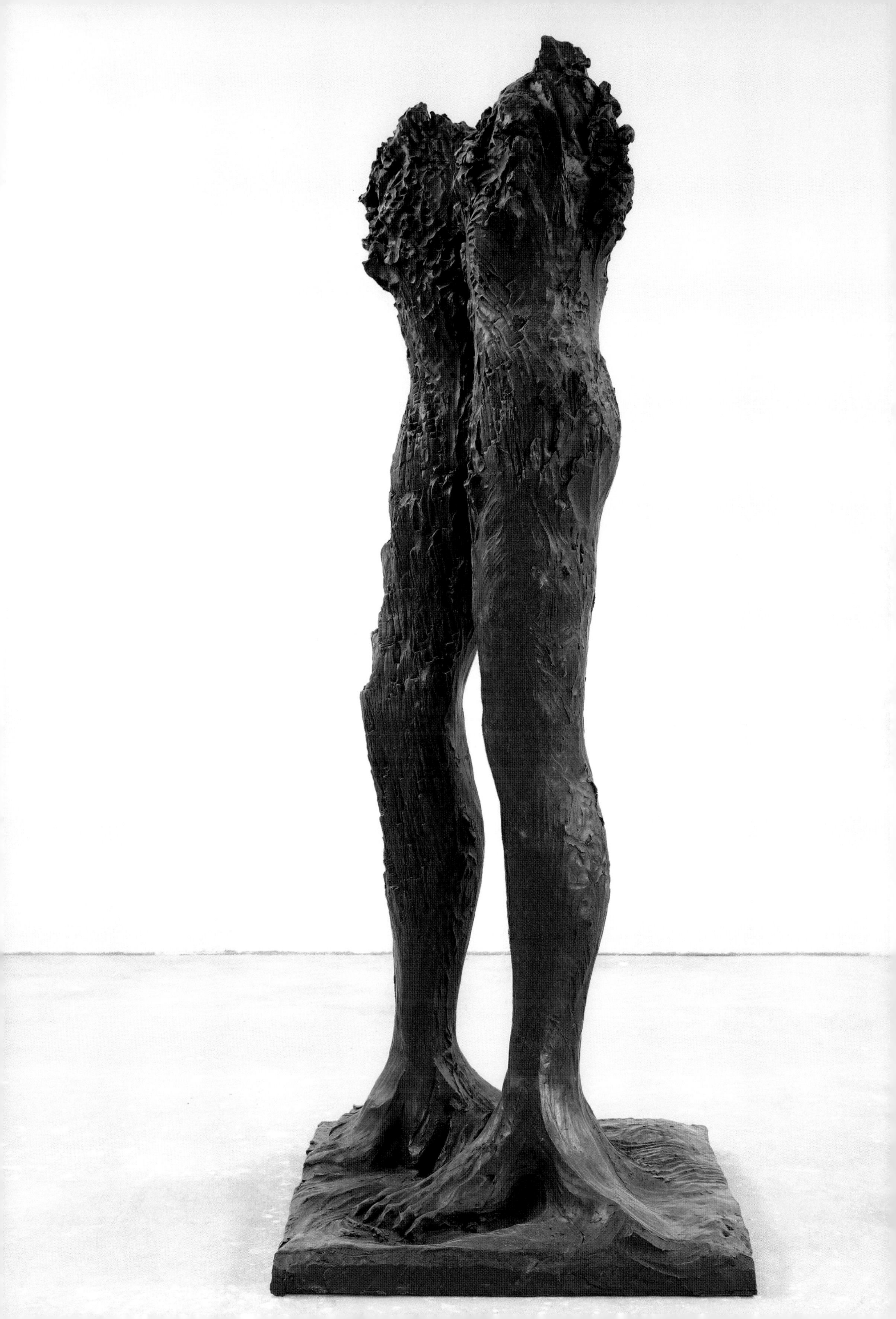

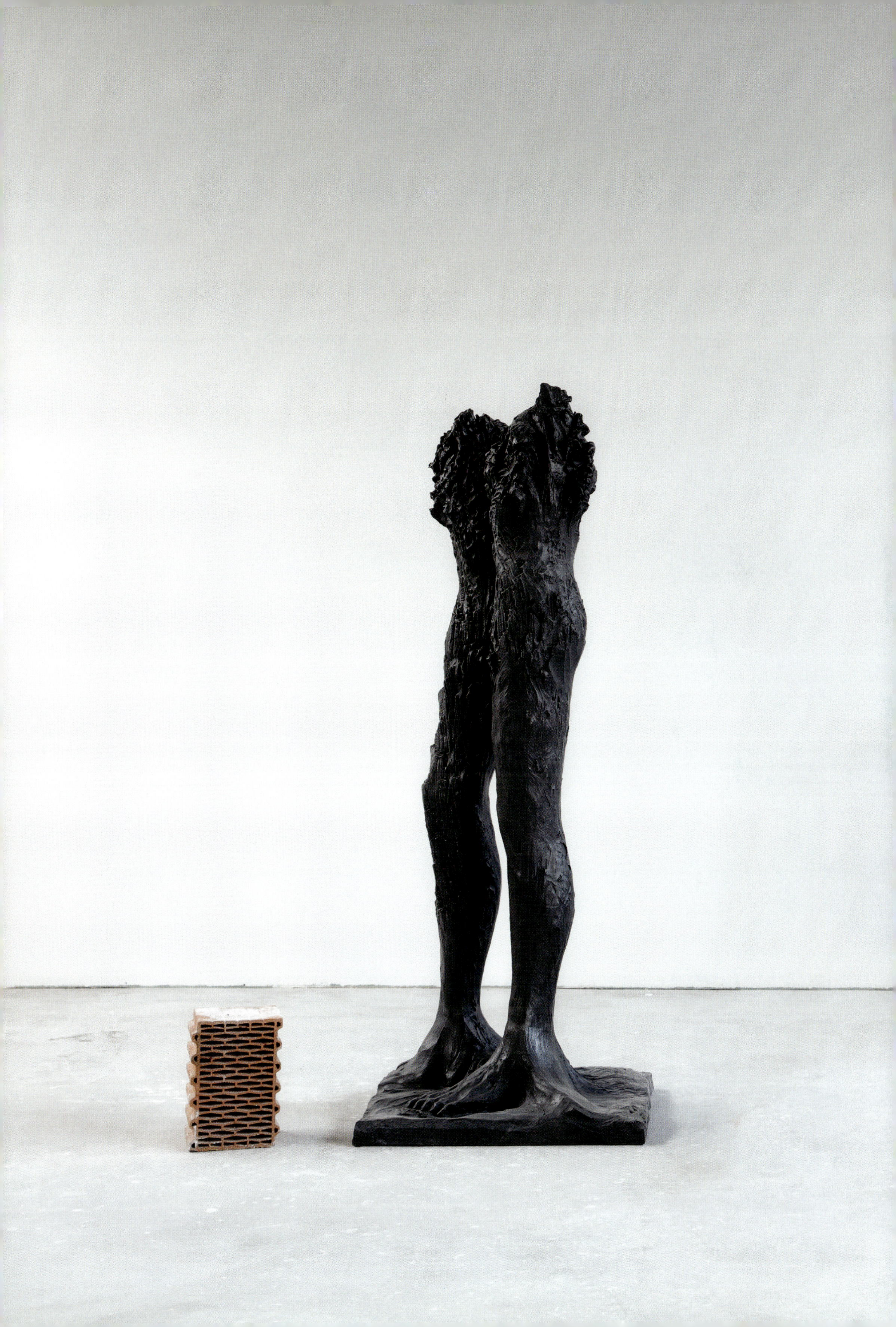

APPENDIX

INDEX OF THE ILLUSTRATED WORKS

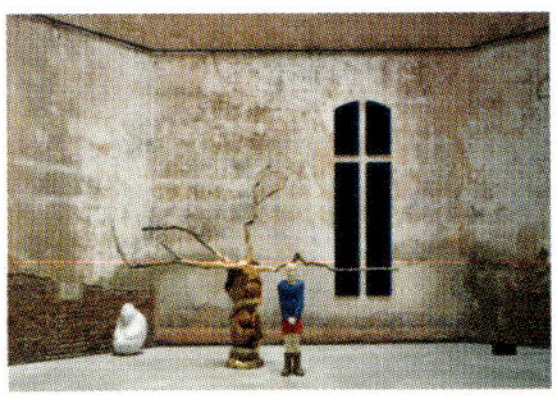

Alexander – 5 Plastiken, 2004
Mixed media
Dimensions variable

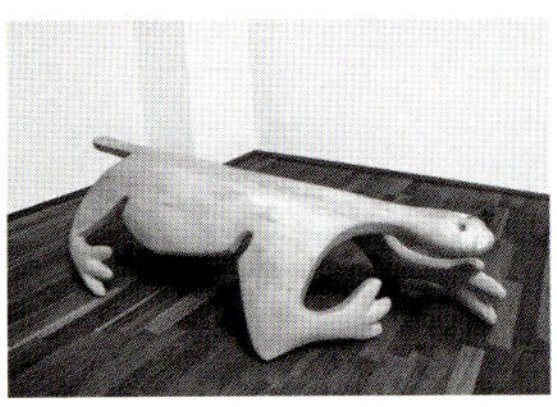

Dämon – the simplicity of a ghost-like beast, 2004
Polyester
60 × 130 × 65 cm

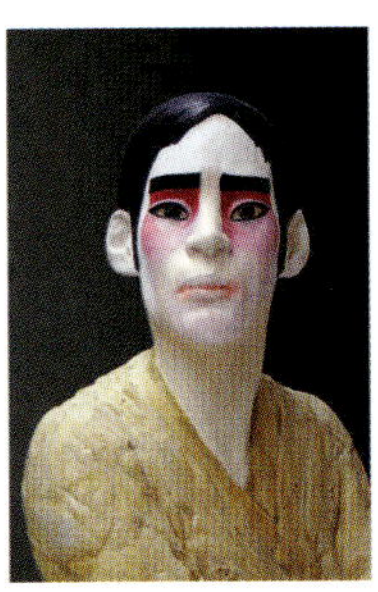

Tatú – for no reason, 2004
Polyurethane, artificial marble, dyed, partial polychromy
175 × 40 × 45 cm

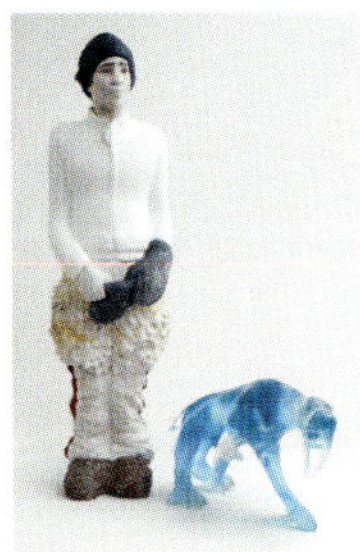

Abel – Bild aus zwei Figuren, 2005

Abel
Marble, limestone, polyurethane, epoxy resin, partial polychromy
173 × 53 × 40 cm

Dämon II
Polyester casting resin
52 × 100 × 47 cm

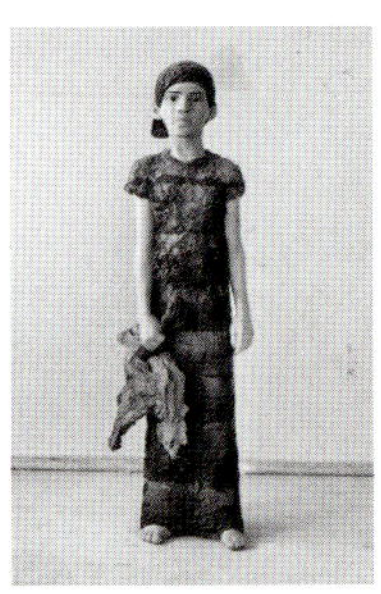

Maria, 2005
Polyurethane, dyed, partial polychromy
152 × 40 × 40 cm

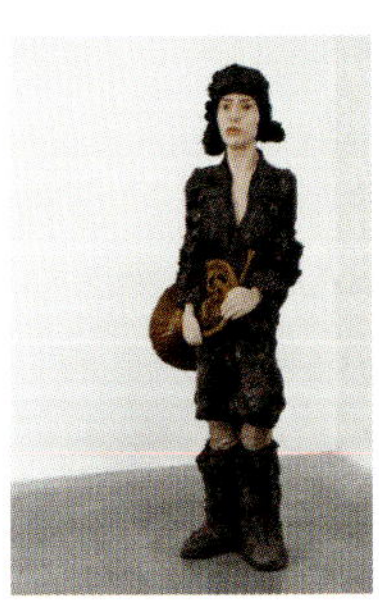

Martha, 2005
Polyurethane, dyed, partial polychromy
165 x 60 x 50 cm

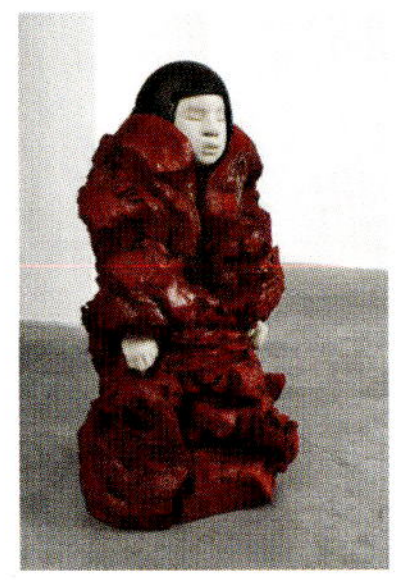

Quinten, 2005
Polyurethane, dyed, partial polychromy
100 × 55 × 45 cm

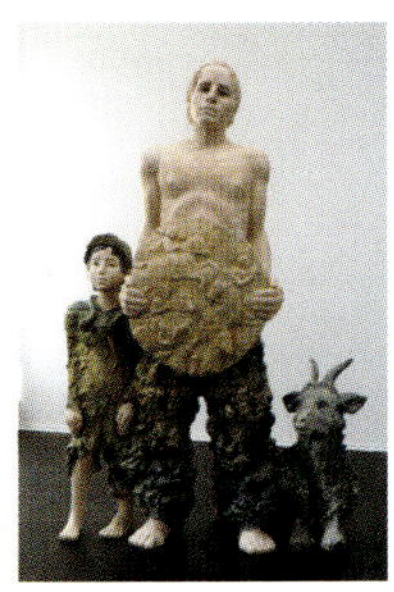

Lawrence – end of time, 2006
Polyurethane, artificial marble, dyed, partial polychromy
190 x 123 x 70 cm

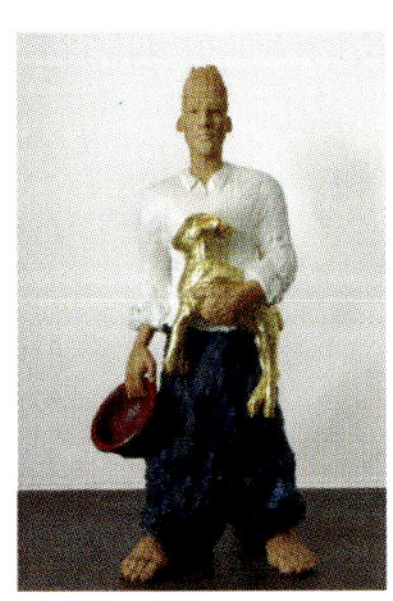

Malik, 2006
Polyurethane, epoxy resin, artificial marble, gold leaf, partial polychromy
190 x 70 x 50 cm

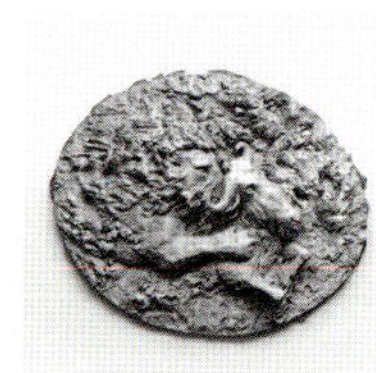

prayer, 2006
Polyurethanes, epoxy resin
140 × 180 × 40 cm

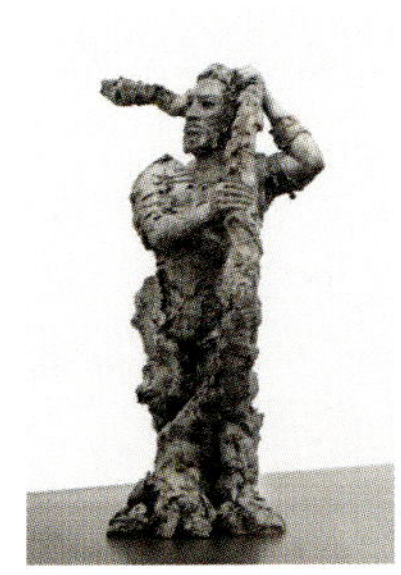

Berserker I, 2007
Bronze, patinated
236 x 153 x 105 cm
Edition: 3
Foundry: Bildgießerei Hermann Noack

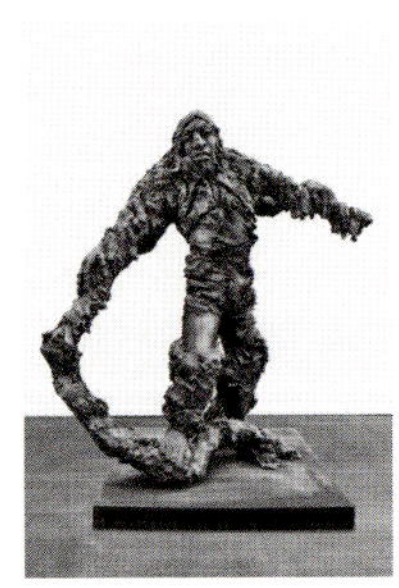

Berserker II, 2007
Bronze, patinated
245 × 260 × 130 cm
Edition: 3
Foundry: Bildgießerei Hermann Noack

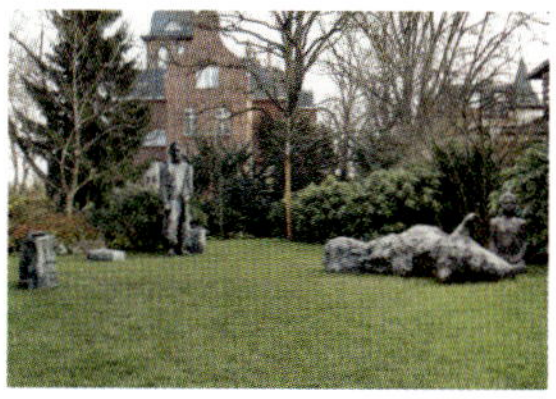

over and out, 2007
Sculptural group of 6 bronzes:
a bull, a child, a man,
three canisters
Bronze, patinated
Dimensions variable
Foundry: Bildgießerei
Hermann Noack

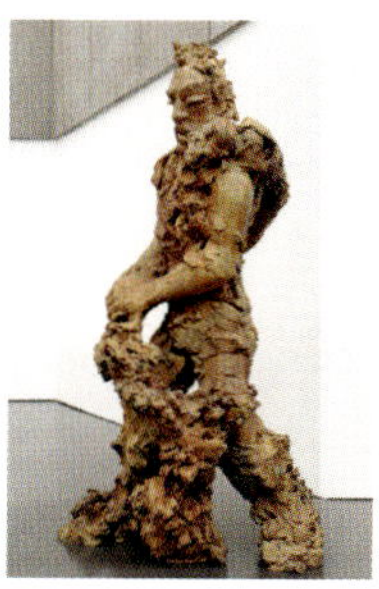

Berserker III, 2008
Bronze, patinated
244 × 150 × 100 cm
Edition: 3
Foundry: Bildgießerei
Hermann Noack

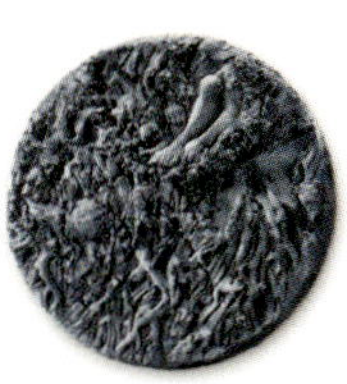

sieben100millionen, 2008
Mineral powder bound
with acrylic resin
∅ 310 cm

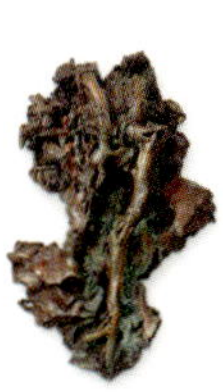

vom Verrecken und der absoluten
Unmöglichkeit zu sterben 1 –
das Tabu, 2008
Bronze, patinated
115 × 80 × 50 cm
Edition: 3
Foundry: Bildgießerei
Hermann Noack

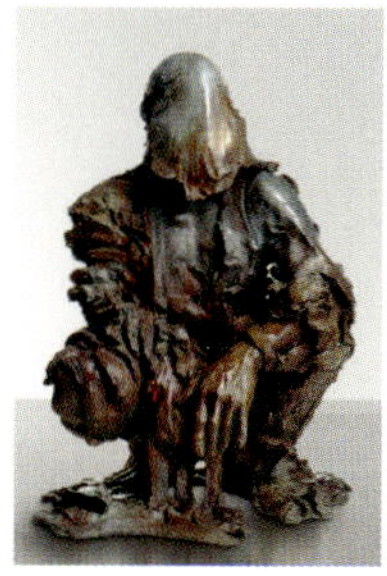

vom Verrecken und der absoluten
Unmöglichkeit zu sterben 2 –
der Gefährte, 2008
Bronze, patinated
114 × 90 × 80 cm
Edition: 3
Foundry: Bildgießerei
Hermann Noack

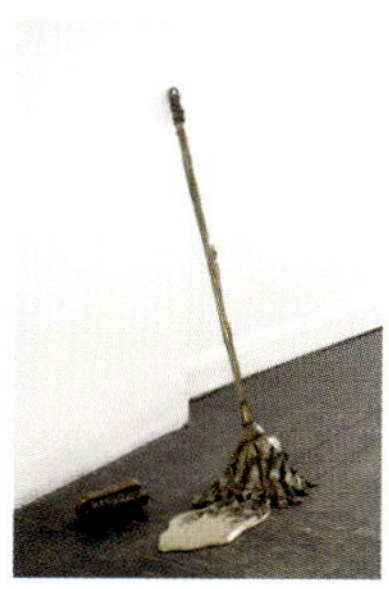

reset, 2009
Bronze, patinated
123 × 98 × 40 / 9 × 22 × 8 cm
Edition: 3
Foundry: Bildgießerei
Hermann Noack

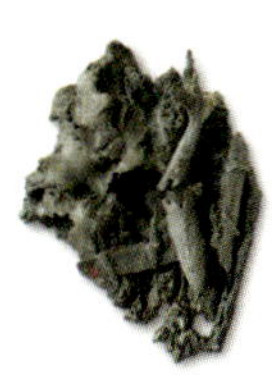

über Land, 2009
Concrete, laminated
120 × 90 × 25 cm

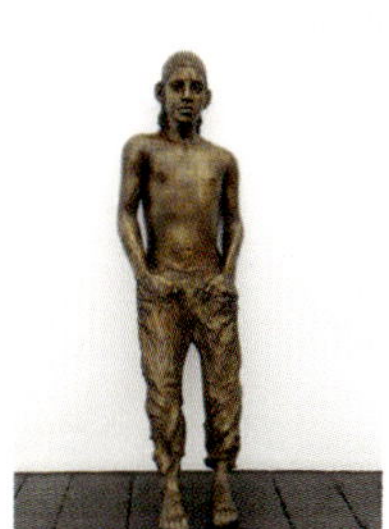

Das Mädchen, 2010
Bronze, patinated
170 × 55 × 60 cm
Edition: 3
Foundry: Bildgießerei
Hermann Noack

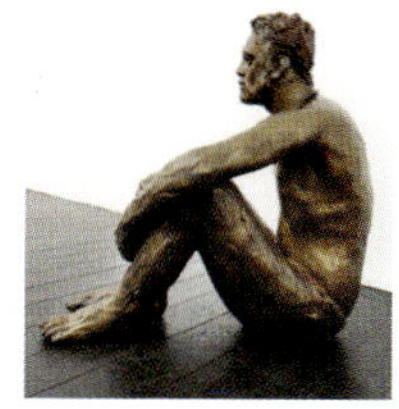

Der Fremde, 2010
Bronze, patinated
107 × 80 × 110 cm
Edition: 3
Foundry: Bildgießerei
Hermann Noack

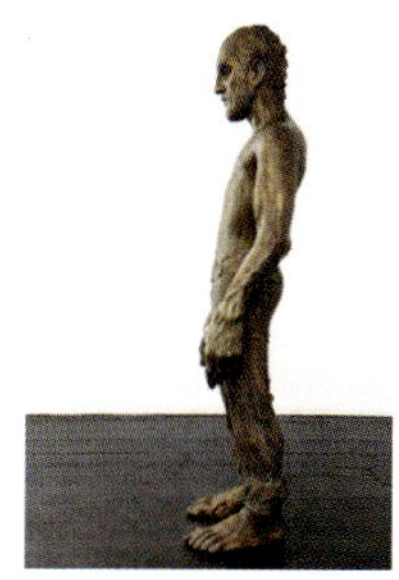

Der Freund, 2010
Bronze, patinated
187 × 70 × 40 cm
Edition: 3
Foundry: Bildgießerei
Hermann Noack

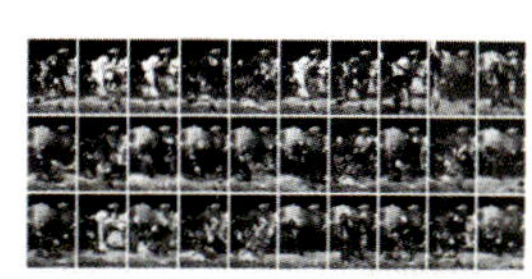

out of season, 2011
Documentation of an action
30 digital prints on
Hahnemühle Fotorag
415 × 185 cm

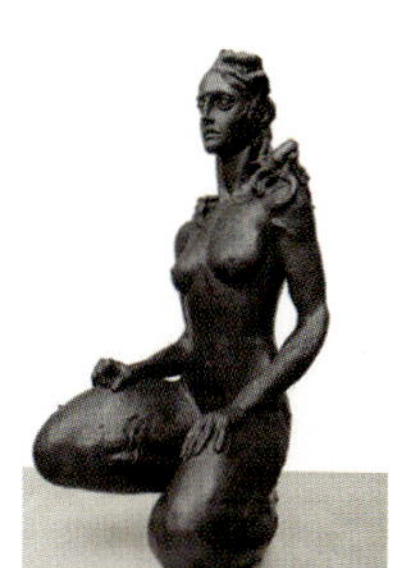

Frau, 2013
Bronze, patinated
195 × 100 × 95 cm
Edition: 3
Foundry: Karl Casper
GmbH & Co. KG

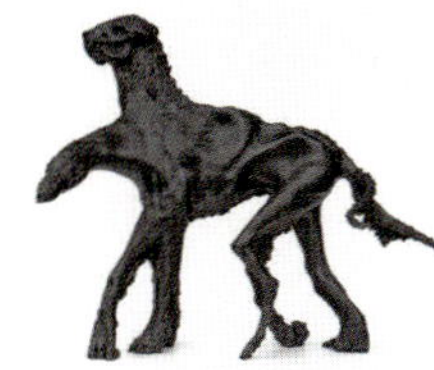

Hund, 2013
Bronze, patinated
230 × 120 × 270 cm
Edition: 3
Foundry: Karl Casper
GmbH & Co. KG

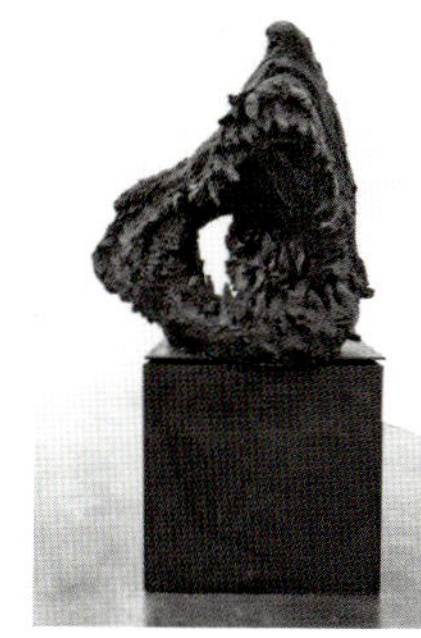

das ist das, 2015
Bronze, patinated
120 × 110 × 110 cm
Edition: 3
Foundry: Skulpturen-
gießerei Knaak

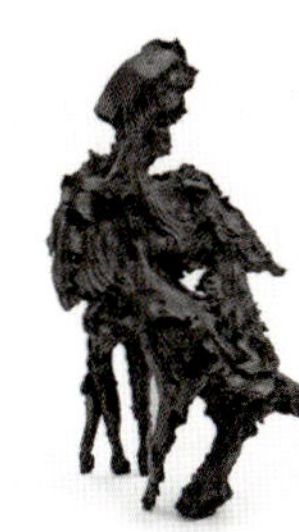

fortune, 2015
Bronze, patinated
125 × 100 × 70 cm
Edition: 3
Foundry: Skulpturen-
gießerei Knaak

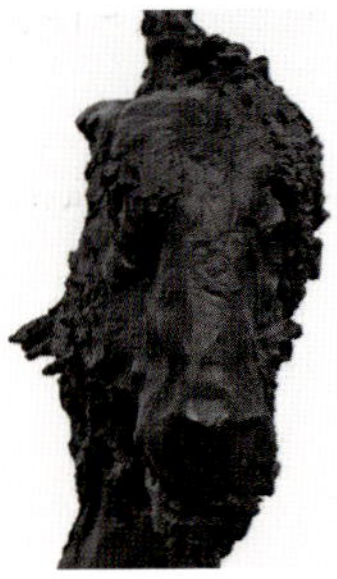

großer Schatten, 2015
Bronze, patinated
107 × 120 × 50 cm
Edition: 3
Foundry: Skulpturen-gießerei Knaak

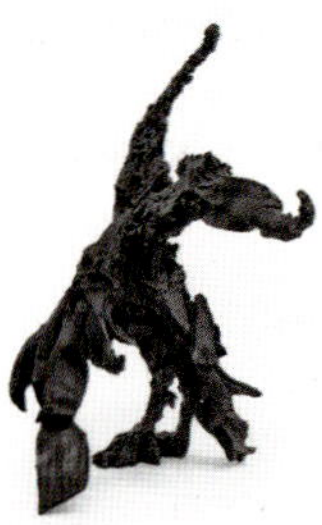

kein Titel (großer Dank), 2015
Bronze, patinated
112 × 120 × 75 cm
Edition: 3
Foundry: Skulpturen-gießerei Knaak

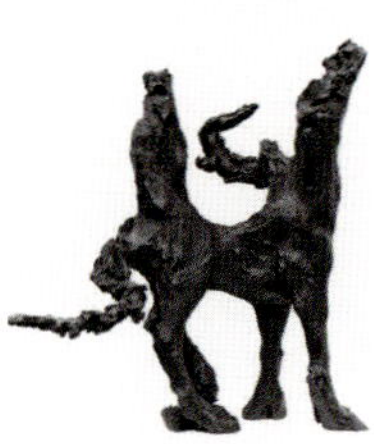

knotty network
(don't think twice), 2015
Bronze, patinated
98 × 60 × 90 cm
Edition: 3
Foundry: Skulpturen-gießerei Knaak

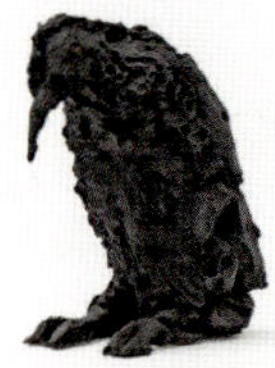

me, 2015
Bronze, patinated
53 × 35 × 45 cm
Edition: 3
Foundry: Skulpturen-gießerei Knaak

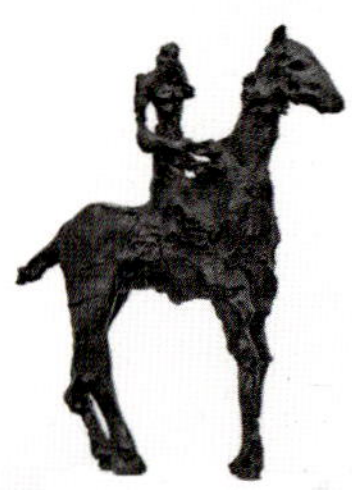

my dear fellow, 2015
Bronze, patinated
110 × 98 × 25 cm
Edition: 3
Foundry: Skulpturen-gießerei Knaak

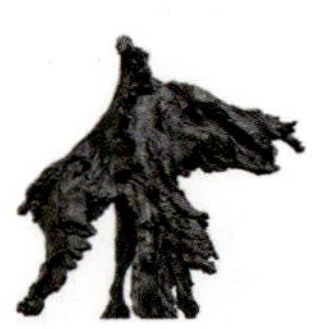

Nacht, 2015
Bronze, patinated
105 × 115 × 60 cm
Edition: 3
Foundry: Skulpturen-gießerei Knaak

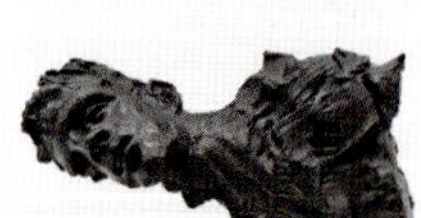

szenischer Ausschnitt (Blitzlicht) 1, 2015
Bronze, patinated
35 × 80 × 38 cm
Edition: 3
Foundry: Skulpturen-gießerei Knaak

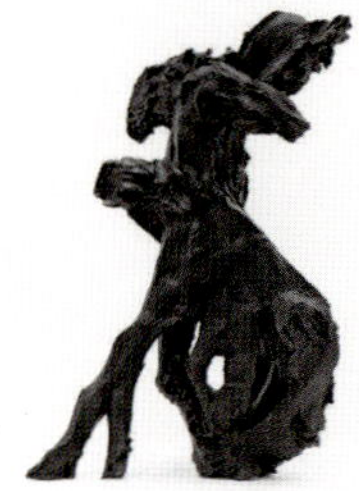

the curve 1 – twilight mountain sculpture, 2015
Bronze, patinated
105 × 70 × 50 cm
Edition: 3
Foundry: Skulpturen-gießerei Knaak

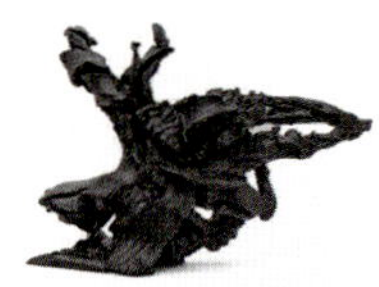

the curve 2 – Stille, 2015
Bronze, patinated
88 × 70 × 140 cm
Edition: 3
Foundry: Skulpturen-gießerei Knaak

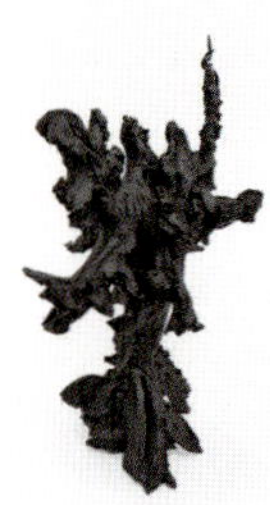

the curve 3 –
echoes in my head, 2015
Bronze, patinated
150 × 100 × 55 cm
Edition: 3
Foundry: Skulpturen-gießerei Knaak

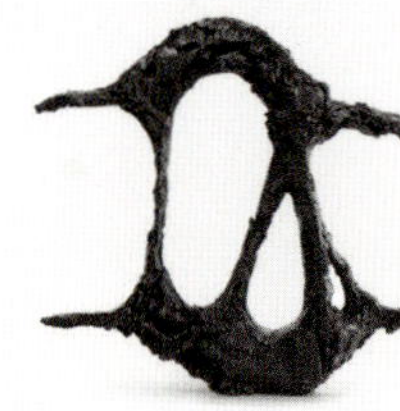

vanishing sculptures – clay 1, 2015
Bronze, patinated
98 × 105 × 17 cm
Edition: 3
Foundry: Skulpturen-gießerei Knaak

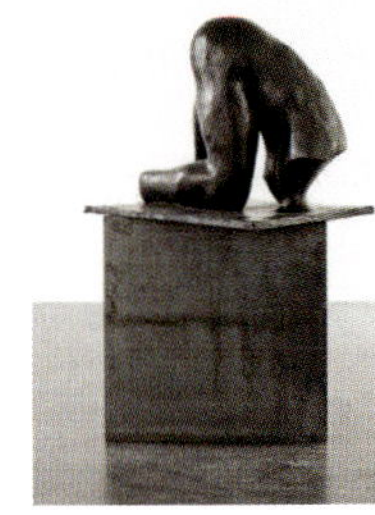

Trance, 2016
Bronze, patinated
90 × 90 × 90 cm
Edition: 3
Foundry: Skulpturen-gießerei Knaak

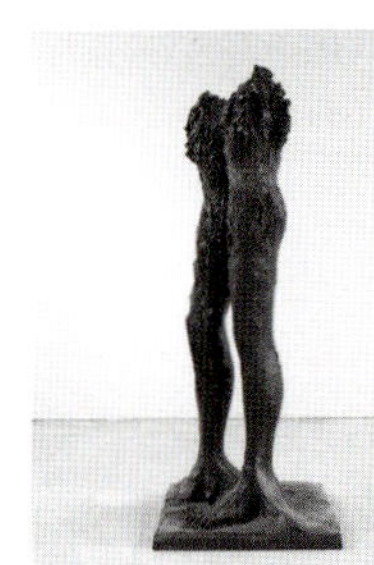

à travers la tête, 2017
Bronze, patinated
235 x 86 x 89 cm
Foundry: Skulpturen-gießerei Knaak

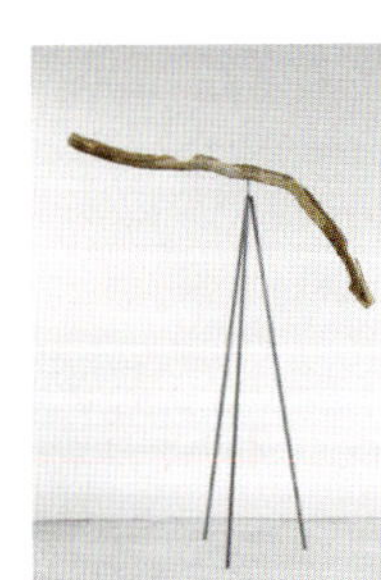

Robinie, 2017
Black locust wood, iron
300 x 300 cm
Supporting tripod,
edge length: 90 cm

STELLA HAMBERG

1975
Born in Friedberg, Hessen, Germany

1998–2004
Studies at the HfBK
(Academy of Fine Arts) Dresden
Diploma, Prof. Martin Honert

2004–2006
Masterstudent, Prof. Martin Honert

Lives and works in Berlin, Germany

PRIZES/SCHOLARSHIPS

2006
Karl Schmidt-Rottluff Stipendium

2001
Skulpturenwettbewerb Dresden

SOLO EXHIBITIONS

2017
à travers la tête, Galerie EIGEN + ART, Berlin

2016
Neutron, Kunstraum Potsdam

2015
Galerie EIGEN + ART, Leipzig

2013
Götter 1, Neue Galerie Gladbeck
WHITEOUT, Galerie EIGEN + ART, Berlin

2012
Stella Hamberg – Plastik, Zeichnung, Fotografie, Kunstverein Ulm

2011
Creature, Mönchehaus Museum Goslar

2010
ghost light, Galerie EIGEN + ART, Berlin

2009
RESET, Galerie EIGEN + ART, Berlin

2008
liebe Hölle, Galerie EIGEN + ART, Leipzig

2006
Lawrence – end of time, Galerie Diskus, Berlin

2005
with or without you, Galerie Diskus, Berlin

GROUP EXHIBITIONS

2016
An der Oberfläche_on surface. Die Oberfläche als Bedeutungsträger in der Skulptur, Lehmbruck Museum, Duisburg
Villa Schöningen, Potsdam

2015
Gute Kunst? Wollen!, offen auf AEG, Nuremberg
Jagdschloss Grunewald, Berlin
Nocturne – Ahnung. Abgrund und Apokalypse in der Zeitgenössischen Kunst, Kunsthalle der Sparkasse Leipzig
Additionen der Gegenwart. Zeitgenössische Kunst aus der Sammlung Frank Hense, Kunstmuseum Bochum

2013
on paper, Galerie EIGEN + ART, Berlin

2012
Berlin.Status, Künstlerhaus Bethanien, Berlin

2010
Galerie EIGEN + ART, Leipzig
Das versprochene Land, Staatliche Kunstsammlungen Dresden, Albertinum
Skulpturengarten, Villa Schöningen, Potsdam

2009
Carte Blanche VII: Prinzip Messe, Galerie für Zeitgenössische Kunst Leipzig

2008
Sommer bei EIGEN + ART, Galerie EIGEN + ART, Berlin
Karl Schmidt-Rottluff Stipendium, Kunsthalle Dusseldorf
abc, Art Berlin Contemporary, Berlin

2007
Wenn der Sonnentau ... Neuzugänge zeitgenössischer Kunst im Kunstfonds von 2005 bis 2007, Staatliche Kunstsammlungen Dresden, Residenzschloss
MAD LOVE ˆ Young Art from Danish Private Collections, Arken Museum for Moderne Kunst, Skovvej, Denmark
open end, Galerie Birgit Ostermeier, Berlin

2006
Full house – Gesichter einer Sammlung, Kunsthalle Mannheim

2005
the collection, Arken Museum for Moderne Kunst, Skovvej, Denmark
quartet, Sommer Contemporary Art, Tel Aviv, Israel
open, Galerie Diskus, Berlin

2004
Skulptur, Galerie EIGEN + ART, Leipzig

2003
in the forest is a monster, Galerie Krausserben, Dresden

2002
Ende November, Ausstellungsreihe JUNG UND GESUND, Königsbrücker Straße, Dresden

2001
Screenings 08, Museum für Moderne Kunst, Frankfurt on Main

WORKS IN THESE PUBLIC COLLECTIONS

Arken Museum for Moderne Kunst
Hort Family Collection
Kulturstiftung des Freistaates Sachsen
Kunsthalle Mannheim
Sammlung Faber-Castell
Sammlung Goetz
Sammlung Sander
SØR Rusche Sammlung
The Rubell Family Collection
Zabludowicz Collection

LIST OF THE ILLUSTRATED WORKS

IMPRINT

Concept: Stella Hamberg and Mick Vincenz
Author: Moritz Woelk
Text p. 150: Galerie EIGEN + ART, Berlin
Project management/publisher: Kerstin Ludolph
Editing: Hannah-C. Grabner, Anne Schwanz
English translation: Russell Stockman
English copy-editing: Chris Murray
Layout, typesetting, and production: Sabine Frohmader
Lithography: Reproline Genceller GmbH & Co. KG, Munich
Printing and binding: Passavia Druckservice GmbH & Co. KG, Passau
Typeface: Brandon Grotesque
Paper: 150 g/qm Hello Fat Matt 1.1

All works by Stella Hamberg courtesy Galerie EIGEN + ART Leipzig/Berlin
www.eigen-art.com

Bibliographical data of the Deutsche Nationalbibliothek: The Deutsche Nationalbibliothek lists this publication in the Deutsche Nationalbibliografie; detailed bibliographic information is available on the Internet at http://www.dnb.de.

ISBN 978-3-7774-2792-8 (English edition)
ISBN 978-3-7774-2786-7 (German edition)

Printed in Germany
www.hirmerpublishers.com

Two limited collectors' editions are being published. For further information please contact the publisher.
ISBN 978-3-7774-2794-2 (Edition 1: Liebe, Edition: 40)
ISBN 978-3-7774-2796-6 (Edition 2: Lust, Edition: 40)
Printing of the etchings: Atelier für Radierung, Leipzig
Paper for the etchings: 340 g/qm Zerkall reinweiß

PICTURE CREDITS

Andres Sune Berg: p. 22

Christian Korth: p. 7

Galerie EIGEN + ART: p. 25

Mick Vincenz: pp. 36, 37, 41, 82/83, 84, 85, 86, 89, 90/91, 92/93, 94, 97, 98, 99, 100, 101, 102, 104, 105, 106, 107, 108, 109, 111, 112, 113, 114, 115, 117, 118, 119, 120, 121, 123, 124, 125, 126, 127, 128, 129, 130, 131, 132, 133, 134/135, 137, 138/139, 142, 143, 144, 146, 147, 148/149, 151, 152, 153, 155

Sommer Contemporary Fine Arts: p. 156

Stella Hamberg: pp. 10/11, 16, 17, 18, 19, 26, 27, 28, 29, 78/79, 87

Uwe Walter, Berlin: pp. 20, 21, 23, 30/31, 35, 38, 39, 42/43, 46, 47, 48, 50, 51, 52, 53, 54/55, 58, 62/63, 66, 67, 68, 69, 70, 71, 72, 73, 74, 75, 76, 77, 156

pp. 8/9:
In an associative pictorial tapestry, Stella Hamberg has collected sources of inspiration in a kind of pinboard. In spite of our best efforts, it has not always been possible to discover the owners of the rights to the pictures. Any justified claims in this regard will of course be recompensed under the usual agreements.

Nos. 1, 3, 5, 7, 8, 9, 17, 19, 20: unidentified
no. 2: nebredaelena.wordpress.com
no. 4: flaminiogualdoni.com
no. 6: cinemathequeip.wordpress.com
no. 10: phippsfilm.com
nos. 11, 12, 14: pinterest.de
no. 13: 3quarksdaily.com
no. 15: Martin Honert (c) VG Bild-Kunst, Bonn 2017, artberlin.de, photo: Graeme Vaughan
no. 16: syndrome-de-stendal.blogspot.de
no. 18: dinca.org